Irish Television

IRISH TELEVISION

The Political and Social Origins

Robert J. Savage, Jr.

CORK UNIVERSITY PRESS

First published in 1996 by
Cork University Press
University College
Cork
Ireland

British Library Cataloguing in Publication Data
A CIP catalogue record for this book is available from
the British Library.

ISBN 1–85918–101–5 hardback
1–85918–102–3 paperback

*For Robin, Molly, and Nicholas
and dedicated to the memory of Ann Burke*

Contents

Acknowledgments

This book would not have been possible without the help of many friends and associates who were kind enough to lend important support and encouragement. On this side of the Atlantic Professor Kevin O'Neill patiently directed my doctoral dissertation offering invaluable advice during its long gestation. In the history department Professors James Cronin and Francis Murphy were kind enough to lend their support in reading drafts of the dissertation and offering constructive guidance. The Co-Director of the Irish Studies Program, Professor Adele Dalsimer, and dedicated Irish Studies faculty such as Philip O'Leary were also tremendously helpful and supportive. The Irish Studies Program at Boston College, its faculty and graduate students, have provided a unique environment which has contributed greatly to the effort required to write this book. Other individuals associated with the history department and the Irish Studies Program who have helped in this regard include David Buckley, Ann Burke, Margaret Kelleher, Patrick Pardy, Joseph Cugini, Barbara Machtinger, and Robert Tarutis.

In Ireland, Pearse Kearney in particular proved not only a great friend but also a generous host and companion. At Radio Telefís Éireann, Brian Lynch was of tremendous assistance in exploring the rich written archives that were critical to this book. Colm Gallagher at the Department of Finance helped identify relevant files that greatly enhanced this study. If not for his patience and flexibility a vital part of this story would have gone untold. At the Department of Communications, Bernard McDonough, Seamus Moran, and Tom Kennington were kind enough to provide access to important files from what had been the Department of Posts and Telegraphs. David Craig at the National Archives and Dr. Phil Connolly at the State Paper Office also provided valuable assistance in this research. Professor Ronan Fanning at University College, Dublin was a great help in plotting research strategies.

Others were also quite generous with their time and therefore deserve mention for their efforts. Paul Warren, John Irvine, Dónall Ó Móráin, Tom Hardiman, the Most Reverend H. R. McAdoo, Áine Ní Cheanainn, Emir Ó Broin, Meave Conway-Piskorski, and Pádraig Ó Rahilly all were kind enough to grant interviews. Dr. Garret Fitzgerald, Eilish MacCurtain Pearce, Coilin O'Broin, Professor Gearóid Ó Tuathaigh, Vincent Finn, T. K. Whitaker, Ian Lee, Jane Hall, John McMahon, Tony Blackwell, William Hammond, Tom Quinn, Ian McCarthy, and the family of Edward Roth were also helpful in making suggestions and providing insights and access to information concerning the development of Irish television.

Much of the research for this book was conducted in the Archives of Radio Telefís Éireann, the State Paper Office at Dublin Castle, the Department of Communications at Scotch House, the Department of Finance at Kildare Street, the National Library, the Archives of University College Dublin, the Trinity College Manuscript Collection, and the BBC Written Archives at Caversham. I owe the staff of each one of these institutions a word of thanks for their assistance and understanding.

Lastly I would like to thank my rather large extended family for their love and support, especially my wife Robin whose patience and understanding has made the endeavor so rewarding.

Introduction

On New Year's Eve 1961, the first broadcast of the Irish television service was made. The initial broadcast featured addresses by the President of the Irish Republic, Eamon de Valera, and the Primate of all Ireland, Cardinal D'Alton. Both men expressed concern over the effect television might have on Irish society. The Cardinal warned parents of the influence that television could have on the young and expressed concern over the possibility of what he termed "TV addiction." However, it was the President who seemed the most uncomfortable with the advent of Irish television. His ominous warning echoed the concerns that had been made by intellectuals, clerics, and "cultural purists" who were concerned with the impact the new service would have on the nation.

I must admit that sometimes when I think of television and radio and their immense power I feel somewhat afraid. Like atomic energy it can be used for incalculable good but it can also do irreparable harm. Never before was there in the hands of men an instrument so powerful to influence the thoughts and actions of the multitude. The persistent policy pursued over radio and television, apart from imparting knowledge, can build up the character of the whole people, inducing a sturdiness and vigour and confidence. On the other hand, it can lead through demoralization to decadence and disillusion.[1]

The President referred to the content of broadcasts, fearing that the demand for a "popular" service would erode what he envisioned as the unique culture of the Irish nation. He hoped that high standards would be employed by the new television service, but was clearly worried that vulgar programs would invade Irish homes. He pleaded with his audience to demand programs of the best quality.

If you insist on having presented to you the good, the true, and the beautiful, you will get this and I for one will find it hard to be convinced that good taste cannot be cultivated. I find it hard to believe for example that a person who views the grandeurs of the heavens or the wonders of this marvelous mysterious world in which God has placed us will not find more pleasure in that than in viewing for example some squalid domestic brawl or a street quarrel. . . . I am confident that those who are in charge will do everything in their power to make it useful for the nation, that they will bear in mind that we are an old nation and that we have our own distinctive characteristics and that it is desirable that these be preserved.[2]

The image of an elderly de Valera warning citizens of the dangers of modern technology quite dramatically illustrates a turning point in the modern history of the nation. Here was "the Chief," the one individual who, more than any other, had come to represent post-independence Ireland, warning of the perils of a medium that was beyond his control. Although he had been able to dominate Irish politics for close to thirty years, he was now presiding over a nation that was being rapidly transformed. Ireland was emerging from the social and economic torpor that had paralyzed the state since its founding. The venerable President had little control over the direction his nation would take. The television camera into which he peered anxiously represented a changing country that would challenge his successors.

Among others who greeted the nation were the Taoiseach,* Sean Lemass, and, oddly enough, a young King Hussein of Jordan. In a gala celebration broadcast from the Gresham Hotel on Dublin's fashionable O'Connell Street, viewers tuned in to witness a curious spectacle. The audience saw a festive gathering which featured politicians and entertainers all assembled to celebrate both the advent of 1962 and the inauguration of Irish television.

Irish television had made its debut. Its impact on Irish society was, and is still, a subject of lively debate. As one historian commented, "The Irish people now had a window on the world never before open to them; and that window opened a strange and exciting vista which neither state nor church authorities could any longer hide from their gaze."[3] Another commentator pointed out that the opening of the service created new challenges. Irish society—"the nationalist tradition, the cultural heritage, the primacy of rural values, the repression of sexuality—was about to meet its most serious challenge since the foundation of the state."[4]

*Taoiseach is the Irish term for premier or prime minister.

The dire warnings issued by the President and the Archbishop illustrate the high level of apprehension held by many individuals, who were acutely concerned with the impact the new service might have. This anxiety had been articulated by numerous organizations and interest groups since the debate over television started to take shape in the early 1950s. While many of the fears and hopes that were attributed to the power of television may now seem exaggerated, they help explain the complexities of Irish culture and society during a period of tremendous change.

In the following pages, I shall examine the process that led to the creation of Irish television, *not* the impact that the service has had on Irish society in the last thirty-five years. I will concentrate on the debate that developed in the 1950s over key questions that concerned television and how a service should be introduced into the country. A number of corporations and organizations expressed a keen interest in building and operating television stations in Ireland. Other groups also stepped forward to make the case that their particular interests should be addressed in any service that was to be established.

At the end of the decade, one can also examine the Lemass Government in action. The issues raised shed a good deal of light on his early administration and demonstrate how policy developed in response to events that were moving at a rapid pace. Lemass's government had been in place for only a short time when it found itself confronted by an explosive issue that could no longer be ignored or postponed.

A coherent television policy had eluded successive Inter-Party and Fianna Fail Governments throughout the 1950s. These conservative governments were concerned over the cost a television service would impose on an already depleted National Exchequer. They feared that the price of a national television service would be beyond the modest means of the country. These same governments were afraid of alienating such powerful forces as the Catholic Church, the Gaelic Athletic Association, Irish-language groups, and professional organizations, all of whom expressed concern over television and its impact on Irish society. Until the close of the decade, these governments lacked the will to adopt a position or policy and see it through to completion. The tremendous amount of time and energy expended on committees and commissions that were set up to examine what shape an Irish service should take hindered the development of television. Every conceivable interest group in the country had a position and an opinion on television, and none were afraid to voice their fears and desires concerning the subject.

The debate that ensued, and the final decision made, must be understood within the context of a nation undergoing a major transformation. Although the term *watershed* can be an overused and simplistic cliché, it seems to apply to this period, which brought tremendous change to Irish society. A generation of politicians were stepping down from the largest political parties and being replaced by leaders who were less committed to the economic, social, and cultural policies of their predecessors. This new genera-tion of leaders would oversee a dramatic shift in the economic and social progress of the country. Innovative policies emerged from a government that endorsed a more "modern" outlook, which encouraged foreign invest-ment and endorsed free trade. These policies challenged the once-sacred creed of self-sufficiency and protectionism. Irish television emerged out of this watershed period and would play an important role in the transformation of Irish society during the 1960s. However, one must remember that through-out the 1950s, Ireland remained a nation troubled by severe economic difficulties. High unemployment and relentless emigration haunted the country. These social ills handicapped the development of a national tele-vision service.

What follows is an examination of the policy that led to the establishment of an independent television authority. To do this, one must first consider the early ideas and schemes that were circulated and what type of service they sought to establish. What clearly emerges is a debate between those who favored a service that would be set up as an independent, commercial entity versus those who endorsed a more "Reithian" concept of a govern-ment-owned and -operated "public" service.[5] Advocates of each of these models or philosophies lobbied strenuously for their respective proposals. Each model found support inside the government, and one can trace the emerging debate as it developed, not only in the press, but within the government itself. The fiscally conservative Department of Finance was horrified at the prospect of a government-owned public service being created, as it predicted a burdensome financial cost to the nation. Finance insisted that a television service should only be established with the clear understanding that no cost should fall on the Exchequer. The Department of Finance would have preferred to see a commercial service modeled on the Independent Television Network in the United Kingdom or even the commercial networks in the United States.

The Department of Posts and Telegraphs was already heavily involved in Irish telecommunications, as it was responsible for the state's national radio service, Radio Eireann. This department would play a significant role in deciding the form of a national television service. Posts and Telegraphs advocated the establishment of television as a "public service," loosely based on the British Broadcasting Corporation. This department maintained that it was imperative, for cultural as well as political reasons, that television be government-owned and -operated. These two powerful departments were lined up on opposite sides of this issue; both would engage in frequent skirmishes in trying to influence the government. Internal government memos that endorsed one alternative or the other offer valuable insight into the machinations and power struggles that ensued within the various national governments throughout the 1950s, as individual ministers and departments pressed their views on governments that were paralyzed by indecision. The arguments culminated in a forum set up by the state to allow those parties interested in television to articulate their proposals and concerns before an official government commission. The Television Commission was established in 1958 to examine the question of how the medium should be introduced into the country. The creation of the commission also provided the de Valera government with important breathing space as it allowed a volatile question to be relegated to a council that deliberated for over a year and called dozens of witnesses before issuing a confused and contradictory final report.

What remained constant throughout the debate, and indeed through the life of the Television Commission, was the basic question of how a national television service should be structured. This was the critical issue that had to be decided, as the adoption of either an independent commercial service or a government-owned public service would determine the content of programs, which was the paramount issue of the debate. Posts and Telegraphs argued that a public service following the model of the British Broadcasting Corporation (BBC) could be an important asset to the nation, as it would broadcast educational and cultural programs that would uplift and enlighten citizens. The seemingly insurmountable obstacle to this type of service was cost. The initial investment for equipment and the day-to-day operating expenses to run a national television service were judged as simply too great for an underdeveloped nation such as Ireland. The alternative was to grant an exclusive license to an independent contractor that would broadcast programs of its own choosing and with the explicit goal of making a profit. These two opposing concepts provided the terrain on which the battle over television would be fought. This dialectical approach might seem somewhat superficial at first, but the Irish television service that emerged in 1960 was a synthesis of these opposing ideas, as it borrowed from both to produce what might be described as an Irish solution to an Irish problem. What follows is an exploration of the process that led to the establishment of a national television service in 1960. The political, cultural, and social issues that were debated will be analyzed to examine how public policy evolved, and how this helped shape the service that opened on New Year's Eve 1961. This public policy determined the substance and character of Irish television as it exists today.

NOTES

1. *Irish Times*, January 1, 1962.

2. Ibid. Although uncomfortable with the unfolding Irish television service, de Valera had proven quite astute in exploiting the medium of radio. Once Fianna Fail formed its first government in 1932 de Valera took to the air waves to address the Irish nation and listeners in the United States. One could argue that some of his most famous speeches were broadcast by Radio Eireann. These would include, *The Ireland That We Dreamed Of*, broadcast on St. Patrick's Day 1943 and his reply to Winston Churchill's attack on Irish neutrality at the conclusion of World War II, *National Thanksgiving*, May 16, 1945. (See *Speeches and Statements by Eamon de Valera 1917–1973*, edited by Maurice Moynihan, Gill and Macmillan, Dublin 1980).

3. Ronan Fanning, *Independent Ireland* (Dublin: Helicon, 1983), pp. 199–200.

4. Luke Gibbons, "From Kitchen Sink to Soap," in *Television and Irish Society*, ed. Martin McLoone and John MacMahon (Dublin: Radio Telefis Eireann, 1984), p. 21.

5. John Reith was the first Director General at the BBC. He advocated radio as a tool for broadcasting educational and cultural programs and not simply as a source of entertainment.

Irish Television

CHAPTER 1

The Department of Finance, Radio Eireann, and the Origins of Irish Television

Before further examining television in Ireland, it is necessary to review the rather unique history of Ireland's national radio service. This is required to understand how Radio Eireann's experience influenced the development of the television service. A survey of the development of electronic communications in Ireland begins, appropriately enough, with the 1916 Easter Rebellion. The Canadian "godfather" of media studies, Marshall McLuhan, has pointed out the role Irish rebels played in the development of radio as a means of mass communications in his 1964 book, *Understanding Media*. He explained that 1916 "was the year of the Irish Easter rebellion and of the first radio broadcast. Wireless had already been used on ships as ship to shore 'telegraph.' The Irish rebels used a ship's wireless to make, not a point-to-point message, but a diffused broadcast in the hope of getting word out to some ship that would relay their story to the American press."[1]

The rebels, with a great deal of foresight and imagination, acted to break the British monopoly on communication and get word to America about the rebellion. In the years following their innovative broadcast, radio developed rapidly, especially in the United States and Britain. However, it would be ten years before Ireland would have a radio service of its own. As the 1920s progressed, "listening in" to the wireless became increasingly popular in the United States and Britain. The receiving sets, though primitive, were cheap, and radio quickly became a medium available to the masses. While radio became increasingly popular in the United States and Britain, the unrest that enveloped Ireland during this period retarded the growth of radio there. In 1922, when the British Broadcasting Company was established, Ireland was in the midst of a tragic civil war.

Once hostilities subsided, the government began to address the question of how to set up a radio service. In many ways, the Irish civil service had remained substantially unchanged, despite the withdrawal of the British.[2] In the United Kingdom, the Post Office was responsible for licensing radio transmitters. Its Irish counterpart also assumed the role of granting licenses, and by default, overseeing the development of an emerging media.

In November 1923, five months after the cessation of civil war hostilities, the Postmaster General, James Joseph Walsh, circulated a White Paper prepared by his department that proposed the establishment of a broadcasting station in the Irish Free State. During the civil war, Walsh had received several proposals from broadcasting firms that were interested in setting up stations in Ireland. Walsh had delayed action on these proposals while the civil war raged. In fact, the Free State Government ordered that all transmitters and receivers be confiscated by the Post Office until hostilities ceased.

Walsh's White Paper proposed the creation of a national radio service modeled on the British Broadcasting Company. It suggested that the applicants who had already approached the government merge into a consortium to form the Irish Broadcasting Company (IBC). Walsh later testified as to the influence of the BBC and explained that although the proposed IBC was not an exact copy of the British organization, "it follows as closely as circumstances will permit on the English model."[3] Walsh revealed that he and his advisers found the BBC an attractive and proven prototype on which to base the IBC. The Irish Post Office had developed a close working relationship with its British counterpart since the establishment of the Irish Free State. In these circumstances, it is not surprising that Walsh and his staff would look to the British Post Office and the BBC when outlining a blueprint for an Irish service.

However, there were serious differences between the companies that drew together to form the BBC and the proposed members of the IBC. The BBC was comprised of a number of large companies with considerable experience in broadcasting and substantial assets. The constituent companies included manufacturers of radio equipment as well as several companies that had been in the broadcast business for a number of years. The Irish companies mentioned in the White Paper were not abundantly qualified in the field of broadcasting. In fact, two were formed by investors interested only in exploiting an Irish radio service as a profit-making enterprise.

Walsh's White Paper created a great deal of controversy when it was circulated in the Dail.* The deputies refused to sanction the document and were clearly not interested in rushing legislation through the Dail to establish a service along the lines proposed by the Postmaster General. Allowing private enterprise to operate a monopoly in the state was a concept that received little support from the deputies. Radio was recognized as a medium with tremendous potential to influence society. Therefore, members of the Dail demanded that the state have strict control over a national radio service. After some debate it was agreed that a committee would be established to investigate Walsh's proposal. This committee was comprised of Dail members and empowered to consider alternatives to the Post Office White Paper. The committee was ordered to conduct a thorough investigation and report to the Dail with a firm recommendation as to how radio could best be brought to Ireland.

When the committee met, a letter to the Postmaster General surfaced from Andrew Belton, a disgruntled business associate of Deputy Darrell Figgis. Belton, whose company was a constituent member of the Irish Broadcasting Company, had written to James Joseph (J. J.) Walsh stating that Figgis had promised to use his influence to assure Belton's company a place in the proposed IBC. Deputy Darrell Figgis, an independent member of the Dail, was accused by his former business partner of what today we might call "influence peddling." Figgis denied the charge, and while he was never censured by the government, the affair did influence the outcome of the committee's work. The fact that he had sought, and been awarded, a place on the committee complicated matters for Figgis. As the proceedings of the committee were not open to the public, rumors of a scandal swept through the press allegedly involving the entire IBC.

To further confound matters for the IBC and Walsh's White Paper, allegations surfaced that questioned the political agenda of both Figgis and Belton. Darrell Figgis strenuously denied the allegations and wrote to President William Cosgrave, denouncing his former business partner as an untrustworthy opportunist and an agent of British interests in Ireland. The Figgis-Belton affair alienated many members of the committee, not only from the proposed IBC, but from the general notion of a privately owned and operated radio service. The deputies were appalled at the prospect of a national service being operated by a tainted group with strong British connections.

---

*Dail is an Irish word that means assembly or parliament. The Irish Dail was the equivalent of the British House of Commons.

The Figgis-Belton episode was not the only factor that estranged the committee from the concept of privately owned commercial radio. Members of the committee were concerned with the type of programs such a service might produce or transmit. Many were impressed with the power of the new medium and keenly interested in how the service would fit into the ideological framework of the Irish Free State. A number of groups recognized that it would be important to control the type of social, political, and cultural programs that would emanate from an Irish service. The Gaelic League lobbied for a national radio service that would help restore the native language, and it found support from educators and intellectuals as well as politicians, who demanded that radio be used as a means of meeting the elusive goals of official government policy. Many of these groups emphasized the need to allow a unique Gaelic culture to flourish unfettered from the oppressive domination of the "foreigner."

One must remember the historical context within which the debate was taking place. The Irish Free State in 1925 was an insecure entity, having survived a war of independence and a civil conflict that had caused a great deal of bitterness and divisiveness within the newly established state. The government of William Cosgrave portrayed itself as an administration committed to the ideals that had been articulated by cultural nationalists such as Patrick Pearse and Douglas Hyde. The government felt insecure on what was generally termed the "national question," having accepted a treaty that partitioned the nation and acquiesced to a status that differed from the cherished republic advocated by nationalists since 1798. One area where it could exhibit its commitment to embracing a unique national identity was a policy of preserving an ill-defined "Irishness."

The final report of the Committee on Wireless Broadcasting, issued in March 1924, was a 600-page tome that contained most of the testimony presented to the committee. The committee recommended that a service be established that would be state-owned and operated. It suggested that the Post Office be responsible for the new state-owned monopoly, which would be financed by a combination of license fees, taxes on the import of receivers, and a limited amount of commercial broadcasting.

The government quickly agreed with the recommendations of the committee and established a state-owned and -operated radio service. In doing so, the model of the BBC was emulated. Although it was realized that the Irish service would require financial support from commercial advertisers, the concept of radio as a public service was accepted. A modified public service model was employed to try and ensure that Irish radio would reflect the unique culture of Ireland and not be dominated by British commercial interests.

It is interesting to note the contradiction here. While the Irish government feared that allowing a commercial service to be established would merely extend British influence in the country, the solution that was adopted was to copy the structure of the British Broadcasting Company. In this regard, the BBC was happy to encourage and assist the Irish service. The director general of the BBC, J.C.W. Reith, attended the interviews of prospective candidates for the job of director of the Irish station. It is obvious that the desires of the BBC were compatible with those of the Irish Free State.[4] Both were interested in encouraging the development of a stable state that would not be susceptible to radical republicanism. The BBC remained very interested in influencing the development of radio and television in Ireland. The persistent efforts of the British service to protect and extend its political, social and cultural hegemony will be chronicled in later chapters.

The reaction to the government decision of the Postmaster General, J. J. Walsh, illustrates the lack of enthusiasm his department had for administering a radio service. He warned the Dail, "If the house determines that the Post Office must differentiate between rival organ grinders, rival tenors and people of that kind and even rival politicians who want to get control and preferential treatment, we will be able to do it at a price and it will be a very dear price."[5] Walsh strenuously objected to the government's decision, as he believed that his department would not be able to provide a satisfactory national radio service. He knew that the Post Office was ill-suited to assume responsibility for the daunting task of setting up and maintaining such a service. He also understood that the civil service would have difficulties creating programs, whether for the purpose of entertaining or educating listeners. It is clear he was disappointed that his own proposal had failed and that his testimony before the Committee on Wireless Broadcasting had been ignored. He feared the service would never become viable if it was to be owned and operated by the government. Walsh was convinced that Irish radio would falter and that its failure would reflect poorly on the government and his department.

Walsh's objections were to prove prophetic as the service struggled as a state-owned and -operated entity. Despite a number of impressive performances, most notably the first national broadcast, which covered the Eucharistic Congress in 1932, the service found it rough going. The Department of Finance was never impressed with the service and held back substantial funding, as it saw the radio station as a waste of scarce resources. Finance seemed to have nothing but contempt for Radio Eireann and adopted a hostile attitude toward the station that endured for many years. At the critical stage in the life of Irish radio, Earnest Blythe was both the Minister of Finance and the Minister of Posts and Telegraphs, a situation that was certainly not conducive to growth at the station. Blythe had never been impressed with the radio service and refused to divert scarce resources to the station. In fact, once Finance realized that the taxes being collected from the importation of receivers provided a good source of revenue, it intervened and collected the tax itself, thus refusing the radio station a critical source of revenue.

Irish radio stagnated as a result of the irrational organizational structure that had been imposed on it. The national radio service was intended to be a public service, which would serve the nation. However, the government refused to grant it adequate funds to attain this goal, which limited its ability to develop an audience that could enjoy popular and innovative programs. The fact that Irish radio was staffed by the civil service furthered the perception that the station was an unresponsive entity, unable to serve as a dynamic innovative source of entertainment and culture. The service that developed was underfunded, understaffed, and, one could argue, unpopular. It is clear that the decision taken by the government to have the Post Office operate the service, as well as the failure of the state to offer financial support, stunted the development of Irish radio. Surveys conducted well into the 1950s demonstrated that listeners consistently chose to tune into the British Broadcasting Corporation, American Armed Forces Radio, Radio Luxembourg and other European broadcasts rather than listen only to Radio Eireann.[6]

Radio Eireann was unpopular for other, more cultural reasons. The service committed itself to the revival of the Irish language. This noble, although futile, effort alienated many listeners, who switched the dial once broadcasts began to be transmitted in the native tongue. Many listeners believed the radio service had gone too far in this endeavor. One was the president, William Cosgrave who complained that the service had become a "vehicle for Irish Ireland propaganda."[7] Cosgrave's anxiety stemmed from what he saw as a general assumption that the service was "an Irish-Ireland institution and there is only abuse awaiting any criticism."[8] The radio service conducted its own surveys which illustrated that less than .5 percent of its listeners tuned into the Irish-language broadcasts. In the 1950s this number would decrease to a depressing .1 percent. In fact, the Post Office and Radio Eireann refused to publish the results of their polls despite demands made in the Dail and the national press. The results were simply too embarrassing.

The service did start to improve in anticipation of the creation of a shortwave broadcasting station that would aim its programs at the east coast of the United States. Desmond Fisher, who has written on the structure of Irish radio, maintains that although the plans for the station were abandoned in 1948, the preparation had a positive effect on the development of the service.[9] An example can be seen in the manner in which news was collected and disseminated by Radio Eireann. Since its inception, the service had "lifted" much of its news material from newspapers and other radio stations. However, the practice ceased with the development of a professional news staff, which was established by 1950. Moreover, it was not until the 1950s that the service began to enjoy a limited degree of independence.

The troubled history of Radio Eireann was not lost on advocates of a national television service. Indeed, many of the controversial issues that defined the 1950s debate over television recalled earlier conflicts involving radio broadcasting in Ireland. The experience of Radio Eireann proved a warning to many both inside and outside government that a new television service would not succeed if it followed the example of the stillborn radio service.

As the debate over television developed, a number of key individuals emerged who exerted a great deal of influence on government policy. Posts and Telegraphs, the department in charge of the nation's radio service, was in a position to influence the government as this debate evolved. The most important person in that department was Leon O'Broin, who as Secretary for Posts and Telegraphs was heavily involved in the development of government policy. The Director of Radio Eireann during the 1950s, Maurice Gorham, was another key figure. Gorham had worked at the BBC and had been responsible for getting BBC television back on the air after the war. A close confidant of O'Broin, he helped the secretary investigate television throughout the decade. Both men shared the same broad Reithian philosophy concerning the role of broadcasting, and both firmly believed in the concept of public service television.

Television had caught the interest of the Department of Posts and Telegraphs as early as 1950. In that year, Leon O'Broin, acting on his own initiative, established an informal committee within his department to investigate the new medium. This group later became the more formal Television Committee, which reported to the government on a number of occasions and influenced the state's emerging television policy. In January 1950, O'Broin wrote to the Department of Finance, seeking funds to purchase a television receiver to allow his committee to observe broadcasts emanating from Britain. O'Broin's request initiated a troublesome relationship between Posts and Telegraphs and Finance over the question of television broadcasting. Throughout most of the 1950s, Finance adopted a hostile attitude toward the establishment of a national television service, fearing the cost that would be incurred by the government in any such venture.

In writing to Finance, O'Broin pointed out that since the end of the war, television had progressed rapidly in Britain, France, and the United States. He noted that television was expanding quickly to other less developed countries and that questions about the new medium were being brought up in the Dail. He contended that his department should initiate research on the subject, arguing, "The question of providing a public television service in this country will have to be given serious consideration before long."[10]

It should be noted here that O'Broin and his associates referred specifically to "*public* television." This is significant as it demonstrates that the secretary and his associates were referring to a specific type of television; a state-owned service that, no matter how ill-defined, was not a private commercial entity. This bias toward public television was not missed by the Department of Finance, which greatly feared the prospect of a project that would require public financing.

O'Broin argued that the British government had made a commitment to expand the range of television and was about to open a new station at Sutton Coldfield in the British Midlands. When the BBC expansion was complete, he explained, there would be nine broadcasting stations in Britain and one in Northern Ireland. Given these developments, he maintained, "Public opinion will press strongly for the erection of a Television Station."[11] It was noted that signals from the new transmitter at Sutton Coldfield could, under the right conditions, be received in the Dublin area. O'Broin predicted that the new station would increase significantly the number of Irish homes able to pick up British transmissions.

O'Broin contended that under these circumstances, his department should receive permission to purchase a television receiver. This would enable engineers at Posts and Telegraphs to measure the range of the new Sutton Coldfield station and allow his minister to provide authoritative replies to inquiries made in the Dail about the reception of the BBC. The memo to Finance concluded by formally requesting a sum of £180 to purchase a television and an aerial.

O'Broin's request was greeted with a great deal of suspicion and skepticism at the Department of Finance. One internal memo, excerpted here, provides insight into the thinking of the department when the issue of television was under consideration. It also provides a view of the embryonic policy that, given the history of Finance and its opinion of broadcasting in general, is not surprising.

It is difficult to have any patience with Mr. O'Broin's minute . . . or indeed to take it seriously. It is extraordinary to find so little appreciation for the Government's desire for economy and still more extraordinary . . . to see a proposal to spend money, even £180, on a Television receiver. . . . If this objection were overcome it would still be ridiculous to think of a Television Service in a country which has manifested no interest in it and whose people would probably be opposed to the spending of considerable sums of public money on such a luxury, available, of course, to a very limited number because of geographical and financial reasons. Mr. O'Broin can be quite certain that, apart for himself and the Commercial Radio Suppliers (who would see in an Irish Television Service further opportunities of enriching themselves), Television is a long way off here.[12]

The hostility displayed in this early memo demonstrates that whenever the subject turned to television, relations between these two departments would become quite tense. This was especially true when funds were being requested or mention was made of a "public service" entity that would involve state expenditure. It should be noted that terms such as "extraordinary" and "ridiculous" would continue to characterize the rhetoric of Finance when the question of Irish television was being discussed. The term *luxury service* would be employed throughout the 1950s by Finance to emphasize the contempt it held for the concept of a service that would require public financing.

A formal response was sent to O'Broin in February 1950 by Sean Moynihan, an assistant secretary at the Department of Finance. Moynihan advised O'Broin that his request had been denied and that the Minister of Finance, Patrick McGilligan, was not interested in supporting television research. Finance did not want to make any gestures that might suggest "the government was sympathetically disposed to the introduction of a luxury service such as television, which is known to be so costly. . . . [McGilligan] would accordingly be opposed, on financial grounds, not merely to a Television Service proper but to expenditure associated with television research."[13] In regard to questions concerning television that arose in the Dail, Finance suggested that the best way to answer any queries would be to state that the government was not prepared even to consider the establishment of a television service, given the cost that would be involved.

O'Broin was not intimidated by this response and quickly demonstrated that he would not back down. He wrote back to Finance asking that his request be reconsidered. The secretary maintained that his department was simply asking to spend a modest amount of money to purchase a television set in order to observe a new form of media that would have a tremendous impact on the country. He argued that the proposed tests would allow the Minister of Posts and Telegraphs to respond intelligently to queries that were being raised in the Dail. O'Broin explained that private manufacturers of communications equipment in Ireland had started to conduct tests of their own to try and determine whether television signals, emanating from Britain, could be received in a dependable manner. He also pointed out that the BBC was scheduled to open a transmitter in Northern Ireland in 1951. The secretary tried to convince Finance that television was an inevitable fact of modern life and that it was in the interest of the state to prepare for it.

Speaking quite frankly there is no use sticking our heads in the sand . . . and pretending that we shall escape the storm by simply saying and doing nothing. Television is coming as surely and as generally as sound broadcasting came and we must face up to that fact as most other countries in Europe are doing by experimentation or preparation of some sort."[14]

O'Broin's memo had its intended effect, as the Department of Finance reconsidered the matter and reluctantly reversed its position. Finance had determined that the request was not as unreasonable as it first appeared and that the state would benefit from the requested research. In writing to his minister, Sean Moynihan pointed out that O'Broin had a valid point in arguing that the government should be informed of developments in television. In suggesting that Finance modify its position, he contended that the most recent communication from O'Broin demonstrated a sincere request to initiate valuable research. He concluded, "We know now that it is not a mere stunt."[15] In April 1950, a reluctant Department of Finance authorized funds that enabled O'Broin's committee to buy a television set. This decision was communicated to O'Broin by Sean Moynihan, who told the secretary that Finance would grant special permission for the expenditure. O'Broin was also informed that Finance expected Posts and Telegraphs to refrain from requesting additional funds to conduct television research.

The episode illustrates both the determination of Posts and Telegraphs and the parsimonious, suspicious attitude of Finance. After all, O'Broin had merely requested £180 to purchase a television set. If he had any hopes of help or support coming from Finance, they were dashed by this initial confrontation. This seemingly rather petty argument initiated what would prove to be a troubled and acrimonious relationship between these departments over the question of television.

O'Broin's informal committee tried to keep abreast of developments in television around the world and endeavored to keep the government advised of recent improvements in a technology that was rapidly expanding. The committee knew that any truly comprehensive study of television and its implications would require the financial and political support of the government. One year after receiving sanction from Finance to purchase a television receiver, O'Broin submitted a formal *Memorandum for the Government* to both the Cabinet and the Taoiseach seeking permission to initiate a comprehensive inquiry into all aspects of television. The document, which was submitted in March 1951, argued that the state should prepare the way for the inevitable introduction of television into Ireland. The Cabinet was urged to develop a coherent policy that would enable the nation to be ready for the new medium. The memo explained that the rapid development of television in Britain had been encouraged by the British government and that this would have a direct impact on Ireland in the very near future. The Cabinet was told that the British government would continue to increase the range of the BBC and that it planned to build a station in Belfast.

The memo asked that O'Broin's informal committee be allowed to become a formal investigative body, which would examine both the programming and technical aspects of television broadcasting. O'Broin asked the Cabinet to provide the financial and political support that, he asserted, was necessary for his committee to successfully complete the proposed research. It is interesting to note the mention of Belfast gaining a station. Later, when trying to persuade the government to build a television service, O'Broin would return to this point. The prospect of a British station broadcasting into the Irish Republic caused a great amount of discomfort to the government. As an early advocate of Irish television, the secretary did not hesitate to exploit this sensitive issue which remained a difficult component of the television debate throughout the 1950s.

Although one can detect a preference for public service television, the submission to the Cabinet assumed that no matter what type of service was established, television would have some sort of a relationship with the Department of Posts and Telegraphs. As O'Broin's department had been involved with Radio Eireann since its inception, he believed it would naturally follow in the steps of its British counterpart and be responsible for a television service. O'Broin also pointed out that it would be up to his department to ensure that television abided by the international regulations governing the proper use of wavelengths.

O'Broin was very sensitive to international agreements that regulated broadcasts and the allocation of frequencies. The desire to avoid breaking international agreements would later be emphasized by the department in order to discredit private commercial proposals that challenged these European treaties. Since the inception of the Irish Free State, the government had endeavored to be seen as a scrupulous supporter of international law. Both the Fianna Fail and the Inter-Party governments throughout the 1950s were anxious to maintain and cultivate the image of Ireland as an upstanding member of the international community. The secretary knew this was an issue to which all governments would be sensitive and did not hesitate to bring it up when he believed Ireland's international reputation was in jeopardy.

O'Broin made it clear that he did not envision an Irish television service being operated by his department. There is little doubt that the experience gained by his department in running the national radio service influenced his attitude toward any relationship that television would have with Posts and Telegraphs. The secretary, like James Joseph Walsh before him in 1925, was not enthusiastic about the prospect of his department running a broadcasting service, in this case television. In spite of this disclaimer, the Department of Finance equated "public service" with an expensive undertaking operated by Posts and Telegraphs. Finance remained obsessed with the issue of cost, fearing that government involvement in television would entail the spending of the scarce public funds it so prudently guarded.

The *Memorandum for the Government* addressed what would be the thorniest issue when it raised the question of the actual ownership and control of a service. It outlined four possible alternatives that it wanted to explore. These included ownership "1) by the state direct, 2) by a public corporation, 3) by private enterprise, 4) by having a combination of these methods, such as having the transmitters state-owned, but the programmes provided by private enterprise."[16]

It proposed that as part of this study, research be conducted abroad to examine how other countries were dealing with the advent of television technology. O'Broin wanted to send an engineer and a programming professional from Radio Eireann overseas to conduct this research. Although these two senior officials would study British and French television, he suggested that they might concentrate their efforts on smaller European nations, which had more in common with Ireland.

It is significant that O'Broin and his minister, James Everett,[17] had intentionally bypassed the Department of Finance by forwarding the document directly to the Taoiseach and Cabinet asking that the proposal be taken up at the Cabinet level.[18] Posts and Telegraphs had sent a copy of its memorandum to the Minister of Finance, but not before the document had been received by the Taoiseach and other government ministers. The desire to circumvent the Department of Finance demonstrates that O'Broin knew that his request would not be appreciated or supported by that department. The move was not lost on Finance, which realized that O'Broin would be a formidable foe who was not above trying to "go over the head" of the department. Commenting on the shortcut taken by O'Broin, Finance complained that their minister had been denied a chance to examine and comment on the *Memorandum for the Government* before it had gone to the Cabinet. Finance protested that O'Broin had violated established procedure and complained that these tactics had given "the proceedings an ugly look."[19]

The Department of Finance remained strongly opposed to the government becoming involved in what it considered to be the quagmire of television. Finance wrote to the Taoiseach and explained that it objected to any government involvement in television, including the proposed research that O'Broin was advocating. The Taoiseach, John A. Costello, was aware of the request for funds made by Posts and Telegraphs and one may reasonably surmise the growing tension between the two powerful departments. Posts and Telegraphs was required to withdraw the formal *Memorandum for the Government* and ordered to follow procedure by submitting a formal request for funds to Finance.

As one might expect, the response of Finance to O'Broin's request for research funding was not positive. Initially, Finance adopted the same posture it had taken on receiving O'Broin's earlier request to purchase a television receiver. The Minister of Finance responded that it would be premature to undertake any research that might imply that the government was preparing the way for the introduction of a "luxury service such as television."[20]

However, by making the Taoiseach and the Cabinet aware of his request, O'Broin had seized the initiative. Finance found itself on the defensive and was soon forced to reexamine its position. J. E. Twamley, a senior civil servant at the Department of Finance, reconsidered the request that had been made by Posts and Telegraphs. Although concerned about the costs that would be incurred in sending staff abroad, he suggested that conditional sanction be given to allow Posts and Telegraphs to complete the requested research. He advised Sean Moynihan that although sending staff abroad would consume scarce public funds, the research was important, as the government would eventually need detailed information concerning television.

Sean Moynihan agreed with Twamley and wrote to his minister, Patrick McGilligan, stating that it would be unwise to adopt a "blankly negative attitude" toward television and the request for research funding.[21] Citing the development of television in Britain, he argued that it would be prudent for Posts and Telegraphs to "be in a position to advise the Government when the need arises."[22] Moynihan suggested that McGilligan approve O'Broin's request with strict conditions to limit both the cost and scope of the proposed study. Both Twamley and Moynihan realized that the request made by Posts and Telegraphs was a reasonable one and that Finance needed to develop a more sophisticated strategy to try and contain the influence of Leon O'Broin.

Finance therefore focused on O'Broin's stated desire to investigate the cost associated with bringing television to Ireland. The department designed a policy that underscored the need for the state to avoid a financial commitment to television. The Minister of Finance understood that the efforts of his department needed to be directed toward minimizing the financial impact a service would have on the exchequer. Therefore, the policy of blanket opposition was modified as the department decided to try and curtail the proposed research by granting conditional permission to O'Broin and his committee. This change in policy was adopted without much enthusiasm. In agreeing with the recommendation of his assistants, Patrick McGilligan advised his staff, "With reluctance and great foreboding I approve Mr. Twamley's suggestions."[23]

Authorization was granted for O'Broin to initiate research, which would include sending staff abroad to study British and European systems. However, a number of strict conditions were imposed to try and limit the scope of the proposed research. One stipulation in particular caused O'Broin so much concern that he rejected the offer of funding extended by Finance. This concerned how "cost investigations" would be pursued. Finance wanted it understood from the start that the government should not become involved in funding a television service. Posts and Telegraphs was told that McGilligan had supported the research with "reluctance, [and had] directed that it should be emphasized that a Television service, if instituted, must pay its way without assistance from the Exchequer and that the costs investigation should proceed on that understanding."[24]

Finance did not want O'Broin to even consider the possibility of a state-run public service. It feared that if O'Broin succeeded in getting the proverbial foot in the door, he would endorse an expensive public service that would be operated by Posts and Telegraphs. O'Broin quickly determined that he could not accept the conditions laid out by McGilligan and denounced them as "virtually unworkable." In rejecting the conditional approval extended by Finance, O'Broin focused on the stipulation that the research be conducted with the understanding that television would not require the spending of public funds. "It is certain that the Post Office will not operate television and its only object in making this proposal was having to assist and save the Government from embarrassment by having expert information at hand when the inevitable pressure for television arises."[25]

The tone of O'Broin's memo illustrates the level of frustration felt toward Finance and the obstructionist policy he believed it had developed. The statement that his department was not interested in running a television station demonstrates his feeling that a government-owned public service should not be operated by his department. O'Broin did not see any contradiction in this position, as he envisioned a separate governmental entity that would operate a television service. However, Finance was unable to reconcile this claim with what it believed was O'Broin's desire to launch an expensive service that would be operated by his department.

O'Broin had recently received correspondence from the Dutch company Phillips, which had expressed an interest in building a television transmitter in Dublin for what were referred to as "experimental purposes." Phillips had also asked to be considered if and when the government decided to allow a television service to be established in the country. A copy of this letter was attached to O'Broin's reply to Finance, and the secretary asked that department

to be good enough to indicate the reply that should be sent to the inquiry. . . . The "reaction" of this Department to the query is that no television should start here until the Government is informed of all the factors. The factors cannot be ascertained without enquiry abroad and this Department is not prepared to undertake any such inquiry on the conditions laid down by you.[26]

O'Broin's response caused Finance to review once again its attitude toward television and to refine its position on what was quickly becoming a difficult subject. The primary concern of Finance remained the fear that scarce public funds would be wasted on what it regarded as a "luxury service." It was clear to Finance that O'Broin had in mind the creation of a public service that would be managed by Posts and Telegraphs and require substantial government funding. In a long internal memorandum, the department reviewed developments concerning television and the requests that had been made by Posts and Telegraphs. Finance examined past communications from O'Broin that proved what it considered was a clear bias in favor of a government-owned public service. It argued that O'Broin had

referred to "providing a public television service," and . . . contemplated strong public pressure for the erection of an Irish Television Station. These references clearly indicate the lines on which [Posts and Telegraphs] was then thinking. . . . The background, as it was in early 1950 is thus clear. . . . [Posts and Telegraphs] was toying with the idea of a public service.[27]

Finance was confused by what it regarded as mixed signals being transmitted by O'Broin. It recognized the preference the secretary had for a public service but equated this type of service with a television station that would be actually operated by his department. Finance was not convinced, despite O'Broin's disclaimer, that he did not want to operate a state-subsidized television service. Responding to the secretary's statement, Finance questioned O'Broin's sincerity and feared a hidden agenda.

Our experience of these expressions of opinion and undertakings from the Department of Posts and Telegraphs in broadcasting affairs is not . . . too happy, and I would not place too much reliance on what I regard as this new change of front. If the statement is genuine, TV would be robbed of many of its terrors so far as we are concerned.[28]

Finance recognized the value of the research that had been proposed but clearly feared that it would be used by O'Broin to advocate the establishment of a costly state-owned television service. The department predicted problems if the research was delayed and warned that in simply postponing the work, "the danger of having a state sponsored TV service under the Department of Posts and Telegraphs control would not be removed permanently. Mr. O'Broin's disclaimer may therefore have been expressed with the possibility that a TV service will eventually be thrust upon the Department of Posts and Telegraphs."[29]

Finance found itself in a difficult position. It supported the proposed research but did not want to encourage O'Broin to think he was gaining sanction to initiate a broad inquiry that might support the establishment of a government-funded television service. In spite of the disclaimer issued by O'Broin, Finance simply did not trust or believe the Secretary of Posts and Telegraphs. J. E. Twamley and Sean Moynihan debated how their department should react to O'Broin's position. It was decided that the ball would be placed back in O'Broin's court. "A way out of the present impasse would be to tell the Department of Posts and Telegraphs that this Department's attitude to the proposal has been altered by the disclaimer. . . . [W]e will see what can be done to reconcile our views with those of Posts and Telegraphs. This should not provoke another display of petulance, but one never knows!"[30]

O'Broin was told that given the statement that it was not the intent of his department to operate a national television service, Finance was now willing to come to an understanding with Posts and Telegraphs. Finance chose to interpret O'Broin's recent pronouncement as meaning that the state need not be concerned about becoming involved in operating a television service. Finance therefore declared irrelevant the question of how "cost considerations" would be investigated.

Posts and Telegraphs responded quickly to Finance and indicated that it was not prepared to back down on the question of "cost investigations." It is clear that at this early stage, the secretary did not wish to limit the scope of the proposed research and that he bitterly resented the obstructionist policies of Finance. He advised Finance that he understood "clearly that any study of television and any subsequent consideration of its complex problems, if undertaken by the Post Office, would have to be carried out with the maximum of criticism and the minimum of assistance so far as the Department of Finance is concerned. . . . [T]he proposal has now been withdrawn."[31] Finance was disturbed at O'Broin's response and perplexed by his recalcitrance, concluding that his "attitude [was] somewhat extraordinary."[32]

The Department of Finance had shown a willingness to try and come to an agreement with O'Broin. However, it was clear that any such accord would require O'Broin to acquiesce to its strict terms concerning costs. Finance remained focused on the question of cost, and McGilligan's March 1951 stipulation that Irish television could not rely on public funding would remain the paramount condition imposed by the department. This stipulation would succeed in keeping a native service out of Ireland for most of the decade.

In spite of the dispute with Finance, O'Broin and his committee began work researching television as had been outlined in their proposal. However the sending of staff abroad was delayed. The committee included Leon O'Broin, Maurice Gorham, the Director General of Radio Eireann, and an engineer at the national radio service, T. J. Monahan. Their work culminated in two reports, the first of which took the form of a thirty-nine-page interim report, which was issued in September 1953. However, before examining the work of this committee, it is important to note certain developments outside government that influenced the emerging debate about television.

While O'Broin's committee met, pressure continued to be applied on the government to come to a decision on television. One interest group that kept the pressure on the government was comprised of manufacturers and retailers. As had been the case with radio in the 1920s, the 1950s saw pressure exerted by those who stood to profit the most from an expanded market. Raymond Williams has pointed out in *Television, Technology and Cultural Form* that manufacturers in both the United States and Britain were powerful pressure groups behind these developing technologies.[33] This was also true in Ireland, where the voice of the manufacturers and retailers was the *Irish Radio and Electrical Journal*. This publication covered recent developments in the electronics industry and offered opinions on related topics. The televisions available on the Irish market were, for the most part, manufactured in Britain. A number of these British manufacturers established Irish subsidiaries and expressed an interest in building assembly plants in Ireland once a station began broadcasting. One such British manufacturer was the Pye Company, which opened an Irish subsidiary, Pye Ireland Limited (Ltd.).

The Chairman of Pye Ireland Ltd. advocated the building of an Irish television service as early as the summer of 1950. In June of that year, Chairman C. O. Stanley addressed a company meeting, an event covered by the *Irish Independent* and followed closely by the government. The chairman stated that he had recently traveled throughout the United States, Europe, and Britain studying television, and he had come to the conclusion that television should be established in Ireland as soon as possible. He emphasized that "when a station operates in Northern Ireland certain large sections of our population here will be able to receive vision programmes. This . . . will create a great deal of discontent amongst the people who want to see television from their own Irish station and cannot."[34] His speech concluded with a call for the prompt building of a small Dublin based station. In addressing the issue of prohibitive program costs, Stanley stated that imported features could supplement a native service. No details were provided of how the service would be organized or financed. The company was simply interested in creating a market for its goods.

Manufacturers realized that the public had to be prodded to demand a service. However, one did not have to simply wait for pressure to grow by relying only on British "fallout" signals as in addition, the appetite of the public was whetted by trade shows and television demonstrations that would target potential customers in the Dublin area.

In April 1951, the first television exposition was held in conjunction with the Spring Show of the Royal Dublin Society (RDS).* Financed by Pye Ireland Ltd., the presentation offered the first public demonstration of television in the Irish Republic. This event and subsequent exhibits proved very popular and received a great deal of attention in the press. At the opening of the show, the chairman of Pye Ireland Ltd., C. O. Stanley, once again renewed his call for the building of a television station in the Dublin area. A correspondent for the *Irish Times* reported, "He did not think that one should have any ambitious scheme, but if, for £40,000 or £50,000, they could have a transmitter in Dublin, with its educational and entertainment value, and its contribution to the arts, they would be offering something to the young people to become acquainted with the many-sided activities that existed in the television world."[35] Stanley told the audience, which included the Minister for Posts and Telegraphs, James Everett, that television could educate "millions" and add something positive to the lives of Irish people.

The television exhibit at the Royal Dublin Society was described by the press as a tremendous success. National dailies reported that thousands of people had attended the exhibition and that the line for admittance stretched some seventy-five yards. The demonstration, coupled with the published address of the chairman of Pye Ireland, created renewed interest in television, which was expressed in the press as well as in the Dail. The *Irish Times* was clearly impressed by both the show at the RDS and Stanley's speech. An editorial argued that the official government position regarding television was now open to question. While in the past the state had simply maintained that cost precluded the building of an Irish station, Stanley's speech had challenged this position. The chairman of Pye Ireland had announced that Ireland could have a television station for as little as £40,000. "Now the fat is properly in the fire; for if, Mr. Stanley's figures are not at fault—and he is a person of the highest eminence in the radio and 'TV' world—the question of expenses ceases to be a hindrance, and there is no reason why a modest station—or even two or three modest stations—should not be set up in the near future."[36]

In the Dail, Minister for Posts and Telegraphs James Everett was asked by Deputy Maurice Dockrell what plans the government had concerning television. Deputy Dockrell referred to the interest generated by the television show at the RDS and asked if the government had made any plans to bring television to Ireland. Everett explained that his department had no

*The RDS was founded in 1731 as an organization dedicated to the arts and sciences. Its headquarters in Dublin remains a center for exhibitions, concerts, and shows.

plans to bring television to the country.[37] The answer of the minister would become an all-too-familiar refrain that would disappoint supporters of television for years to come. While the government may have been made uncomfortable by Stanley's pronouncements, and especially his emphasis on the reception of British programs in the country, it did not respond to his call for building a station. The Department of Finance was clearly not impressed, referring caustically to "the clamour of manufacturers [e.g., Pye Ltd.], whose sole interest is, of course, their own enrichment."[38]

In January 1952, the question of television broadcasting came up again in the Dail. This time, the former Minister of Posts and Telegraphs, Deputy James Everett, questioned Erskine Childers, the new minister, about the status of television in the Republic. In doing so, he highlighted an aspect of television that caused a great deal of discomfort to the government: he asked "whether [Childers was] aware that in districts along the east coast television broadcasts are being received from another country and whether, in view of the cumulative damaging effect which these broadcasts may have on our national culture, he [would] take the necessary steps to introduce television broadcasting in the Republic of Ireland with a minimum of delay."[39]

Childers replied that he knew of the broadcasts that were being received along the east coast. He emphasized that it was his belief that the reception was sporadic and limited to a small number of homes. He continued by stating that due to the cost of setting up a service, "television in this country will not be practicable for a number of years."[40]

The subject of television continued to haunt the government and created pressure for the state to develop a coherent policy. In 1953 the area receiving what were termed fallout signals expanded with the introduction of BBC Northern Ireland. In May the BBC began broadcasting from a small temporary transmitter in Belfast. This enabled viewers in Northern Ireland and part of the Irish Republic to witness the coronation of Elizabeth II, a fact that was certainly not lost on the Irish government. The timing of the station's opening was intentional and certainly helped promote the sales of televisions and licences in Northern Ireland. It should be pointed out that it was clear from the start that the Belfast station would be a relay service and would not produce its own material.[41] The BBC station in Northern Ireland did not provide its own programs until 1959. In that year, studio facilities were built that allowed the first weekly program, *Studio Eight*, to be produced and broadcast from Belfast.

Shortly after the Belfast station began broadcasting, the *Irish Times* and the *Irish Independent* began publishing the schedules of BBC television.

The fact that there was a "foreign" service broadcasting into the Irish Republic was a constant reminder that television was a problematic issue that would not fade away. The political and cultural implications of the situation were not lost on the government or on parties advocating the establishment of a national television service in Ireland.

One of the earliest and more interesting proposals supporting the establishment of a television service was broadcast by Eric Boden on Radio Eireann in February 1953.[42] Boden had been employed by Radio Eireann as the host of a popular radio program and described himself as a "television enthusiast." His proposal was not a formal submission but an attempt to challenge the prevailing sense of apathy that permeated the government. He tried to debunk the "official" reasons that had been used to explain why Ireland could not afford a service. Boden argued that with the support of the state, a national service could be up and running in one year. Moreover, like many other advocates of television, he believed the country could not afford to delay its introduction.

Boden contended that a properly managed television station would serve the nation and have a positive impact on Irish society. He argued that television could be exploited to promote the work of the church and spread the word of God throughout the country. This was an aspect of the medium that he believed had not received adequate attention. His emphasis on the evangelical possibilities of television implied that it would be both irreligious and immoral for any God-fearing Irish Catholic to oppose his appeal. He asserted that a national television service was needed to fill the airwaves with programs that would reach out to troubled souls and enhance Christ's message.

Boden addressed a number of issues that would dominate the debate on television for years to come. His comments on television programming and the role the church might play in a national service were topics that would create a great deal of controversy in Irish society beyond the service's initial broadcast. It would be easy to dismiss Boden, as his ideas at times appear bizarre.[43] This would be a mistake. His ideas caught the attention of the Department of the Taoiseach, and the fact that he was able to use a national platform, the radio service, to articulate his concerns illustrates that he was taken quite seriously. His thoughts helped highlight some of the more problematic issues created by television and contributed to the growing debate.

In September 1953, Posts and Telegraphs presented to the government a document titled, *The Interim Report of the Television Committee*. The report was kept secret, not only from the general public, but also from members of Dail Eireann. O'Broin regarded the document as much too sensitive to be shared with the public or deputies in the Dail and was very concerned that the report would be exploited by political or commercial interests intent on pursuing a particular agenda. The Television Committee included in the report its own proposal for an Irish television service. As might be expected, the committee strongly endorsed the concept of public service television as opposed to a private, commercial enterprise. The prediction of the Department of Finance, that O'Broin would support such a service, had been proved correct. The *Interim Report* outlined all the options that were available to the government and endorsed its own plan as the only option capable of adequately serving the nation.

The committee made it clear that in their view, television could have a positive effect on the nation if it was properly exploited. In commenting on the power of the medium, one can sense the same discomfort that would be expressed by President de Valera in a speech that opened the service in 1961. "While it is probably true that television is not essential to our national life, it is nevertheless an invention of enormous potentiality for good as well as evil and, if we could afford on financial grounds to have it, the proper course would be to take the invention and exploit it, under proper control."[44]

The report noted that if and when a decision was made to introduce television, the structure and form of the service would have to be determined. The options available were described as either a government-financed public service or a commercial entity that would be privately owned. According to the report, it was necessary to determine which of the two options would best satisfy the "primary objects of television," which were defined as the ability to entertain, inform, and educate an audience. The committee reported that in a small nation such as Ireland, there was room for only one television station; therefore, the service that was to be established would have to be a monopoly. Such a service, according to the committee, would be very powerful and naturally must be a carefully organized enterprise.

Under these exceptional circumstances, the committee concluded that television would have to be a government-owned public service. The key issue for the committee was one of control. A public service owned and operated by the state would be able to regulate what was broadcast. On the other hand, in the opinion of the committee, a privately owned commercial service, by its very nature, would not commit itself to meeting high standards, especially in the areas of education and culture.

It would inevitably seek to make money for its owners by providing widely popular programmes at the lowest possible cost, and the chief source of such programmes would be British, American and other foreign television . . . films. The station would presumably depend for its income on advertisers, who would also want to obtain a bulk audience at the lowest possible cost per viewer per minute.[45]

The committee believed that a privately owned commercial service could easily become a force for evil. The report argued that a television station should seek to avoid "foreign" influences that might contaminate what was regarded as the unique culture of the nation. Commercial television was seen as a foreign intrusion that would disrupt the isolation in which the country had been immersed since at least the 1930s. Ireland in 1953 was still a nation very much secluded from the outside world. In this report, one can see either a perceptive committee predicting the perils of what would later be termed "cultural imperialism" or, perhaps, a reactionary clique of bureaucrats afraid to expose an unrealistic, idealized version of Ireland to what was perceived as the corrupt and decadent modern world. Like radio before it, television was viewed as a medium that was simply too important to be trusted to a private company. A commercial service would not, according to the committee, promote and celebrate Irish culture but would simply broadcast popular foreign programs that would undermine a frail national heritage.

The influence of the British Broadcasting Corporation can be seen in the advocacy of a public service. It should be remembered that O'Broin admired and respected Maurice Gorham, a member of the Television Committee and the Director General of Radio Eireann. Gorham had worked for the BBC before accepting the post at Radio Eireann and fully supported the concept of public service radio and television. O'Broin's own background was one that would lead him to favor a service that shared the broad Reithean philosophy of the BBC. His son, Emir, has recalled his family gathered by the radio listening, not only to BBC broadcasts, but also to those other European stations that were committed to public service broadcasting.[46]

The Television Committee realized the financial difficulties inherent in establishing a public television service. Consequently, its report maintained that because of its prohibitive cost, television would have to wait before making its debut in Ireland. In spite of the desirability of a public service, the committee reported, "It appears impracticable at present on strictly financial grounds."[47]

However, there were other important considerations to be contemplated according to the report. The committee first explained that it was not in a position to evaluate the political ramifications of delaying the introduction of a television service. Nevertheless, it did not hesitate to emphasize a troublesome consequence of this policy of postponement. It argued that government would have to take into consideration "national prestige, with which may be coupled the attitude to be adopted towards the Six-County area in which television is already a reality."[48] Because the nation's dignity was at stake, the committee explained that it had drawn up a scheme that would establish an Irish station at the lowest possible cost.

This is a very telling passage. It is interesting to note that the committee, which was comprised of three civil servants, initially maintained that political considerations were beyond its scope, stating that it would be inappropriate for the Television Committee to comment on sensitive political matters. After mentioning that it was in no position to evaluate the political repercussions of a policy of procrastination, O'Broin and his associates cited "other grounds" to justify the promotion of a service that it believed the government should adopt. The committee was well aware that there were sensitive political issues involved in simply delaying the introduction of television to Ireland. It recognized that these problems caused a great deal of consternation in government circles and might be exploited to gain support for the type of service that the committee advocated.

Perhaps the best financial argument against the creation of a television service was not all that convincing when national prestige was at stake. The reference to television broadcasting from Northern Ireland can be construed as an attempt to embarrass the government into action. It was hoped that in this instance, the Cabinet would ignore the orthodox economic conservatism articulated by the Department of Finance and commit itself to building a television service. Because television was up and running in the "Six Counties," the committee felt that it was necessary to provide a detailed proposal to bring television to the Republic. The committee had touched on, and would exploit, a very sensitive issue in addressing television coming to Northern Ireland.

The fact that televisions in the Republic could receive British broadcasts from Belfast created a dilemma for a government that continued to pay lip service to the cherished ideal of unification. The Irish Constitution and the Irish Government continued to claim jurisdiction over the six counties that comprised Northern Ireland. A perception that the six counties might be experiencing a higher standard of living than the Republic presented another difficulty for the Irish Government. The prospect of the nation's lost "fourth green field" enjoying a television service as a British province, while citizens of the south could only receive "fallout" signals from these broadcasts, was emphasized by the Television Committee.

The committee preferred the establishment of a pure public service that would follow the structure of BBC television and cover the entire state. However, it understood that given the financial constraints that restricted the nation's spending, this was not a feasible option. The Television Committee proposed a hybrid of sorts, a state-owned public service that could avail itself of income by adopting a commercial format. This, of course, was a significant departure from the model of BBC television and recalled instead the commercial structure of Radio Eireann.

The service the committee outlined indeed seemed to resemble the organization of Radio Eireann, however, the similarities were superficial. The report argued that even a government-owned and -operated "public service" could be commercial in that it would accept advertising. This would enable the organization to have a source of revenue beyond the traditional license fee that served as income for the BBC. The most significant departure from the model of Radio Eireann was the call for the establishment of an independent authority to run the service. In the opinion of the committee, it was imperative that television have explicit statutory independence. This would free it from the constraints of both the civil service and the Department of Posts and Telegraphs. The committee envisioned an independent public corporation that would be responsible for both sound broadcasting and television.

The service outlined by the committee would not be a national one but rather would be limited to the metropolitan Dublin area. This decision contradicted a passage in the report that had dismissed such an option as untenable. However, the committee decided that the expense involved in building a station forced it to propose a very limited service. The committee maintained that a service for Cork could not be considered until experience had been gained in operating a Dublin station.

The Dublin station would be a small one, limited to broadcasting approximately eighteen hours a week, and would include what was described as "a varied and cultural programme, in harmony with the national aspirations of the people."[49] The service would need studios and facilities for outside broadcasts in order to transmit distinctly Irish programs and avoid relying on "canned" imports. However, the committee admitted that the service being proposed would be a very limited one and would be unable to broadcast a large amount of native material. It recognized that foreign programs and films would have to be employed. Therefore, the committee suggested that the BBC be approached as a source of programs in hopes that the British service might make material available to an Irish public service at a greatly reduced rate.

The committee realized that broadcasting BBC programs might create political problems. Thus, the report stated that while consideration had been given to building a permanent link with the BBC station at Belfast, this was not considered a viable option. While the idea of having a permanent link to the BBC was attractive financially, it was dismissed as being unworkable for political reasons. The committee predicted that such a link would cause unending complications and be criticized for broadcasting material that might be regarded as, "offensive to Irish sensibilities, moral and political." This might include "news reels displaying royalty or royal occasions."[50] The committee therefore recommended that an Irish service limit BBC relays to special occasions and instead try to purchase programs from other countries.

While addressing the sensitive topic of programming, the role of the Irish language was also considered. This was an issue that would later cause a great deal of controversy as various proposals were considered by the government. The inclusion or, some might say, exclusion of the native language from television programming remains a contentious topic. The report did not provide much detail when addressing the amount of material that would be broadcast in Irish by a state-owned service. It is obvious that the committee did not believe that even a public television service could employ a large amount of Irish-language material. Radio Eireann was cited as a service that had provided programs in the Irish language,

out of all proportion to the position of Irish in the life of the country. . . . [M]ost of these programmes are not being listened to. . . . It would not be practicable to lay down a minimum proportion of Irish language programmes to be televised by a public service television station, bearing in mind the high cost of television programmes and the need for obtaining the maximum number of licenses.[51]

The report did suggest that the Irish language could find a place in the service being proposed. Examples were cited such as broadcasts of Gaelic games and occasions when Irish music and dancing or ceilis were featured. The committee intentionally departed from the policy of Radio Eireann as it searched for what it considered a more reasonable middle ground. The report emphasized that an independent commercial service would ignore the language, whereas in a public service, the Irish language would have its place. This line of reasoning remained constant throughout the decade.

The scheme generated by the committee slowly developed to become one of the most influential proposals submitted to the government. Although the position and philosophy endorsed by O'Broin and the Television Committee would wane as the 1950s progressed, it would make a dramatic comeback at the end of the decade. On September 4, 1953, *Interim Report of the Television Committee*, marked "secret," was received by the Taoiseach's office. In a cover letter to the Taoiseach's Department, Posts and Telegraphs tried to emphasize how sensitive the document was. It asked that all seventeen of the copies that were made for a cabinet meeting be strictly monitored. O'Broin was clearly concerned that the report might be leaked to the press or other members of the Dail.

This confidential document would be the only serious work completed by the government or any of its departments until the Television Committee submitted an updated report, titled the *First Supplementary Report of the Television Committee*, in March 1956. In the intervening thirty months, television remained an issue that generated a great deal of interest and activity from a number of different sources. This will be examined in the following chapters.

NOTES

1 Marshall McLuhan, *Understanding Media* (London: Routledge and Kegan Paul, 1964), p. 304.

2. On this point see Fanning's *Independent Ireland* (Dublin: Helicon, 1983).

3. Robert J. Savage Jr., *The Origins of Irish Radio*, (Unpublished master's thesis, University College Dublin, 1982), p. 21.

4. See Desmond Bell, "Proclaiming the Republic: Broadcasting Policy and the Corporate State in Ireland," *Broadcasting and Politics in Western Europe*, 8, no. 2 (1985): 27.

5. Quoted in Savage, *Irish Radio*, p. 46.

6. Archives of Radio Telefis Eireann, 105/58, no. 1, Listenership Surveys. Four were conducted, two in 1953 and one each in 1954 and 1955.

7. Fanning, *Independent Ireland*, p. 79.

8. Ibid.

9. Desmond Fisher, *Broadcasting in Ireland* (London: Routledge and Kegan Paul, 1978), p. 22.

10. Department of Finance, S104/1/50. Memo from Leon O'Broin to the Department of Finance, January 24, 1950.

11. Ibid.

12. Ibid., internal memo addressed to McHenry, February 23, 1950.

13. Ibid., memo from Moynihan to Leon O'Broin, February 27, 1950.

14. Ibid., memo from Leon O'Broin to Moynihan, April 21, 1951.

15. Ibid., internal memo from Moynihan, April 25, 1950.

16. Department of the Taoiseach, State Paper Office, S14996A. Memo from Posts and Telegraphs to the Taoiseach, March 15, 1951.

17. Everett was a member of the Labour Party from Wicklow. He was minister in the first Inter-Party Government (1951–1954).

18. This was a clear violation of government and civil service procedure. The Department of Finance would ordinarily review any submission requiring the spending of public funds before it went to the Cabinet. It would have the opportunity to comment by either amending the *Memorandum* or submitting a separate document that would articulate its position on the issue at hand.

19. Department of Finance, S/104/1/50, May 10, 1951.

20. Ibid.

21. Ibid., memo from Moynihan to McGilligan, March 1951.

22. Ibid.

23. Ibid., memo from Patrick McGilligan, March 1951.

24. Ibid., memo to O'Broin, May 2, 1951.

25. Ibid., memo to Finance from Leon O'Broin, May 7, 1951.

26. Ibid., letter from Leon O'Broin, May 9, 1951.

27. Ibid., Department of Finance, memo of May 10, 1951.

28. Ibid.

29. Ibid.

30. Ibid.

31. Ibid., letter from Leon O'Broin to Finance, May 23, 1951.

32. Ibid., internal memo, Department of Finance, June 21, 1951.

33. Raymond Williams, *Television, Technology and Cultural Form* (London: Fontana, 1974).

34. *Irish Independent*, June 29, 1950.

35. *Irish Independent*, April 30, 1951.

36. *Irish Times*, [editorial], May 1, 1951.

37. *Dail Debates*, 125 (May 1, 1951): col. 1704.

38. Department of Finance, S/104/1/50, memo of May 10, 1951.

39. *Dail Debates*, 129 (January 31, 1952): pp. 217–218.

40. Ibid.

41. See Rex Cathcart, *The Most Contrary Region, the BBC in Northern Ireland, 1924–1984* (Belfast: Blackstaff Press, 1984).

42. Department of the Taoiseach, State Paper Office, S14996A, Radio Eireann broadcast of Eric Boden, February 9, 1953.

43. For example, he suggested that television could get "on the air' quickly by transmitting signals from an aircraft that would continually circle the midlands.

44. Department of the Taoiseach, State Paper Office, S14996A, *Interim Report of the Television Committee*, September, 4, 1953.

45. Ibid., p. 28.

46. Interview with Emir O'Broin, Dublin: December 14, 1990.

47. Department of the Taoiseach, State Paper Office, S14996A. *Interim Report of the Television Committee*, p. 38.

48. Ibid., the term "Six Counties" had been used by the Civil Service since the Irish Free State was established as a means of rejecting the cold reality of partition. The Civil Service was able to refer to "Northern Ireland" in January 1966, after Sean Lemass had traveled to Belfast for a meeting with the prime minister of Northern Ireland, Terence O'Neill. See O'Broin, *Just Like Yesterday* (Dublin: Gill and Macmillan, 1985), p. 211.

49. Department of the Taoiseach, State Paper Office, S14996A, *Interim Report of the Television Committee*, p. 39.

50. Ibid, p. 36.

51. Ibid., p. 33.

CHAPTER 2

The Department of Posts and Telegraphs and the Television Committee

In the general election of May 1951, the Inter-Party government, headed by John A. Costello, was defeated and Fianna Fail returned to power. Erskine Childers (the son of Erskine Robert Childers, who had been Minister for Publicity in the Republican Government of 1919–1921), was named Minister for Posts and Telegraphs. Childers's father was an English-born Irish Republican, who had been executed during the Civil War by the Free State Government. Convicted of possessing a revolver, he was shot while his case was on appeal. His execution has come to symbolize the bitterness that tore at the fabric of the country during the Civil War. His son would hold a number of ministerial portfolios and become President of the Irish Republic in 1973.

Maurice Gorham, who was hired as the director of Radio Eireann under Childers, noted that Childers was an energetic and innovative minister with a strong interest in broadcasting.[1] John N. Young's rather pious biography of the minister provides some insight into the difficulties he experienced in his new position. Young addresses the relationship between Childers and the powerful secretary who had dominated the department since his appointment in 1946:

From the beginning Minister and Secretary were frequently at variance after the former made it clear on day one that he had no intention of merely acting as a rubber stamp, [and] was fully capable of judging departmental issues for himself. . . . O'Broin did not appreciate Erskine's broad culture and overtly saw him as an Englishman who simply could not be expected to understand the Irish people.[2]

Young's description of the relationship between the two men is interesting, if somewhat simplistic. O'Broin himself was a man of "broad culture," a well-read intellectual, with a strong interest in classical music, who had demonstrated a gift for writing Irish history.[3] O'Broin also demonstrated an impressive ability to administer the huge Department of Posts and Telegraphs in an efficient manner. There most certainly was tension between the two men, and "nationality" may have complicated their relationship. In his autobiography, *Just Like Yesterday*, O'Broin commented on this issue. "Father and son were both very English. Though young Erskine had spent most of his life in Ireland he was, I always thought, more English than Irish, and his speech betrayed this. People spoke about his Oxford accent, but 'you know,' he said . . . 'it's not Oxford but Cambridge,' as if that, in the circumstances, made any difference."[4]

O'Broin regarded Childers as a threat to his department and viewed him as an appointed politician with no real understanding or appreciation of the complexities of Posts and Telegraphs. After all, Childers, like ministers before him, would last perhaps three or four years, while O'Broin, as the senior civil servant at the department, would remain at the helm much longer. The new minister did try to make innovative changes at Radio Eireann. Besides hiring Gorham, he established the Comhairle Radio Eireann an appointed board that was intended to give the radio service a degree of independence. This group was established to advise the minister of matters concerning broadcasting and was intended to free the national radio service from the control of the civil service. In spite of Childers's efforts, the Comhairle never became a dynamic vehicle of independence for Radio Eireann. Without clear statuary sovereignty, the Comhairle was little more than an advisory group that was unable to wield any real power. Radio Eireann continued to operate as an appendage of Posts and Telegraphs, unable to chart its own course or grasp control of its own destiny.

O'Broin was highly critical of Childers's efforts to involve himself in the affairs of Radio Eireann. His autobiography recounts a minister who was obsessed with the radio service and the details of its day-to-day operation. The secretary regarded his minister's fixation with Radio Eireann as unproductive and commented: "It was sometimes tempting to ask him why he had taken the trouble to install a new regime and a new director if he wished to run the service himself. And when he operated independently he was by no means as competent as he probably thought he was."[5]

Childers's active interest in radio carried over into television. In June 1953, he asked the Minister of Finance for permission to retain, as a consultant, an engineer from Radio Eireann who had recently retired.

Childers maintained that it was imperative that qualified personnel be available to help investigate proposals received from private companies that were interested in television broadcasting. Ignoring the sentiment expressed by O'Broin and the Television Committee, he argued that the commercial proposals coming into his department required careful examination. Although the minister did not advocate the establishment of a commercial service, he wanted this alternative to be carefully considered. O'Broin and the Television Committee had already asked the government for permission to deny the requests of these applicants.[6]

In the meantime, BBC television experienced financial problems that were blamed on the cost of producing television programs. Articles from the British press with headlines such as "Why the BBC Is Broke" were copiously collected by the Department of Finance. These reports confirmed the fears of a department that was alarmed at the cost of a national public television service. Other collected articles outlined the difficulties experienced by the Canadian Broadcasting Company in trying to purchase American programs. This compilation of material illustrates the departmental obsession with maintaining strict controls on spending and a prudently balanced budget.[7]

In September 1953, Childers reported to Finance that he intended to travel to Britain to study developments in television. The Minister for Posts and Telegraphs travelled, not only to London, but to Brussels and Paris as well in order to investigate television broadcasting in Europe. On his return he wrote to O'Broin telling him to "finalize the 'position with regard to television.' As a source of adult education . . . it is the last weapon we possess if we are to remain reasonably distinctive in character and temperament."[8]

In November, Childers addressed the Dail on broadcasting and explained his government's thinking on television. The minister dismissed speculation that the state was about to enter into an agreement with a company that was interested in building a commercial station. He argued that any service that was established would have to be truly national and available throughout the country. The minister cautioned that any such service was years away and emphasized the need for deputies to be patient, warning, "Nothing will be gained by hasty decisions."[9] The language employed by the minister was carefully constructed, as he did not wish to commit himself or his department to any one type of service. The Television Committee had presented its report to the government, and Childers understood the basic recommendations contained in the document. However, in his Dail address one can detect a bias that favored a public service television as the minister referred to a station that would require "heavy subsidies."

Childers told the Dail that he was not overly concerned with the increased reach of BBC broadcasts. "The range of foreign television over the Twenty-Six Counties [of Ireland] is unlikely to extend in the next few years, so as to by itself compel a decision on home television."[10] This was wishful thinking. The BBC had begun broadcasting from Belfast in May 1953, months before Childers' remarks in the Dail. In 1955 the power of the Belfast transmitter would be increased, enabling British programs to penetrate well into the Irish Republic.

In January 1954 Posts and Telegraphs wrote to the Cabinet asking permission to clarify its position on television. Childers' statements given in the Dail had done little to satisfy critics of the government who wanted a commercial service established quickly. Realizing the difficult position the minister was in, and perhaps fearing the pressure building within the country for a commercial service, Posts and Telegraphs decided to ask the government to accept the recommendations outlined in the 1953 *Interim Report*.

A formal *Memorandum for the Government*, clearly initiated by Leon O'Broin, urged the government to come to a policy decision on television. O'Broin argued that there were a number of reasons that required the state to approve a declaration of policy. First and foremost was the fact that a number of companies had approached Posts and Telegraphs asking for a concession or license to operate a television station in the Republic. The department wanted to give commercial applicants a definitive answer to queries concerning building stations in Ireland. Accordingly, it was imperative that the government make a decision on what type of service would be established, the options being either a "private company or public corporation."[11] A firm decision by the government would also allow the Television Committee to make adequate long-term plans for the future of Irish television.

If Childers had harbored any doubts about public service television, they had vanished as he threw his support behind the recommendations made by the Television Committee, which were highlighted in this document. The *Memorandum for Government* emphasized that the entire subject had been carefully reviewed by the Television Committee and the minister, who had become closely involved in studying the development of television throughout Europe. Posts and Telegraphs concluded by asking the government to formally endorse the *Interim Report* of the Television Committee as official state policy.

This submission to the government provoked a sharp response from the Department of Finance. The request by Posts and Telegraphs initiated a thorough review of television inside Finance. A lengthy policy memo was prepared for Sean MacEntee, who had succeeded Patrick McGilligan as Minister of Finance. The document explained that since the department had first entered into discussions with O'Broin in February 1950 it had adamantly opposed spending public funds on what it had termed a "luxury service." Although there had been a change in government, the Department of Finance maintained a policy of forcefully opposing the creation of public service television. Two senior civil service officers at Finance, Louis M. Fitzgerald and J. E. Twamley, prepared a memorandum for MacEntee, that articulated their department's concerns to O'Broin's formal memo. Both Fitzgerald and Twamley had worked with Patrick McGilligan in opposing O'Broin in the past and both would help devise a policy of obstruction that would be embraced by the department for most of the decade.

It was noted that the Minister of Posts and Telegraphs, Erskine Childers, had made a number of statements in the Dail that Finance viewed as problematic. Specific mention was made of the statements that promised that any service introduced would be a national one, capable of being received throughout the country. Finance was also concerned by the reference Childers had made to the state incurring "heavy subsidies" in a national service and complained that the self-supporting stipulation demanded by Finance had been ignored.

Finance was also anxious that proposals from private companies receive adequate attention and not be quickly dismissed. It is clear that the department was interested in examining commercial proposals in the belief that private capital should be used to build a television service. The department summarized its position, which would be embraced as incontrovertible policy for years to come.

From the narrow Exchequer point of view there is clearly strong objection to rejecting any reasonable proposals for commercial television because it now appears that there is no hope of a state television service being other than a heavy drain on the Exchequer. . . . It is accordingly recommended that Department of Posts and Telegraphs be reminded of this Department's policy that a luxury service of this kind must be self supporting.[12]

The Department of Finance determined that the requests of Posts and Telegraphs and the Television Committee had to be aggressively challenged. Finance believed that Posts and Telegraphs had issued a confused and contradictory report, and was convinced that its conclusions could be exploited to discredit the work of the Television Committee.[13] If Posts and

Telegraphs or the Cabinet demanded the department to provide a detailed reply to the submission, Finance was prepared to vigorously attack the Television Committee's *Interim Report*, which it considered inconsistent. The Department of Finance had thoroughly researched the *Interim Report* and seemed resigned to locking horns with Posts and Telegraphs. It appeared that confrontation was imminent.

While this conflict was unfolding, the Fianna Fail Government started to experience problems. It had introduced a harsh, unpopular budget in 1952 and adopted strict deflationary economic policies. In late 1953 and early 1954, the party lost a number of by-elections, and Eamon de Valera called a general election for May 1954. As an election was upcoming, Childers decided that the entire question should be postponed until after a new government was formed. The *Memorandum for the Government* from Posts and Telegraphs that had forced the Department of Finance to evaluate and refine its position regarding television was therefore withdrawn.[14] Television was, for the moment, relegated to a back burner of government.

The election brought back a coalition government, which remained in power until 1957. The new Minister for Posts and Telegraphs was Michael J. Keyes, a Labour deputy from Limerick who was brought into the Cabinet by the Taoiseach, John A. Costello. Keyes contrasted sharply with Childers. He was much more willing to accept the advice of the secretary of his department, and was therefore a welcome change to Leon O'Broin. Keyes and O'Broin worked well together, as the new minister quickly endorsed the work that the Television Committee had completed.

Keyes was first questioned about television in the Dail during a debate on his department's budget in June 1954. The minister was asked when Ireland could expect a television service. The answer was not surprising and demonstrates that no matter who was in power, a commitment that endorsed a comprehensive television policy would not be made. Keyes replied that he had not had the opportunity to closely examine the subject. However, he made a number of points that simply reiterated the position that his department had officially adopted whenever queried on the subject in public.[15] He explained that his department had been conducting a detailed investigation of television for a number of years and that he intended to encourage it to continue its research.

Posts and Telegraphs contacted the Department of Finance once again in June and November 1954 to ask the department to reconsider its position on retaining T. J. Monahan, an engineer, at Radio Eireann. Erskine Childers had tried unsuccessfully to retain the services of this senior engineer while he had been minister the previous year. Posts and Telegraphs argued once again that Monahan had valuable experience and had contributed greatly to the Television Committee. In November 1954, Finance relented. Louis Fitzgerald urged his minister, Gerard Sweetman, to allow Posts and Telegraphs to retain Monahan.

I think that in view of the television pressures and the heavy expenditures which might be thrown on the state if the Department of Posts and Telegraphs were stampeded into television it is well to have the services of this wise and recognized authority on the subject at our disposal. . . . In any event the pressure is *now* and the Department really needs someone who can give them the right reasons for saying "no."16

Finance had come around to supporting Monahan, as it was felt that the former Engineer in Chief at Radio Eireann would act as a brake on what was considered an overanxious Department of Posts and Telegraphs. There was no reason to believe that Monahan would be inclined to oppose the general philosophy of Gorham and O'Broin, with whom he had chaired the Television Committee. Finance most probably felt that the engineer could offer helpful criticism on technical aspects of proposals that were arriving at Posts and Telegraphs.

While television received little attention within government circles for several months, it found its way into the press on a regular basis throughout the summer of 1955. The BBC station broadcasting out of Northern Ireland once again started to intrude on political and cultural sensibilities in the Republic. In July 1955, a new transmitter was installed on the top of Divis Mountain, outside Belfast. This greatly increased the range of the BBC and estimates indicate that the new transmitter offered coverage to 80 percent of Northern Ireland.17

While the range of the service inside Northern Ireland was increased, the new transmitter also penetrated deep into the Republic. In July, the *Irish Times* ran a story concerning television reception in the twenty-six counties and the expansion of the Irish television market. It was reported that with the opening of the new transmitter at Divis, reception had greatly improved in the Republic. Letters to the editor testified that the new transmitter had increased the number of homes able to receive the broadcasts of BBC Northern Ireland. This development provided a boon to television retailers, who had changed their policy in regard to sales. Retailers in the northern half of the country were actively marketing television sets and featuring attractive "lease to own" plans that made it easier for customers to bring home receivers. It was reported that this was a new development in the television trade. "Up to now the radio dealers discouraged people from purchasing television sets on the grounds that they could not guarantee that the viewer would see the programmes transmitted from the B.B.C. stations in England at all times. Direct signals from the Belfast transmitter are now being received from Sligo across to Dublin, and as far south as Tulla-more."[18] The secretary of the Wireless Dealers Association, T. J. Reynolds, declared that retailers had enjoyed a surge in sales since the new Belfast transmitter had gone on the air. Even if one were to dismiss such hyperbole from Reynolds, there was no denying the fact that the penetration of the BBC now extended well into the Republic.

The expansion of the British service created added pressure on the Irish Government to make a decision on a native service, though the extent of that pressure is difficult to measure. One vocal group that tried to exploit this issue was the association of manufacturers and retailers of televisions in Ireland, the Wireless Dealers Association. The small Irish television industry knew that the opening of a station in the Republic would create a demand that would increase sales dramatically. However, in spite of the increased range of the Belfast transmitter, the position of the government remained unchanged. This was made clear by the Minister for Posts and Telegraphs, who addressed the Wireless Dealers Association in September 1955. Michael Keyes told the association that he doubted there was a growing demand for television in the country. He explained that the nation had more important issues to consider before it would deal with television. He was, of course, referring to the cost of an Irish service, which he maintained was prohibitive. Keyes argued that a television station would require more than the initial capital costs to build the necessary infrastruc-ture and indicated that costs for maintaining a television station would be a drain on an already depleted Exchequer. Using figures for program costs obtained from the BBC, he pointed out that one hour of programming could cost as much as £900.

It is significant to note here that Keyes, in emphasizing the cost of a service, had accepted the recommendations of the secretary of his depart-ment, Leon O'Broin. The report of the Television Committee provided a framework that was accepted inside the department, and pronouncements made by the minister took for granted that some form of state-owned service would be established. O'Broin and the Television Committee had suc-ceeded in convincing a succession of ministers of the need for public service television. At this juncture, the option of accepting a commercial proposal was simply not considered a desirable alternative.

The President of the Wireless Dealers Association, W. B. Dalton, made it clear that the industry rejected the government's position. He pointed out that every time the BBC expanded its range, an increase in sales occurred in Ireland. The *Irish Times* quoted Dalton as politely disagreeing with Keyes by pointing out that when the Holme Moss station in the north of England was opened, as many as 2,500 television sets were sold in the Republic and that a further 1,000 sets were sold when BBC Northern Ireland began broadcasting on its new transmitter:

"We feel . . . that in the next 12 months from 12,000 to 15,000 sets will be sold in the Republic. That indicates there is a latent, if not articulate, demand on the part of the people of Ireland for television in this country." He went on to say that, sooner or later, the people of the south would begin to ask why the people of Northern Ireland were getting something that people here were not getting.[19]

Dalton had raised, but not fully exploited, a thorny problem that troubled the government. The fact that Northern Ireland could boast of having television while the Irish Republic could not was a constant source of embarrassment for the Irish government which was loath to admit that the living standards in Northern Ireland might be higher than in the Republic. The fact that an intrusive British service was making further inroads into the Republic added fuel to the growing demand for an Irish service. As the reception of British programs extended south of the border, broader questions concerning the political and cultural content of these broadcasts became a topic of growing debate. In October 1955 Keyes was questioned in the Dail about his department's attitude toward television and gave a reply that echoed that of Childers two years earlier. Noting that his department had been watching developments closely, Keyes maintained that television would not receive serious consideration until a service could be delivered that would be "distinctively Irish" without being a burden on taxpayers. Like Childers before him, Keyes emphasized the cost and quality of an Irish service, implying that a commercial station would fail to provide uniquely Irish programs.

Deputy Jack McQuillan, an Independent member of the Dail, asked a more difficult question:

Is he aware that at the present time there are a large number of television sets throughout the rural areas, that the people who have these sets have now to watch amusements and so forth that have a completely British slant and does he not think that the way to counteract that is to provide television programmes in Ireland with an Irish slant?"[20]

This dilemma had been explored by the Television Committee, and Keyes would have understood both the problem and the solution proposed in the *Interim Report*. Keyes replied that he was aware of the difficulties that had been caused by the BBC broadcasts but that the government simply was unable to provide a national television service.

The British press examined the political consequences of this problem, describing an incident that occurred in November 1955. The *Observer* reported that "the screens of Britain and Ireland presented . . . the Prime Minister of Northern Ireland, Lord Brookeborough [, who] made a discon-certingly successful appearance in the B.B.C.'s 'Press Conference.' "[21] The reporter described the awkward predicament this created for the Irish Government.

It has suddenly been realised that here is a medium which can jump across frontiers and laugh at censorship. Shows that would never pass the vigilant film censor may be seen and enjoyed on the television screen; and the anti-anti-partition propaganda of Northern Ireland can be carried with bland and smiling assurance, into the parlours of the south. These two facts are exercising a good many minds in the Republic.[22]

The journalist for the *Observer* had cleverly highlighted the awkward position in which the government found itself. The reality of uncensored material polluting the hearts and minds of Irish citizens concerned the government and, one might assume, the Irish bishops. This was an issue that caused a great deal of consternation in government circles and put added pressure on the state to respond by building a television station that would defend the nation's political and cultural sovereignty.

The Irish-language publication *Comhair* addressed this dilemma in a September 1955 editorial. *Comhair* argued that an Irish television service was needed to counter the influence of the British media.

Now England has a medium to mold the public mind . . . [through] the [television] screens in thousands and thousands of houses throughout Ireland. . . . For the first time ever, life, as it appears in England will be projected . . . to every Irish hearth. Can we afford . . . to do nothing to neutralise this baneful influence? Are we satisfied to let England win the last fight so easily?[23]

Comhair argued that the government was being shortsighted in main-taining that building an Irish television service was simply too expensive to consider. A truly Irish service could help sustain the efforts of the language revival and protect Ireland from the insidious effects of British cultural imperialism. The editorial complained of other British influences that were steadily eroding Ireland's cultural identity and predicted that, "television will put the 'KIBOSH' on our efforts to extricate ourselves from Brittania unless the Government takes a decisive step with regard to television within a few years."[24] The issues raised by *Comhair* would become a recurrent theme as the debate concerning television evolved.

In March 1956, the Department of Posts and Telegraphs submitted to the government the *Supplemental Report of the Television Committee*.[25] In the three years that had elapsed between the initial report and this revised and updated document, the issues that would form the debate over television had come into focus. The powerful Department of Finance remained strongly opposed to the Television Committee and its desire to establish a state-owned public service, while O'Broin and his department continued to exert a great deal of influence on the television question. Their suggestions regarding a state-owned service had evolved into strong convictions that would be more clearly defined in the 1956 report.

The governments that had been in power during this time exhibited a great deal of ambivalence and confusion over television policy. Cultural and political groups were beginning to articulate strong opinions and concerns on the subject. These positions contributed to a growing debate that would consider television for years to come. The *Supplemental Report of the Television Committee* marked a milestone in the development of television policy in Ireland and will be closely examined in the next chapter.

NOTES

1. Maurice Gorham, *Forty Years of Irish Broadcasting* (Dublin: Talbot Press, 1967), p. 201.

2. John Young, *Erskine Childers, President of Ireland* (Buckinghamshire: Colin Smythe), p. 109.

3. O'Broin's publications include, *The Unfortunate Mr. Robert Emmet* (Dublin: Clonmore and Reynolds, 1958), *Dublin Castle and the 1916 Rising* (Dublin: Helicon, 1966), *The Chief Secretary, Augustine Birrell in Ireland* (London: Chatto and Windus, 1969), *Fenian Fever* (New York: New York University Press, 1971), *Michael Collins* (Dublin: Gill and Macmillan, 1980), and *Frank Duff* (Dublin: Gill and Macmillan, 1982). He was the editor of *In Great Haste: The Letters of Michael Collins and Kitty Kiernan* (Dublin: Gill and Macmillan, 1983).

4. Leon O'Broin, *Just Like Yesterday, An Autobiography* (Dublin: Gill and Macmillan, 1985), p. 179.

5. Ibid., p. 181.

6. Department of Finance, S104/1/50, memorandum from Childers to MacEntee, June 2, 1953. Finance refused Childers's request.

7. Ibid.; articles from the *Financial Times*, the *Economist,* the *Observer*, and the *Listener* were added to the file.

8. Young, *Erskine H. Childers*, pp. 115–116.

9. *Dail Debates* (November 10, 1953): col. 1771–1772.

10. Ibid. "Foreign television" was code for British television.

11. Department of Finance, S104/1/50, memo from Posts and Telegraphs to the Government, January 1954.

12. Ibid., Department of Finance draft memo, March 5, 1954, p. 6.

13. Ibid., memorandum to Fitzgerald, March 10, 1954, p. 1.

14. Ibid., Twamley to O'Doherty, March 12, 1954.

15. *Dail Debates*, 146, no. 7, pp. 776–777.

16. Department of Finance, S104/1/50, Fitzgerald to Sweetman, November 25, 1954.

17. See Rex Cathcart, *The Most Contrary Region, The BBC in Northern Ireland 1924–1984* (Belfast: Blackstaff Press, 1984).

18. *Irish Times*, July 27, 1955.

19. *Irish Times*, September, 15, 1955.

20. *Dail Debates*, 153 (October 26, 1955): col. 24–26.

21. *Observer*, November, 27, 1955. This was included in the television file of the Department of the Taoiseach (S14996A).

22. Ibid. The *Observer* estimated that there were over 4,000 television sets in Ireland and that sales exceeded 150 per week.

23. *Comhair*, September 1955.

24. Ibid.

25. State Paper Office, Department of the Taoiseach, S14996A, Television Committee, *First Supplemental Report*, March 1956.

CHAPTER 3

The Department of Finance, Leon O'Broin, and the Television Committee

In March 1956 O'Broin's committee completed a document for the government titled *The First Supplemental Report of the Television Committee*. The report is significant as it illustrates the development of the policy endorsed by Leon O'Broin and his associates at Posts and Telegraphs. The document provides insight into the thinking of the committee and explains how members of the group, especially O'Broin, evaluated and reacted to commercial proposals received from private companies. As has been noted, the only coherent study that had been sanctioned by the government came from the Television Committee. Although at times the influence of the committee would wane, it would in the end prove to be an influential voice in the debate concerning Irish television. Therefore, a close examination of the report is necessary.

The thirty-six-page report reviewed developments involving television since the committee's initial report, which had been issued in 1953. In reporting on the worldwide growth of television, the committee noted that in 1956, twenty-three European nations had television services. The number of sets in these countries ranged from 5,170,070 in the United Kingdom and an estimated 1 million in the Soviet Union to a mere 12 in Poland. Outside Europe, the United States had the largest number of sets, with an estimated 36 million. The committee emphasized that it was not only wealthy nations that enjoyed television, as countries such as Argentina, Brazil, Mexico, and the Philippines also had television stations. The report stressed the rapid growth of television worldwide, noting that in the United States and Great Britain the expansion had been tremendous. In the short period of three years since the first report had been issued, the number of receivers had increased in the United States from 23 million to 36 million. In the United Kingdom, the number had more than doubled in this same period.[1]

The report emphasized that throughout Europe, states were either already enjoying television or taking steps to bring the medium to their citizens. The exceptions were Finland, Portugal, and Ireland. It was pointed out that Portugal was studying television and expected to begin experiments in the near future. The committee was anxious to illustrate the degree of isolation that enveloped Ireland whenever television was concerned. If the 1953 report had been ambivalent about the establishment of an Irish service, the committee argued that the situation in 1956 had changed dramatically.

The committee examined the establishment of the commercial television service in the United Kingdom and the British Television Act of 1954. It explained the structure of commercial broadcasting in Britain, noting that the newly formed Independent Television Authority (ITA) would compete with the "public service" British Broadcasting Corporation. The committee explained that the ITA hired independent program contractors to provide programs for transmission. It was also noted that the ITA was interested in expanding quickly and planned to open a Belfast station in 1957 or 1958.

It is important to note that the Television Committee, and the government in general, were aware that there was a clear alternative to the "public service" model preferred by O'Broin. The ITA provided a prototype whose signal could be received in parts of Ireland and compared with the older "public service" model, the BBC. O'Broin was concerned with the success the ITA enjoyed and feared that this prosperous commercial station might help those who advocated that a similar service be established in Ireland. In fact, the committee did its best to discredit the content of the ITA's programs and the overall concept of commercial television. It was conceded that when the service first came into operation, the programs that were broadcast were of a high quality. However, the committee reported that after operating for several months, the ITA had responded to the pressure of advertisers and started broadcasting only what it termed "popular programs" at peak times. It pointed out that educational and news programs had been relegated to peripheral time slots and that this change in programming had resulted in the resignation of the Editor-In-Chief and his assistant. The committee stressed that "reliable critics" had not been impressed with the actual programs broadcast on the ITA. It was reported that while the new commercial service had not introduced many new or original programs, it had experienced tremendous success in broadcasting American imports.

According to the committee, this had affected the BBC in a number of ways. The BBC had expanded its hours, devoted more resources to "popular programs" and sporting events, and generally abandoned the type of broadcasts that it had traditionally offered. It is clear that the committee believed the BBC was being compromised by the new commercial service and forced to feature what it considered unrefined but popular programs.

Advocates of a commercial station in Ireland were encouraged by the success of the ITA and considered it as a natural model to duplicate at home. The ITA represented a serious threat to O'Broin and his committee and to their elitist vision of what an Irish service should be. To the Television Committee, the success of the ITA and the effect it was having on the programs at the BBC jeopardized the recommendations they had made in their 1953 report. When combined with the realization that commercial television, broadcasting from Belfast, might soon be available in many Irish homes, a new sense of urgency was created in the eyes of O'Broin and his associates.

The committee addressed developments in Northern Ireland, and explained how the expansion of the television service in the north would affect the Republic. As has been seen, in July 1955 a new powerful transmitter had been built in Belfast. The committee noted that the new transmitter was thirty times more powerful than the original and was intended to reach over 1 million citizens in the province. It stated that the number of televisions in Northern Ireland had expanded from 5,000 in 1953 to over 38,000 in 1956. The report also maintained that the BBC had recently indicated that it intended to build a second transmitter in Derry.

The expansion of BBC Northern Ireland had an immediate effect on the television market in the Republic. The committee reported that reception of signals from the new transmitter extended as far south as Dublin and into the midlands and the west. The decision of the manufacturers and retailers to encourage the purchase of sets in the Republic was noted, and the Wireless Dealers Association's estimate of 7,000 sets having been sold in the Republic was mentioned. The committee pointed out that these circumstances had combined to create a strange situation, as Ireland, a nation without its own domestic service, had more televisions than "small but rather wealthier countries such as Denmark, Norway, and Sweden."[2] According to the committee the new Belfast transmitter, when combined with transmitters from the British mainland, combined to penetrate well into the Irish Republic. This meant that reception was possible for as many as 1 million citizens.

The report made it clear that the committee was concerned with the consequences of what it saw as an intrusive expansion of British culture. This unwelcome "fallout" was viewed as a challenge that required action on behalf of the Irish government. In order to impress on the government their concern, the committee explained that it had studied the content of BBC broadcasts and concluded that the programs that were being received by over 7,000 families in the Republic were undesirable. While acknowledging that many of the documentaries and sports programs that were broadcast were of a very high quality, the committee believed that for the most part, the programs were not suitable for Irish viewers. It complained that the British service was "governed by ideas that are wholly alien to the ordinary Irish home."[3] When analyzing the programs the report considered offensive, it explained:

Some are brazen, some "frank" in sex matters, some merely inspired by the desire to exalt the British royal family and the British way of life. This last element naturally runs through a wide variety of programmes. . . . [T]here is constant emphasis on the British way of life, the British view of world affairs, and the British (including Six County) achievements. The B.B.C.'s resources are lavishly expended on reporting every movement of the royal family at home and on tour.[4]

The annoying attention paid to the royal family was not the most serious problem created by these programs. In a telling passage, the more puritanical concerns were expressed. The sexual content of the broadcasts was seen as being highly objectionable and injurious to Irish sensibilities. The BBC attitude toward sex was defined as "quite alien to this country. It includes exploitation of semi-nudity, 'blue' jokes in comedy shows, documentaries . . . of the unmarried mother[,] . . . plays hinging on the theme of adultery . . . and even films showing in detail the sex activities of animals."[5]

The committee made it clear that it believed that these types of programs would pollute the minds of Irish citizens. Again it should be stressed that one has to understand the historical context within which the committee was writing. Ireland in 1956 was still very much an isolated, conservative society, which embraced traditional Catholic values emphasizing the importance of the family and the sacraments. Censorship was a fact of life as books, plays, and magazines were routinely banned by an active national Censorship Board.

The committee also feared the power that television appeared to exert over the viewer. The possibility of "tv addiction" was a serious concern, which had to be addressed. "Television is notoriously hard to switch off, and householders who would not themselves want to continue watching a programme that offends their taste may easily feel reluctant to turn it off if others are apparently enjoying it, especially when friends are visiting for the purpose of seeing television."[6]

The Television Committee had come to the firm conclusion that due to the expansion of British broadcasts, it was imperative that a native service be established. The committee explained the alternatives open to the government, stating that a choice would have to be made between supporting a publicly or privately owned service. As has been seen, a number of private companies had approached the Post Office asking for a license to broadcast in the country. The committee reported to the government on these proposals, offering a summary of each submission and suggesting that all be rejected.

The first proposal to be received came from an American identified as Charles Sweeney of the London-based Federated Trust and Finance Co. Ltd. The original proposal had been submitted in May 1953 by Sweeney and General Sean MacEoin, a hero of the War of Independence and a Fine Gael member of the Dail. Federated Trust asked for the right to establish an exclusive commercial station in the Dublin area. The company had hired General MacEoin to lend the company credibility in its dealing with the Department of Posts and Telegraphs. General MacEoin was a member of the Dail while he was lobbying for Federated Trust. It was not uncommon for members of the Dail to work for companies interested in gaining an exclusive broadcasting license from the government.

The committee was clearly not impressed by Federated Trust's proposal, which asked that the state grant the company an exclusive license to broadcast in Ireland. The scheme required the government to collect a license fee, which would be paid to the company. The government would have to buy airtime from the company at standard rates, but Federated Trust would supply news and commercial programs. In the eyes of O'Broin's committee, the proposal had little appeal. The committee indicated that Sweeney had expressed renewed interest and that financing was available in "dollars."[7]

The committee also reviewed a proposal from the Radio Corporation of America (RCA) which had been received in April 1955.[8] This proposition was taken more seriously. The RCA proposal was seen as a comprehensive one; however, it was considered unworkable as the company advocated the use of American equipment, which would not be compatible with English-made sets or, indeed, the television sets being assembled in Ireland. Another flaw in the proposal concerned the wavelengths that RCA considered using. The Stockholm Agreement, of which Ireland was a signatory, had not assigned Ireland the television bands that RCA wanted to use. However, the technical suggestions for the plan to cover the entire twenty-six counties were viewed as comprehensive and technically sound. The committee had written to RCA and requested further information on the company's concept of using radio links to afford coverage that would include the entire country.[9]

The RCA proposal estimated that the cost for providing a national service would be approximately £720,000, a figure much lower than the £2 million that the committee employed in its own projections. The committee dismissed the difference in cost estimates, maintaining that there were undefined "uncertain factors" in the calculations made by RCA. An offer by RCA to set up a free, low-powered station in Dublin for six months had been declined by the committee. The reason stated was that the committee did not want to "prejudice in any way a Government decision on television."[10] It is clear that the committee did not want to grant RCA an opportunity to gain a foothold in the country.[11]

A comprehensive proposal, which received serious consideration by the committee, was made by an English organization, the Pye Company. This proposal had gained a good deal of attention before the Television Committee issued its report in March 1956. In February, Michael Keyes wrote to the Taoiseach to advise him that the Pye Company had hired Deputy Erskine Childers as an agent to represent the company's interests in Ireland. Keyes advised the Taoiseach and the Cabinet that they should, "be made aware of the likelihood . . . of a proposal from Pye Radio for Commercial Television . . . being circulated to individual Ministers by Deputy Childers."[12] The memo continued by stating that since the Television Committee was about to submit a report to the government, no action should be taken until that report had been studied.

It is, of course, significant that the Pye Company had hired a former Minister for Posts and Telegraphs to lobby on their behalf. Erskine Childers tried to influence Cabinet ministers and members of the Dail by directly lobbying on behalf of his employer. He was certainly an asset to the Pye Company, as he could provide important information on the thinking of the Television Committee and the strength behind O'Broin's support of a "public service" television. In fact, the Pye proposal was tailored to try and address the unique concerns of the state.

Pye was a well-established British company that had been involved in manufacturing television and radio equipment in Britain for a number of years. The committee recognized the company as a huge English corporation, which controlled fifty-six companies. In its proposal Pye indicated that it was forming a subsidiary, Pye Ireland Ltd., to conduct business in Ireland. The company explained that it had an established relationship with a number of British programming companies, as it was associated with the Independent Television Authority. This affiliation would give the company access to what were described as mainly commercial programs. The company indicated a willingness to produce and broadcast government programs at cost during non-peak hours. It also offered to broadcast such programs during "prime time" for its standard rate for a maximum of two hours per day.

Pye also expressed a willingness to help the Irish Government build its own public service station. This would operate separately from the Pye station and allow the state to broadcast cultural and educational material. The company stated that the commercial station it envisioned would have a transmitter situated on the hill at Howth and a range extending twenty miles from the center of Dublin. The company explained that it would establish a link to Cork within three years of opening. It maintained that a service that would provide national coverage could cost up to £3 million.

The committee analyzed the Pye proposal and recognized that the plan was the first detailed effort that had tried to take into consideration the unique conditions that existed in the country. The committee concluded that the company was asking for a great deal and not offering much in return. The provision of airtime to the government at special rates at off-peak hours did not impress the committee, which was also troubled with the rather vague plans to expand the service beyond the Dublin metropolitan area. O'Broin and his associates stated that they wanted to be sure that any service that was established could eventually be received throughout the entire state.

The committee expressed concern about the programs that would be featured on a commercial station and believed that the government would have little power to control the material that would be transmitted by a privately owned service. The report contended that if the purpose of establishing a native service was to counter the "alien" broadcasts reaching the country, then the Pye proposal was not a solution. The report therefore recommended that all the proposals, including Pye's, be rejected and once again stressed that when television came to the country it was imperative that it be under both public control and public management.

The Television Committee provided a detailed reassessment of the need for television in the country. Much had changed since September 1953 when the committee had issued its initial report. It is clear that the one development that most influenced the committee was the continued expansion of British television. In pointing out that British broadcasts penetrated deep into the Republic, the committee argued that building a native television service had become a national priority.

The committee reported that a native station, broadcasting from Dublin, could expect to generate more revenue than had been predicted in 1953. One consequence of the increase in power of BBC Northern Ireland was that many more television receivers had been purchased in the Republic than had been anticipated by the 1953 report. The committee had estimated in 1953 that after one year of broadcasting, there would be only 4,000 sets in the Republic. However the number of sets in January 1956 was already 7,000 and increasing, according to the Wireless Dealers Association. The committee believed that this would translate to an increase in the revenue a native service would generate. The report also maintained that an Irish station could attract new programs and advertisers if the service expanded its hours and was permitted to accept advertisements from non-Irish firms.

The report concluded by noting that dramatic changes had forced the committee to alter its previous position. This change was made more palatable by the estimate of increased revenue. The committee advised the government, "The need for an Irish television service has become considerably greater since 1953."[13]

The Television Committee laid the groundwork for a revised plan proposing that the state establish its own television service. As has been noted in 1953, the Television Committee had argued that television, while not essential, would be desirable if it became affordable. The committee had reported that given the cost of public television and the state of the nation's finances, television appeared impractical. It then argued that there were "other grounds," defined as national prestige, that might compel the government to build a television station and outlined a scheme for a limited public service. In 1956 the Television Committee outlined a more detailed proposal indicating that it believed that its plan was not only feasible but also very attractive.

The revised proposal of the Television Committee illustrates that O'Broin and his associates had become convinced that the rather vague plan outlined in 1953 could be refined into a comprehensive scheme that would provide the country with a state-owned and -operated commercial service. The station envisioned in 1956 would extend its hours and depend much more on revenue from advertisers while remaining committed to delivering programs of high quality. The committee's proposal specified that the state-sponsored service it was recommending would cater only to the Dublin metropolitan area. The Dublin station would depend on films as well as material purchased from other countries and be supplemented by programs that would be produced in Ireland. These Irish productions would include game shows, sporting events, and special informative programs designed to appeal to children, farmers, and women.

Although the service would charge a license fee, advertisements would provide the most important source of revenue. The scheme targeted the government's protectionist policies which restricted Radio Eireann's ability to accept foreign advertisements. The committee argued that this policy would have to be scrapped as television would need to aggressively pursue customers who were willing to purchase time for commercials. In accepting advertisements, the committee acknowledged that relying on commercial broadcasting would blemish the state service, as some of the programs broadcast would be distasteful, "popular" programs. This was seen as a small price to pay for maintaining control of a medium as powerful as television. The committee also believed that a state-sponsored public service would be in an excellent position to deal with the BBC and continental public stations in obtaining the quality programs at a reasonable rate.

The issue of Irish-language programs was mentioned but not addressed in detail. The question would present an emotional and complex problem, which continues to torment the government today. The 1953 report had briefly commented on the need for an Irish service to help nurture the native language. In 1957 the committee renewed its support of the language but also explained the difference between carrying programs in Irish on television as opposed to carrying them on radio. Since its inception, Radio Eireann had offered listeners a substantial amount of Irish-language broadcasts. However, Radio Eireann's own surveys indicated that there were few listeners to these programs. The Television Committee believed that making a commitment to a significant percentage of Irish-language television broadcasts would be a mistake for a service that was dependent on revenue generated by advertisers for survival. The reference to the role of the language in an Irish television service was intentionally vague. To supporters of the language, the tone of the committee's statement might have indicated the lukewarm support that would be offered in the future. This is an area that will be addressed as the development of Irish television is chronicled.

Cost projections that the committee prepared indicated that the proposed service would run a deficit. The cost to run the Dublin service was projected at £500,000 per year, while the capital cost for erecting the station itself was expected to be £400,000. The committee also projected that the revenue collected from the sale of licenses would help offset these costs. Referring to the experience of Northern Ireland, where in 1956 there were 38,000 licensed sets, it predicted that in the first two years of operation, a Dublin service could expect to license 30,000 sets, with an additional 5,000 a year thereafter. It was also estimated that the proposed service would generate an additional £100,000 per year in advertising revenue. The committee estimated that revenue would cover expenses after approximately six years.

The report admitted that although the figures employed had been developed with the best information available, they were tentative. In fact, the projections used by the committee would change a number of times over the next few years. The committee was not in a position to offer more accurate estimates because it had not made the necessary inquiries, nor had it conducted an aggressive investigation into what type of expenses would be involved. This failure to develop more precise information concerning costs left the committee exposed to attacks from the Department of Finance, which remained very concerned over the burden television would exact on the Exchequer.

The proposal was problematic for a number of reasons. In recommending that a station be established to serve only the metropolitan Dublin area, the committee contradicted itself. It had earlier criticized commercial proposals that had not made a firm commitment to a national television service. However, if the state were to own the service, the committee believed it would have to be a relatively small one. "The choice would be between beginning with a single station in or near Dublin and postponing a decision indefinitely."[14] One can only wonder how this might go over in areas "remote from Dublin" such as Cork or Galway. The committee proposed a service that would be financed by taxpayers across the country yet only be available to those living in the Dublin metropolitan area. The Television Committee was either simply out of touch with the political realities of the country or arrogant in assuming that such a limited service would be acceptable.

In its conclusion, the report once again maintained that, despite the elaborate proposal that had been prepared for the government, the Television Committee was not in a position to dictate policy. However, it was obvious that the committee believed that television had become an urgent national priority, maintaining that a decision "at this stage rests largely—and to a much greater degree than before—on national and moral grounds. The possible effects on Irish viewers of continued and exclusive viewing of television programmes originated outside our jurisdiction is no doubt a matter of concern to the Government."[15] The Television Committee asked for a prompt commitment from the government to support its scheme. It argued that further delay would only enhance a powerful British influence in Ireland at the expense of a frail native culture.

As might be expected, the strongest objection to the report of the Television Committee came from the Department of Finance. The efforts of Finance to oppose any form of state-sponsored television became even more pronounced after the 1956 *First Supplemental Report of the Television Committee* was issued. In April 1956, Leon O'Broin had sent the Department of Finance an advance copy of the report. In a cover letter to the secretary of the Department of Finance, Owen J. Redmond, O'Broin advised that it was the intention of Posts and Telegraphs to formally submit the report to the Cabinet, "with a view to getting decisions on policy in regard to television."[16] One month later, O'Broin wrote to Redmond again asking for his observations on the report and a draft *Memorandum to the Government*. The two-page document offered a synopsis of the Television Committee's substantial report and was intended to accompany the report when it was submitted to the Cabinet.[17]

The draft memo revealed that the Minister for Posts and Telegraphs, Michael J. Keyes, although sympathetic to the committee's position, did not fully endorse its recommendation. Keyes did not want to commit the government to the immediate financing of an expensive public television service. He indicated that although he did not propose that the state spend public funds on television in the immediate future, he did want a decision made concerning what type of service would eventually be established in Ireland. Keyes fully supported the desire of the Television Committee to reject the proposals that had been submitted by private companies interested in establishing commercial stations in Ireland. He advised the Cabinet that he wanted permission "to announce that when conditions permit of a television service being established here, it will be a service based on public ownership and management."[18]

As a member of the Cabinet, Keyes was familiar with the priorities of the government and understood that in spite of the negative consequences of not having a service, television was simply not, in the eyes of the government, a national priority. In spite of this, the Minister of Posts and Telegraphs, at the behest of O'Broin, requested that an important policy decision be made by the government. Both Keyes and O'Broin fully understood that once the state made a commitment to public television, substantial public spending would eventually be required. Both realized that receiving such a commitment would represent a major policy decision on the part of the government and an important victory in the department's efforts to gain a public television service.

The Department of Finance was concerned about the Keyes memorandum and the *Supplemental Report of the Television Committee*. Finance examined both documents and once again reviewed the position it had staked out since Leon O'Broin had first asked for funds to buy a television set in 1950. The matter was discussed among several individuals at Finance, who carefully reviewed the submissions that O'Broin and his Television Committee had made over the past six years. Throughout the 1950s these same civil servants at Finance advised J. J. McElligott, who was Secretary of the Department of Finance until April 1953; O. J. Redmond, who served as secretary through May 1956; and T. K. Whitaker, who succeeded Redmond in 1956. These senior civil servants formulated strategy that remained constant during most of the decade. J. E. Twamley usually conferred with and reported to Louis M. Fitzgerald, the Assistant Secretary in the Establishment Division at Finance. Both were seasoned veterans of the department, Fitzgerald having been appointed in August 1925.[19] Fitzgerald reviewed the comments and analysis of Twamley and reported directly to both the secretary and the minister. Inside the Department of Finance a strategy developed that was supported by ministers from both coalition and Fianna Fail governments throughout the 1950s. The consensus that emerged within the department adamantly opposed public television and set an important parameter that helped frame the contentious debate on television that would last to the end of the decade.

After reviewing Keyes's memo and the Television Committee's latest report, Twamley prepared a minute for Louis Fitzgerald and Gerard Sweetman who, in 1956, was the Minister of Finance. The state-owned service outlined by the Television Committee had a number of flaws, according to his report. Twamley argued that both the projected revenue and the estimated operating costs employed in the committee's report were overly optimistic. He also criticized the desire of O'Broin and the committee to dismiss the commercial proposals that had been received, especially the scheme developed by the Pye Company.

Finance remained intrigued with the idea of a commercial enterprise building and operating a television station, as it would free the state from funding the type of service that the committee had outlined. Twamley criticized the argument used by the Television Committee to discredit as unsound proposals from private entrepreneurs. Instead it was argued that "outside interests" should be given a chance to set up a service as long as safeguards were in place that ensured there would be no financial risk to the state. Twamley suggested that rather than discourage commercial proposals, the government should invite all parties interested in setting up a television service to submit their plans to the government.

Twamley and his associates at Finance understood that the long-term financial repercussions of Posts and Telegraph's request had to be fully considered. It was understood that Keyes was asking the Cabinet to make a commitment to public service television which would be built "when conditions permit." Twamley realized the consequences of making such a pledge and believed that any such promise should be avoided. He advised his department to oppose the request of Posts and Telegraphs and also argued that Finance should demand that commercial proposals submitted by private companies not be rejected without further consideration.

Louis Fitzgerald agreed with his assistant and sent Twamley's minute to Sweetman, with his own supportive comments. In writing to Sweetman he advised his minister that Finance should support the concept of television being established in Ireland by private capital,

on the clear understanding that if the venture fails the state will not pick up the pieces. Such an outcome, viz. failure commercially, [would] be a complete answer to pressure that the state [should] undertake t.v. Why should the taxpayer foot the bill for what . . . [has] proved to be commercially unprofitable? I agree with Mr. Twamley's view . . . of the [Post Office] memo[;] though it appears innocuous [it could] be dangerous financially.[20]

Fitzgerald also criticized the arguments that had been made by the committee concerning the impact of British broadcasts. He was not convinced that an Irish service would be preferred by Irish viewers. O'Broin had spoken directly with Fitzgerald about television and argued that the Irish Catholic Church might become involved in the debate due to what O'Broin considered the objectionable material transmitted by British stations:

Mr. O'Broin stated that pressure might be expected from ecclesiastical authorities. Viewed solely from that angle I fail to see what benefit Irish t.v. [would] confer. Short of some form of jamming, the Irish t.v. owner will remain free to take whatever programme he chooses. The assumption that he will take the Irish programme in preference to any other is quite unrealistic."[21]

The Minister of Finance accepted the advice offered by his staff and directed Fitzgerald to inform Posts and Telegraphs that it was his opinion the Cabinet should only be asked to decide between a private commercial station or no television at all. In a formal minute labeled "secret" and addressed to O'Broin, Fitzgerald articulated his department's view:

The Minister sees no prospect of it being possible for the Exchequer in the foreseeable future to undertake the expense of setting up and maintaining a state television service. In these circumstances he thinks it preferable that the Government should not be asked to commit itself in even the vaguest way to the proposition that any television service established here would be based on public ownership and management.[22]

It soon became clear that Finance believed that even a private commercial service needing no public funding was problematic. The department was concerned that scarce private capital would be drawn to the venture, draining resources that might be invested in projects it considered more important. Finance also feared that television would aggravate the weak Irish economy by upsetting the country's balance of trade, as it predicted there would be an increase in the sale of imported television sets. The department was also concerned that personal savings would be undermined by a binge in consumer spending that would accompany the establishment of a television station. The consequences would subvert the efforts to encourage capital accumulation among the public.

Finance and Posts and Telegraphs reached an impasse as neither could agree on the content of the formal *Memorandum for the Government* that O'Broin had proposed. This was a critical document intended to introduce the Television Committee's report to the Cabinet. As compromise proved impossible, O'Broin revised the *Memorandum for the Government* by simply incorporating the objections of Finance while retaining the recommendations of the Television Committee and the request of the Minister of Posts and Telegraphs.

O'Broin forwarded this revised memo to the Department of Finance, asking that it be approved quickly so the entire issue could be taken up at the Cabinet level. Inside Finance the new submission was received with a degree of annoyance.

In the circumstances it seems somewhat unreasonable for the D/P&T [Department of Posts and Telegraphs] to be attempting to rush matters . . . [it was] stated that the urgency arose from the fact that the M/P&T [Minister of Posts and Telegraphs] desires to obtain an early decision to enable him to reply to outside organizations . . . which are pressing for a decision on their proposal.[23]

The reference to outside pressures almost certainly concerned the scheme that had been submitted by Pye Ireland and was being lobbied for by Deputy

Erskine Childers. The Pye organization tried to increase the pressure on the government by revealing its proposal to the Irish press.

After some discussion, a reluctant compromise was reached on the content of the *Memorandum for the Government.* Finance inserted in the document a paragraph that outlined its strong opposition to the request being made by Posts and Telegraphs. Despite repeated efforts of O'Broin and his department, Finance refused to dilute the tone of the paragraph that was included in the document and forwarded to the Cabinet. Disregarding the objections of Finance, Posts and Telegraphs formally requested that Michael Keyes be allowed to make a public statement that would commit the government to a television service that would be both publicly owned and managed. The document also asked for permission to reject the proposals of Federated Trust, RCA, and the Pye Company.

The memorandum was submitted to the Cabinet and reviewed on July 6, 1956.[24] It was decided that Keyes should make an announcement in the Dail stating that the government supported the establishment of television as a "service based on public ownership and management; and . . . that, at the present time, the establishment of such a service would involve expenditure beyond the resources available to the state, regard being had to other commitments, and would, furthermore, be undesirable on the ground that it would encourage imports of luxury goods, to the detriment of our national economy."[25] Posts and Telegraphs also received permission to reject the proposals it had received.

The government supported Posts and Telegraphs by making a firm commitment to public service television and by allowing the department to reject the proposals submitted by private companies. This was an important victory for O'Broin and his associates in the quest to introduce public television to Ireland. The concession to Finance was the inclusion of language that stated that given the state of the country's economy, such a service could not be introduced at any time in the near future. Finance might have lost the battle over television to O'Broin, but the war between the two departments was far from over. As will be seen, the powerful Department of Finance still wielded considerable influence in cases where the spending of public funds was an issue.

NOTES

1. State Paper Office, Department of the Taoiseach, S14996A, Television Committee, *First Supplemental Report*, March 1956.

2. Ibid., p. 10.

3. Ibid., p. 11.

4. Ibid.

5. Ibid.

6. Ibid.

7. Ibid., p. 12.

8. State Paper Office, Department of the Taoiseach, S14996 (annex).

9. Ibid. The RCA report had included a map illustrating where transmitters would be located. The map only detailed the twenty-six counties of the Irish Republic, the six counties of Northern Ireland had been erased, showing an island that appeared to have a large bay where the northeast was located.

10. State Paper Office, Department of the Taoiseach, S14996A, First Supplemental Report of the Television Committee, p. 12.

11. RCA had a great deal of experience in television broadcasting and had built television stations in a number of foreign nations, including Mexico and Peru. If the company had succeeded in gaining a license to broadcast in Ireland, it would have sent a Boston native, Edward Roth, to oversee the building of the service. Roth had organized television services in Mexico and Peru and at the end of the decade would play a critical role in bringing a native television service to Ireland. Moreover, Roth would become the first director-general of Irish television in 1960.

12. State Paper Office, S14996A, Department of the Taoiseach, *Confidential Memo to the Office of the Taoiseach from the Minister of Posts and Telegraphs*, February 4, 1956.

13. Ibid., p. 20.

14. Ibid.

15. Ibid.

16. Department of Finance, S104/1/50, O'Broin to Redmond, April 9, 1956.

17. Ibid., *Memorandum for the Government*, from the Office of the Minister for Posts and Telegraphs, May 1956.

18. Ibid.

19. See Ronan Fanning, *The Irish Department of Finance 1922–1958* (Dublin: Institute of Public Administration, 1978), p. 77.

20. Department of Finance, S104/1/50, Twamley to Fitzgerald, May 28, 1956, p. 3.

21. Ibid.

22. Ibid., Fitzgerald to O'Broin, June 2, 1956.

23. Ibid., Twamley to Fitzgerald, June 9, 1956.

24. State Paper Office, Department of the Taoiseach, S14996A, Memorandum for the Government, from the office of the Minister for Posts and Telegraphs, June 13, 1956.

25. Ibid., Cabinet Minutes, July 6, 1956.

CHAPTER 4

The Contribution of Sean Lemass

In March 1957, the Fine Gael–led Inter-Party government collapsed when a partner in the coalition, Clann na Poblachta, withdrew its support. In the election that followed, Fianna Fail won a majority in the Dail and Eamon de Valera, at age seventy-four, returned as Taoiseach. Neil Blaney was named Minister of Posts and Telegraphs, and Sean MacEntee, who had been the Minister of Finance in the previous Fianna Fail Government, moved to the Department of Health and Welfare. Dr. James Ryan became the new Minister of Finance. The change in government coincided with growing public pressure demanding that an Irish television service be established. This created a new sense of urgency as television once again became a contentious subject.

In the summer of 1957, the Irish and British presses published details of specific television proposals that private companies had made to the government. By the end of the year, fifteen different offers had been received by the Department of Posts and Telegraphs. The fact some of the schemes had begun to surface in the press, contributed to the pressure that continued to build in support of television.

Two proposals proved controversial and therefore deserve close consideration. The Paris-based Michelson Group submitted a proposal in December 1956, and an American firm, the McLendon Investment Corporation, presented an offer in April 1957. These two proposals were unique as they offered to build, at no cost to the state, a national television network in exchange for being granted the right to establish international commercial radio stations in Ireland. McLendon and Michelson were primarily interested in the lucrative field of international commercial broadcasting. Both were willing to underwrite the cost of building and operating a national television service if they were granted the exclusive right to operate an international commercial radio service from Irish territory. The McLendon and Michelson proposals were in many ways similar. This suggested to the Television Committee that the plans were financially viable and that there was a tremendous amount of money to be made in international commercial broadcasting. Both proposals were initially rejected and later reconsidered as the government tried to find the service that would best address the complex needs of the nation. The issues that these proposals raised dominated the debate concerning Irish television over the next eighteen months.

The more remarkable of the two proposals was that of a company based in Paris and headed by a Romanian expatriate, Charles Michelson. Michelson submitted an impressive proposal that gained support from a diverse number of parties with an interest in Irish television and radio. Michelson's proposal was striking for a number of reasons, and deserves to be examined in detail.

The Michelson Group proposed to build an extensive television network for the state. This would be comprised of two separate stations: the first would broadcast as a public service, while the second would be a commercial channel. Michelson's company intended to build and operate both these stations and emphasized that the state would not have to risk any capital. The company suggested that the public service station broadcast educational and cultural material and not include any advertisements. The commercial channel would broadcast entertainment programs and accept advertisements from sponsors. The income from this station would one day support its noncommercial counterpart and allow Michelson to disengage completely from Irish television. The proposal envisioned the creation of a government body that would be established by the state to work with the private company. In an effort to placate concerns about the material that would be broadcast, the scheme stipulated that the Irish government would have full control over the program content of both stations.

Television was not the only benefit to be gained by the state, as Michelson was prepared to assist Radio Eireann by building new facilities, including a network of three very high frequency/frequency modulation (VHF/FM) stations. This would enable the radio service to be received in a dependable manner throughout the country, a task that continued to elude Radio Eireann, much to the consternation of citizens in the more remote parts of the country.

Although the outlined benefits would not consume scarce public funds, there was a price that would have to be paid. In return for providing the network described, Michelson's group required rights to set up a number of high-power international, commercial radio stations. This commercial radio network would broadcast directly into western Europe, and particularly into Britain. Michelson also hoped to operate a medium-wave commercial service that would one day broadcast to the East Coast of the United States, as well as a shortwave commercial radio station that, he hoped, could be received worldwide.

The proposal was problematic for a number of reasons, but it was particularly troublesome as the company had not been allocated a wavelength that would enable it to broadcast from Ireland. This was a problem for the Irish government, as it had been party to an international agreement designed to regulate radio wavelengths. While both the Michelson group and its competitor, the McLendon Corporation, were not overly concerned with the treaty, the Irish Government was, especially Posts and Telegraphs. The government was a signatory to the 1948 Copenhagen Plan, which assigned specific radio wavelengths to European nations. The treaty had experienced mixed success, and the entire issue of wavelength regulation had become confused as a number of countries who were not signatories had ignored the agreement entirely and established high-powered radio stations that could be heard throughout Europe. The most important of these stations was Radio Luxembourg, a commercial station that broadcast popular music from Luxembourg, which had not been a party to the Copenhagen Agreement. Radio Luxembourg had a large British audience and the station had proven to be a huge financial success. Michelson and the American McLendon Corporation were impressed by its success and excited at the possibilities that commercial radio offered in Europe.

Michelson had built and operated a commercial service, Europe Number One, which, like Radio Luxembourg, had ignored the Copenhagen Agreement. The station had been established in 1952 and broadcast from the Saar while it was under French administration. By establishing his radio station in the Saar, Michelson avoided being in direct violation of the Copenhagen Agreement. Michelson had cleverly set up a powerful commercial radio station in an area that had not been clearly defined by the treaty. However, Europe Number One created difficulties, and Michelson soon found himself embroiled in disputes with both the German and French authorities. The station had "appropriated" a wavelength that caused interference with a number of European radio stations that were broadcasting in accordance with the Copenhagen Agreement. Finland, Denmark, Sweden, and Norway all protested that Europe Number One was interfering with their national radio stations, which were broadcasting on wavelengths assigned by the treaty. These protests resulted in a decision by the authorities in the Saar to buy out the station, which had been established as a legal enterprise. Europe Number One was scheduled to be closed down in July 1958. In these circumstances, Ireland appeared to offer Michelson the opportunity to get back on the air.

Michelson's proposal contained a legal brief on the issue of wavelengths written by an internationally renowned scholar based at the University of Brussels. Dr. Henri Rolin submitted a written legal opinion arguing that the Copenhagen Agreement was a seriously flawed document. He also pointed out that the treaty featured an escape clause, which would allow the Irish Government to withdraw from the agreement after providing a one-year notice. This would permit Ireland to accept Michelson's proposal and legally establish an international radio station.

Maurice Gorham, the Director of Radio Eireann and a member of the Television Committee, had examined the proposal in detail. In reviewing the proposal for the committee, he addressed the attributes of the scheme but also recognized the wavelength problem, maintaining that the proposal made no mention of how this obstacle would be overcome. Gorham was suspicious of the proposal, which, he concluded, seemed "too good to be true."[1]

The Television Committee met with Charles Michelson in March 1957 and Matthew Doherty prepared a memorandum, detailing the discussion that took place. Doherty was a senior civil servant who worked at Radio Eireann and had become closely involved with the work of the Television Committee. (Leon O'Broin was not present.) Michelson answered a number of specific questions but was evasive when the subject of wavelengths was raised. He maintained that the appropriate wavelength could be obtained through bilateral negotiation with an unnamed European state. Doherty indicated that he believed Michelson would simply appropriate a wavelength for use by the proposed radio station. In spite of this, it is evident that Michelson impressed the members of the Television Committee. Doherty described Michelson as:

a man of considerable ability with a tremendous amount of knowledge about radio. . . . Only for his background (which it would appear must be the dominant factor) he is the type of man one would look for to carry out a programme of this sort if the state were prepared to engage in international commercial broadcasting and was not squeamish about international wavelengths etc.[2]

The Television Committee was interested in Michelson's proposal but concerned about his past business dealings; this explains the comment about his "background." Stories concerning his previous financial exploits in broadcasting had accompanied him to Ireland. Posts and Telegraphs initiated an investigation into Michelson's background and compiled a dossier on his past business activities. When the investigation was complete, O'Broin qualified the document by emphasizing that although the information gathered had come from a variety of sources, his department was unable to confirm it as factual.[3]

Charles Michelson's background certainly influenced the government's decision concerning his proposal. The investigation by Posts and Telegraphs was done with the help of the Gárda Síochána (the Irish police), and Michelson was aware that inquiries concerning his background were made by the state.[4] The investigation compiled contained a report of a 1955 Sub-Committee of the French Parliament and information that had been provided to the Gárda from unidentified sources. A collection of newspaper articles that reported on Michelson's business exploits on the Continent were also collected. The report provides information that sheds some light on this successful but mysterious entrepreneur.

Charles Michelson had been involved in electronic communications since 1939, when he formed Société Tangeroise de Radio—Diffusion, a company intended to operate a commercial radio station in Tangier and turned over to the French Government one year later as a "gift," although Michelson kept a financial interest in it. During the war, Michelson's relationship with the Vichy Government deteriorated, forcing him to flee to the United States. After the war Michelson sued the French Government to recover his interest in the radio station, which had been appropriated by the French authorities and renamed Radio Imperial. He was successful in his action against the French Government and was awarded 98 million francs.

The judgment embarrassed the French state and earned Michelson enemies in high places in the postwar French Government. In 1949 Michelson further alienated the government by disputing the disbursement of the award. He agreed to settle his claim when the French Government replaced part of the award with a grant of television and shortwave radio rights in Monaco. This settlement caused dissension within the French Government, and the French Minister for Information tried to void it. However Michelson prevailed once again in the courts as the settlement was upheld. Michelson then ceded his rights to Prince Ranier of Monaco while keeping a financial interest in a company he had formed.

Michelson was the principal shareholder in Images et Son, a company formed to exploit the concession he had been granted by the French Government in Monaco. The commercial radio service in Monaco ran into problems in 1955 when the French Government rescinded the concession that had been granted to Michelson in 1949. This created problems for the principality, as the national bank of Monaco, the Société Monégasque de Banque et de Métaux Précieux, had invested heavily in Images et Son. The value of the shares in the company plummeted, forcing the government to take measures to protect depositors at the bank. The crisis had political repercussions in the principality, as the entire Cabinet resigned. The troubled national bank was saved only with the intervention of Aristotle Onassis. The entire affair was an embarrassment to Prince Ranier and, once again, to the French government.

In 1952 Michelson formed a company, Société Sarroise de Télévision, that was established to build and operate a television and radio network in the French-administered Saar. Michelson had been a major shareholder in Europe Number One, the high-power commercial radio station he had formed, which broadcast popular commercial programs throughout western Europe from the Saar. As has been described, Europe Number One antagonized several neighboring countries, who complained that the station not only violated the Copenhagen Plan, but interfered with their radio stations. When the complaints were made, the Saar was still under French administration, so protests from these countries were delivered to the French government. As one might suspect, the French authorities were disturbed and once again embarrassed by Michelson. Paris subsequently launched an investigation into his business activities.[5]

Michelson had demonstrated an impressive ability to build radio stations in Europe, stepping gingerly around agreements that tried to discourage the type of radio service he concentrated on developing. This proficiency antagonized the French Government, which was clearly annoyed at his efforts. In 1955, Paris took the extraordinary step of exiling Michelson to the Mediterranean island of Corsica, an event that was reported in the investigation completed for Posts and Telegraphs. (As a refugee, Michelson did not enjoy the rights of French citizenship, and the government took advantage of his "alien" status to banish him to the remote Mediterranean island.)

Michelson appealed the order to the French Committee for Refugees and Stateless Persons and succeeded in having the decree rescinded. He also protested the findings of the Parliamentary Sub-Committee that had launched an investigation into his activities. He complained that he was being unjustly persecuted by the French Government and maintained that a competitor of his was behind what he regarded as harassment by the French Parliament. Michelson accused Radio Luxembourg of being the instigator of the investigation, stating that the owners had friends in high places in French political circles.

During the course of the investigation, O'Broin had received a number of impressive documents from Michelson that were intended to prove him the victim of a malicious campaign to discredit and defame him. In France Michelson had gone to a great deal of trouble to clear his name, and he appears to have succeeded in doing so. Supporters of Michelson were satisfied that he was an honest entrepreneur. However, his past business dealings remained a concern for the Television Committee and, in fact, prejudiced his efforts in Ireland.

It would be an obvious understatement to say that Michelson had ruffled a few feathers in his continental undertakings. It should be noted that all charges that had been made against Michelson by the French authorities had been dropped, a fact recognized by Maurice Gorham, who advised O'Broin not to "attach too much importance to the . . . reports. . . . These seem to be the result of the vicissitudes in French politics."[6]

Michelson's group had done a good deal of research in Ireland and was able to gain the support of Aer Lingus, Board Fáilte Éireann (the Irish Tourist Board), Córas Tráchtála (the Export Board), and the Hospitals Trust. Each one of these bodies was promised free access to the international commercial radio service that Michelson hoped to build. These influential supporters of the Michelson Group testified on his behalf and submitted letters arguing that the state would benefit by making a deal with the Romanian expatriate.

A separate proposal from an American company confirmed that the offer being made by the Michelson Group was, in fact, feasible, at least in the eyes of investors. The McLendon Corporation, a large, Texas-based communications company, was able to put together an offer much like Michelson's. The McLendon Corporation was also anxious to broadcast commercially from Ireland into Britain and Europe and promised to build and operate an Irish television service in return for obtaining such a concession. The company had an established track record in America and owned radio and television stations across the United States.

The president and founder of the company, Gordon McLendon, had been involved in radio broadcasting since 1947, when he purchased a half interest in station KNET in Palestine, Texas. His interest in radio grew with his founding of the Liberty Broadcasting System, which expanded to include over 400 stations in the United States. McLendon has been credited with developing innovative radio programs that helped revive an industry in decline. During his long career in communications, he developed the "top forty" hit song format, along with creative news and sports reporting. The Texas millionaire was co-owner of the largest chain of drive-in theaters in the American Southwest, and he was also a substantial shareholder in Subscription Television of America. His publications included such titles as *Understanding American Government, How to Succeed in Broadcasting* and *Get Really Rich in the Coming Super Metals Boom.*[7]

Gordon McLendon organized a demonstration of American television programs at the Shelborne Hotel in Dublin in June 1957, which Maurice Gorham attended. Gorham reported to the Television Committee that the two 30-minute programs were interrupted a number of times by commercials for the Dr. Pepper soft drink and the Ford Motor Company. The Director of Radio Eireann was not overly impressed by the presentation. He reported that McLendon had explained that the shows were not expensive, first-quality programs but rather what he defined as the type of programs an Irish television service could afford.[8]

During the 1950s submissions made to the government had been forwarded to the Department of Posts and Telegraphs and examined by the Television Committee. With the exception of the Pye proposal, these schemes had been kept confidential, as individual companies and the state avoided publicity that might jeopardize negotiations between interested parties. This changed in May 1957 when the *Irish Times* published a story reporting that the McLendon Investment Corporation had approached the government, offering to build a television service at no cost to the state. The paper did not provide extensive details about the plan but did report that the Texas company was engaged in active negotiations with the government. The article indicated that the Texas company was prepared to build a station worth approximately £400,000, while the government would not be required to make any investment. It was reported that a representative of the company was in Dublin, "to be on the spot while talks with various interested parties are taking place."[9] Noting that the Minister of Posts and Telegraphs, Neil Blaney, had recently stated that television was a "must" for Ireland but added his concern about the cost of a service, the *Irish Times* speculated: "The Minister may have been speaking with knowledge of this offer. . . . [A]t any rate, the fact that such a proposal has been made to the Government is not now in dispute."[10]

The press reports of the McLendon offer prompted Pye Ireland to issue a statement to the press announcing that it had made a £3 million proposal to the state in February 1956, which had been turned down. Dillon Digby, the director of Pye Ireland, told the *Irish Press* that the proposal was refused as the government maintained that when television came to Ireland, it would be operated by the state.[11] Pye was anxious to gain sanction from the Irish Government to build a station. The company had employed the former Fianna Fail Minister for Posts and Telegraphs, Erskine Childers, to lobby on their behalf. The overanxious Childers sent so many memos extolling the virtues of Pye that he managed to alienate members of the Television Committee and the staff at Posts and Telegraphs.

Television received additional coverage in the *Irish Radio and Electrical Journal* in the summer of 1957. In June, the magazine, which represented television retailers and manufacturers in Ireland, reported on the scheme that had been submitted by the Pye Company. A month later a representative of the McLendon Corporation outlined his company's proposal in an interview published in the magazine. Ronald J. Kahn stated that his company was interested in building a service that could cover the entire country in as little as six months. Kahn revealed that the proposed service would transmit television signals to Britain. He stated that it was the aim of his company to "provide Ireland with a powerful television transmitter which will not only give the country its own programme but will penetrate into England from London to Glasgow and compete with the I.T.A."[12] According-ing to Kahn this station would reach and exploit a market of over 48 million people. When queried about the technical problems in building a service that could reach into Britain, Kahn explained that these obstacles had been mastered and that the McLendon Company would have no difficulty transmitting deep into Britain from Ireland.

Kahn maintained that the proposal would provide jobs for Irish workers. American technicians were said to be waiting to make the trip to Ireland to build the station. These technicians would build the station and train Irish nationals in all aspects of television broadcasting. Kahn reminded the readers that Ireland was surrounded by British television and warned that new stations would be opening in Northern Ireland. "Expression can only be given to Irish culture, and the Irish Republic can only expect to counteract all this incoming television . . . by erecting a powerful station to transmit its own news and views to the world outside."[13]

On direct questioning, the McLendon representative gave assurances that if the station failed for technical reasons to transmit over the distances proposed, the company would continue to operate the service. He also stated that the station would eventually be ceded to the state free of charge, "so that you have everything to gain and nothing to lose!"[14] Kahn concluded his interview by explaining that there were certain details of the scheme that could not be disclosed.

The interview given by Kahn is extraordinary. There had not been any indication that television broadcast from an Irish station could penetrate into Britain from "Glasgow to London." The company spokesman was either ill-informed, confused, or intentionally trying to mislead the Irish public. It may have been that the McLendon Corporation sincerely believed it could erect a television transmitter that would reach into Britain, but given the company's technical sophistication, this is difficult to accept. Kahn may have confused radio and television or the range of the two commercial stations his company wanted to build. It would be difficult to assume that the McLendon group had intentionally tried to mislead both the Irish government and television industry in Ireland, as the company would have been aware that all proposals would be closely scrutinized. The interview added a bizarre twist to events and remains a mystery.

Pye Ireland Ltd. was quick to criticize the proposal. C. O. Stanley, the chairman of Pye, responded to the McLendon scheme by dismissing it as incredible. He described the scheme as "technically so fantastic, unrealistic and misleading that we don't wish to be mentioned in the same breath, in case our company should be identified with some of these ludicrous propositions."[15] Several months later, the McLendon Corporation advised the *Irish Radio and Electrical Journal* that its plan called for a commercial *radio* service that would broadcast into Britain, making no mention of a television service that would attempt to do the same.

While individual commercial proposals surfaced in the press, an intense debate heated up inside the Fianna Fail Government. There was a shift in the new government's thinking on television as the Minister of Posts and Telegraphs indicated a desire to consider the various proposals that had been sent to the department by commercial companies. Neil Blaney had asked O'Broin and the Television Committee to reconsider all the proposals that asked for concessions to establish both television and international radio stations in the country. Blaney was impressed by a number of the proposals, especially those of the Michelson Group and the McLendon Investment Company. O'Broin understood this and recognized that the change in government might mean a change in the policy that he had helped cultivate over the previous six years. Both he and Maurice Gorham strongly opposed the "new thinking" of the Fianna Fail Government. They understood that this threatened to undermine the commitment the previous government had made to a publicly owned and operated television service.

The Television Committee drafted a comprehensive *Memorandum for the Government* in June 1957, which considered international broadcasting and television. The memo sparked anew the debate that considered the structure of Irish television. O'Broin wrote a cover letter to Neil Blaney which accompanied the document and set the tone for the memo. He explained to his minister that the Television Committee had conducted an exhaustive investigation of all the proposals received by the government to date. It was reported that this study had taken into consideration Ireland's "obligations under international conventions, and Government responsibility in regard to finances and prestige of the state."[16] The memo was intended to point out the more problematic aspects of the commercial proposals and suggest yet another option that might be taken up by the government. Unfortunately, it was a confused, contradictory effort on the part of the Television Committee. The document was most likely hastily written by O'Broin and his associates, who feared Blaney would open negotiations with either Michelson or McLendon.

O'Broin asked his minister to review and approve the committee's memorandum, noting that it would be examined by a number of departments before it could be formally submitted to the Cabinet for a decision. The three departments involved in the television issue that had to sanction the memo were Finance, Industry and Commerce, and External Affairs. Surprisingly, Blancy did not object to the document, nor did he seek to revise its contents, thus, the poorly written memorandum was circulated to all three departments. The first part of the memo considered the state of Irish radio and what steps were required to improve the service. Radio Eireann, and radio in general (though not the primary focus of this work), were closely involved in the development of Irish television. The proposals of McLendon and Michelson underscore this point.

At this juncture, Leon O'Broin and the Television Committee suddenly exhibited a newfound desire to enhance the national radio service. They argued that this could be done by increasing the power of the main Radio Eireann transmitter at Athlone. In a startling departure from its earlier work, the committee argued that increasing the power of the Athlone transmitter was of paramount importance to the nation. The committee maintained that a more powerful transmitter would enable Radio Eireann to be received throughout Ireland and by the large Irish population living in Britain. The emphasis on reaching Irish nationals living in Britain quickly became an issue that obsessed Leon O'Broin and his staff. Increasing the range of Radio Eireann had not been a factor mentioned in any of the previous reports or memoranda that had been written by the committee. This omission was changed, not coincidently, after O'Broin and his staff had reviewed the proposals submitted by Michelson and McLendon and recognized how profitable their schemes might be.

The committee maintained that if Radio Eireann was allowed to increase the power of the Athlone transmitter, other changes would have to be made to allow the station to exploit its newfound range. O'Broin and his associates targeted the restrictions placed on Radio Eireann that prohibited the station from accepting advertisements from "foreign" companies. The reference to "foreign" companies concerned mainly British firms, which had been barred from advertising on Radio Eireann since 1934. The committee argued that this protectionist economic policy had hurt the development of the radio service and asked that these regulations be rescinded. The committee maintained that a more powerful Radio Eireann that was willing to accept British advertisers, would attract more sponsors, listeners, and revenue. This would allow the service to increase significantly its rather paltry annual receipts of £657,000.

One serious obstacle stood in the way of the committee's scheme. The committee admitted that unilaterally increasing the power of the Athlone station would violate the international treaty that governed radio wavelengths in Europe. The memo explained that the only way domestic radio coverage could be expanded within the parameters of the Copenhagen Agreement was by building an extensive and very costly network of VHF transmitters throughout Ireland. This would improve domestic reception dramatically but still leave the Irish in Britain out of range of Radio Eireann. The committee therefore argued that unless the Athlone transmitter could increase its power, and thereby its range and revenue, Radio Eireann was destined for eternal stagnation.

The committee also addressed the two television proposals that involved commercial radio. As might be expected, the committee was hostile to all commercial proposals, and especially those submitted by McLendon and Michelson. The committee was emphatic in stating that if either one of these two proposals were approved, the radio station would illegally "appropriate" a frequency. It argued that if the government accepted such a proposal, it would "flout [Ireland's] international obligations."[17]

The plans offered by Michelson and McLendon and the interest expressed by the new Fianna Fail government in these proposals caused a great deal of concern to the members of the Television Committee. The committee decided to try and assume the high moral ground by arguing that the international prestige of the country was at risk. It argued that the damage that would be done to the country's proud reputation as an upstanding member of the international community would be irreparable should the government choose to accept either one of these proposals. This point was driven home by. O'Broin, who emphatically asserted that the government should not withdraw from the Copenhagen Plan and enter the field of international commercial broadcasting.

This same memo formally requested permission to increase the power of the Radio Eireann transmitter at Athlone to 200 kilowatts. After spending considerable effort denouncing the McLendon and Michelson plans for advocating the violation of the Copenhagen Agreement, the committee asked that the Cabinet approve a plan that would allow Radio Eireann to ignore the same international agreement! The committee reasoned that increasing the power of the Athlone transmitter would be a lesser violation of the Copenhagen Plan, and therefore acceptable. It explained that it was not advocating simply "grabbing" a wavelength but only increasing the power of one it already possessed.

There is an obvious double standard here. The Television Committee had opened itself up to charges of inconsistency, if not outright hypocrisy. How could the committee take the high moral ground when considering Michelson and McLendon, only to abandon the commitment to principle when its own proposal was being discussed? It is tempting to argue that what really motivated O'Broin and his committee was not so much the principle of national honor, as the distaste for a commercial, foreign company estab lishing a commercial television and radio network in Ireland. This crusade became problematic when the committee decided that Radio Eireann should get into the business of broadcasting commercially into Britain.

Before considering television, the committee added to the confusion by admitting that even with such a high power transmitter at Athlone in operation, a network of VHF transmitters would be needed to ensure adequate radio coverage throughout the country. This statement contradicted an earlier passage indicating that the VHF transmitters would not be needed if the Athlone transmitter was allowed to increase its power.

Although the committee still supported the notion of a state-owned public service, the memo maintained that television "does not seem to the Minister to be so urgent as the problem of making sure that an Irish sound broadcasting service can be well received throughout Ireland and by the Irish in England."[18] This is surprising as the committee had, in its 1956 supplemental report, argued that Ireland urgently required a television service as a matter of national prestige. The committee was suddenly satisfied to wait for the day when circumstances would allow the establishment of a service based on the model it had proposed. The committee refused to consider seriously that a private commercial service might be the solution for which the government should opt. Sensing that the Fianna Fail government was attracted to such an option, O'Broin's committee decided to de-emphasize the importance of television in fear that a private company would be awarded a concession.

The committee accentuated the negative as much as possible, providing a gloomy forecast for television in the country. The Television Committee acknowledged that, given the state of the economy, the expenditure of state funds for a state service was out of the question. It argued that even if a private commercial service was established, the Irish economy would be adversely affected. "The public would be encouraged to buy television sets. They would be encouraged to buy foreign goods advertised on television."[19] The committee sounded confused as it employed the rhetoric of its historic nemesis, the Department of Finance.

The Television Committee concluded its formal memorandum by asking the government to support yet another proposal it had developed. This was a poorly planned and confused scheme that called for the establishment of a television service to be built and operated by a private company but owned by the state. The committee also requested permission to formally deny the proposals of Michelson and McLendon, whose schemes it found most abhorrent. Blaney offered no opposition to this formal memo, which was therefore forwarded to the Departments of Finance, External Affairs, and Industry and Commerce in July 1957. One can only speculate why Blaney had allowed this flawed, contradictory memo to circulate. Perhaps he simply failed to study the document in any great detail or was content to allow his secretary to dictate department policy concerning television.

Once the memo had been circulated, the one minister who was most critical of the document was Sean Lemass, the Tánaiste,* and Minister for Industry and Commerce. While in the past, O'Broin had tangled primarily with the Department of Finance, the Department of Industry and Commerce now became an important player in the debate within the government. As Tánaiste, Sean Lemass wielded considerable power in the last administration of the aging de Valera. Lemass was clearly disturbed by what he believed was an ambiguous, incoherent document. He expressed his concerns in a sharply worded letter sent to Neil Blaney in July 1957. In this correspondence one can, for the first time, observe the future Taoiseach express his opinion concerning television. The letter also sheds some light on the management style that characterized Sean Lemass.

*Tánaiste is the Irish term for deputy prime minister.

The Tánaiste was quick to take Blaney to task for what he regarded as an inferior effort on the part of his department. He complained, "The Memorandum is unsatisfactory from many viewpoints. It is just the type of Memo which, as a member of the Government, I hate to get because it does not convey a clear picture of the problem and appears to be, in some respects, self-contradictory."[20] Lemass focused in on the issue of radio and the confusing references and requests that had been made by Posts and Telegraphs. He criticized the document as being insincere in explaining the department's intentions:

The section of the memo dealing with Commercial Broadcasting also strikes me as being somewhat less than frank. Am I right in assuming that what is really being sought is increased coverage in Britain, plus a withdrawal of restrictions on accepting British advertisers, so as to get more revenue from this source? If so, why not say so?[21]

Lemass's penchant for concise, accurate information can be seen in this exchange. He recognized that the committee was interested in allowing British firms to advertise on Radio Eireann and realized that the true motive of O'Broin and the committee was enhancing the income of the station. The newfound desire of the committee to reach the Irish in Britain was one that Lemass regarded with suspicion. The Tánaiste told Blaney that the memo was highly suspect. "The references to serving Irish people in Britain rings a trifle phoney."[22]

Another point that caught Lemass's eye concerned the consideration that the committee had given to the Copenhagen Plan. He recognized the inconsistencies in the memo concerning the wavelength question and asked why the Irish government did not simply take the legal option of denouncing the Copenhagen Treaty. It is obvious that the confused submission by Posts and Telegraphs annoyed Lemass, who wanted a more concise, conclusive memo. Lemass understood the selective argument that had been made by Posts and Telegraphs. He also knew that Posts and Telegraphs was primarily interested in discrediting the commercial proposals of McLendon and Michelson and promoting its own incoherent plan. The Television Committee, O'Broin, and Blaney certainly made an impression on the future Taoiseach—a very poor one, considering his highly critical review of the memo.

When Lemass examined the portion of the memo that dealt with television, he became even more annoyed. He suggested a much more concise statement be made to the government, unlike the muddled, inconsistent submission that Posts and Telegraphs had produced. He told Blaney that the memo needed to be rewritten and that the issue should be put before the Cabinet in a clear fashion. "I suggest that you should put the T.V. issue to the Government in the following clear form:—(1) A state T.V. service is ruled out on grounds of cost. (2) A T.V. service must, therefore, be based on commercial advertising, and be provided by private enterprise."[23]

Lemass suggested that Blaney and his department outline for the Cabinet the requirements to which any prospective applicant would have to conform:

My suggestion is that you should seek authority from the Government to make a public announcement that proposals for a commercial T.V. service to be provided and operated by private enterprise will be considered subject to the following conditions: (1) No cost to the Government. (2) Suitable machinery for the supervision and control of programmes. (3) Free time for Public Services. (4) Nation wide coverage. (5) Encouragement of the Irish language.[24]

Lemass wanted the government to have the luxury of a concise summary that would make a specific and coherent request. The thirty-seven-part, seventeen-page document that he had reviewed from the Department of Posts and Telegraphs was simply too convoluted to enable the Cabinet to take decisive action. The management strategy Lemass adopted in this instance would again be employed when he became Taoiseach. Rather than be burdened with a complex, contradictory submission that would confuse and frustrate members of the Cabinet, Lemass wanted an explicit memorandum that would recommend a clear option. The government then could debate the submission and come to a decision.

In concluding his letter to Blaney, the Tánaiste suggested that, once adequate guidelines had been established, the department should quickly identify the one proposal that it thought was the most suitable. Blaney was told that he should then request the government's permission to make a commitment to that company. Lemass wanted a decision made by the government and a commitment given to a private commercial company that would allow a service to begin broadcasting. He certainly appreciated the argument that favored a public service, but he believed that the costs involved were beyond the state's resources. He saw no point in endless debate on the issue and was annoyed at the confusing memo produced by the Television Committee and Posts and Telegraphs.

The Department of Posts and Telegraphs responded to the Tánaiste's memo but failed to address the issues that he had raised. Rather than contest or object to specific points that Lemass had addressed, the letter tried to portray Posts and Telegraphs as being in general agreement with the

Tánaiste. It should be pointed out that although de Valera was the Taoiseach, much of the day-to-day business was being handled by his heir apparent, Sean Lemass. Therefore, neither Blaney nor O'Broin desired to openly challenge him. Blaney's reply suggests that the author was O'Broin, as its tone was careful and diplomatic, if not apologetic. It explained that Posts and Telegraphs was redrafting the memo that considered the complex issue of television and its future in Ireland. Though "grateful" for Lemass's "valuable" views on television, Posts and Telegraphs still maintained that it would be a mistake to allow a private commercial service to be established without substantial state control.

The Department of Finance had also received a copy of the confusing *Memorandum to the Government* that the Television Committee had produced. Finance remained very anxious about the cost that might be involved in any venture involving television. The department certainly did not surprise any of the interested parties when it announced that it opposed any service unless it was fully self-supporting.[25]

The Department of External Affairs wrote to O'Broin on July 29, 1957, responding to the Television Committee's memo. It supported the request to deny the proposals of McLendon and Michelson, the private companies that wanted to initiate international commercial broadcasting. Sean Murphy, the secretary of the Department of External Affairs, stated that his minister was not in favor of plans to simply take a wavelength in violation of the Copenhagen Plan, as this would damage the international reputation of Ireland. External Affairs was less concerned with the request by O'Broin and the committee to increase the power of the Athlone transmitter. It admitted that it understood that "while the increase from 100 to 150 kw. is a breach of the Plan, the minister agrees that, as the wave-lengths given cannot be altered in the next two or three years, your Department, if the government so agrees, would be justified in the circumstances, in experimentally increasing the power."[26]

Again, the Copenhagen Plan was open to selective interpretation. External Affairs recognized that simply taking a wavelength would create huge difficulties for the state. However, it was not concerned about violating the agreement if the government was only interested in increasing the power of the Athlone transmitter. Although such an increase would be a clear violation of the plan, External Affairs did not indicate that it saw this opinion as contradictory. On the specific question of television, External Affairs had no comments to make. The Department of External Affairs would not be an important player in the developing debate concerning television.

The three departments that were involved in these discussions agreed to meet to review the issues that had been raised by Posts and Telegraphs in the June 1957 memo. The gathering took place in July at the Department of Finance. Those attending included Leon O'Broin, who represented his department and the Television Committee, the Deputy Secretary of the Department of Industry and Commerce, T. Murray; and T. K. Whitaker, the Secretary of the Department of Finance. Sean O'Droma, an assistant to O'Broin, took the minutes of the meeting. Whitaker had become secretary at the Department of Finance on May 30, 1956, upon the retirement of Owen Redmond, who had been in that position since late 1953. Whitaker has gained a reputation as an innovative secretary who helped transform the Irish economy in the late 1950s and early 1960s. However, in 1957 he opposed bringing television to Ireland, thus embracing policies that had been developed by his predecessors.[27] Whitaker and Murray had agreed to meet with O'Broin in an attempt to allow a frank exchange of views and consider objections that Finance and Industry and Commerce had raised concerning the Television Committee's memo.

The meeting briefly considered the request of the committee to increase the power of the Athlone station. All parties agreed that the power should be increased, although Whitaker suggested that the countries that might be affected should be notified in advance. O'Broin was impatient, telling the two men that this was really an issue that fell under the jurisdiction of his department and not a subject that should concern them. One might assume that O'Broin did not want to dwell on what might be regarded as a thorny issue, which contradicted the rationale he had employed to discredit both the Michelson and McLendon proposals.

The discussion moved on to the question of cost as Finance expressed concern over the impact of the expansion of radio and the development of television on the weak Irish economy. Whitaker initially reported that his department was not concerned with the recommendation that the McLendon and Michelson proposals be rejected, as this was regarded as a matter of policy for Posts and Telegraphs. The Secretary of Finance was most concerned about what was regarded as the expensive proposal for the state to build a VHF network for Radio Eireann. He argued that investing further in Radio Eireann would be a mistake as he doubted it would produce an increase in the size of its audience.

If O'Broin had hoped that Finance might adopt a more compassionate attitude toward radio and television broadcasting, he was mistaken. He complained to Whitaker that he was tired of answering this sort of questioning of broadcasting needs by the Department of Finance; he had expected a more sympathetic approach at this stage. The broad facts were that broadcasting had been starved of funds . . . that it was only since the amount of money provided for programmes had been increased in recent years that it had been possible to have the programmes taken seriously and get a larger listening audience.[28]

It is difficult to understand why O'Broin had expected a more "sympathetic approach" from Finance, for the department had not given any indication that it had reconsidered its position on radio or television broadcasting. O'Broin pointed out that even if the power of the Athlone transmitter was increased, large sections of the country would still be unable to receive Radio Eireann. He argued that the government had an obligation to ensure national coverage and that increasing the power of Athlone and building the VHF transmitters were important for the prestige of the state. As these exchanges demonstrate the relationship between the two departments remained strained in spite of the change in governments and the arrival of T. K. Whitaker at the Department of Finance.

The discussion moved on to television and the most recent proposal by the Television Committee. O'Broin complained that Industry and Commerce had not given its opinion on the Television Committee's request concerning "foreign advertising." The secretary "pointed out that one of the most important aspects was that any television service established [in Ireland] without crippling cost to the state would have to be based on commercial advertising of foreign goods and he had expected the Department of Industry and Commerce to comment officially on this but they had not done so."[29] O'Broin asked the assistant secretary if his department was prepared to alter regulations that had been part of the state's protectionist economic policy which had recently come under revision.[30] Murray admitted that his minister had not commented directly on this question but stated, "It was clear by implication that he accepted that television would have to be based on advertising of foreign goods and his Department's 'no comment' could be interpreted as no objection in principle to the proposals."[31]

Whitaker expressed skepticism that a commercial company would be interested in accepting the latest scheme outlined by the Television Committee. The doubt he expressed was certainly warranted, as this new scheme had been quickly outlined in the rather weak memo that had produced the harsh critique by Sean Lemass. O'Broin recognized this and told Whitaker that the committee was drafting a new memorandum for the Cabinet which would propose that the government build facilities for a television service and then find suitable programs to broadcast on it. This was a return to the type of structure the committee had envisioned in its 1956 report to the government. The plan would require government funding for the construction of infrastructure and purchase of equipment. O'Broin acknowledged that he was looking to the independent television service in Britain as a model, explaining "that the state should bear the capital cost as the I.T.A. does in Great Britain. It would then be in a far stronger position of control vis-à-vis the contractor than otherwise."[32]

O'Broin maintained that he did not simply propose an Irish version of the ITA, and he indicated that the service he had in mind should also have access to noncommercial BBC programs. O'Broin appeared to have accepted the notion that Irish television was going to be dominated by British material. The agents of that domination would be the Irish government. This, it was suggested, would make such an arrangement more palatable.

Whitaker, for his part, must have surprised those at the meeting when, at the conclusion, he indicated that "his Department would raise no objection to the recommendation proposed. They recognized that television would have to come sooner or later and he personally could not imagine a television service in this country without a good deal of public control."[33] The Department of Finance still did not see any urgency in bringing television to the state. In spite of the positive tone that emerged from Finance at the meeting, it soon became apparent that no significant change in policy had taken place.

Shortly after this meeting, O'Broin had what he described as a productive meeting with Sean Lemass. The men discussed the scheme that O'Broin had mentioned to Whitaker and Murray and the earlier memo from Posts and Telegraphs that had initiated the most recent round of discussions concerning television. Writing to Blaney after his meeting with O'Broin, Lemass indicated: "I was considerably impressed by his views. I gather from him that a revised memo will be circulated shortly."[34] Sean Lemass had recognized that when it came to radio or television broadcasting, Leon O'Broin, and not Neil Blaney, was the person at Posts and Telegraphs with whom to confer. After meeting with Lemass, O'Broin set out to revise the draft memo that had initiated the flurry of meetings concerning radio and television.

The revision was done by O'Broin alone, without the input of the Television Committee. The draft of the new memo suggests that the secretary had thought out his department's options and had come to form a more coherent opinion of what steps might be taken to bring television to the country. The revised document covered some of the same ground as the original memo. Again O'Broin stated that bringing television to Ireland would not be difficult. The problem was that doing so would primarily bring commercial British programs to the country, with only a small amount of Irish material. He also returned his attention to Northern Ireland, for the first time since the 1956 *Supplemental Report*. He pointed out that with the imminent introduction of an ITA station, Northern Ireland would have the luxury of enjoying both commercial and public television.

In these circumstances, he argued, it was important that an Irish station be able to broadcast programs from a respected public service station, the BBC. O'Broin had always admired both BBC Radio and Television. He once again raised the possibility of entering into an arrangement with the British that would allow BBC television to be received in Ireland. While before he had seemed resigned to commercial programs purchased from ITA sources, he now saw this arrangement as being detrimental to the state. He argued that an Irish television service should make a concerted effort to obtain programs from the BBC as the British public service offered superior programs. "If we are going to submit ourselves as a nation to further outside influence by having TV, we had better go for the good, as well as for the less good programmes."[35]

O'Broin continued by outlining the structure of such a service, incorporating ideas he and the Television Committee had proposed earlier and some of the concepts he had seen in the commercial schemes he had reviewed. He argued that a public corporation should be established to handle both radio and television. He believed that the television segment of the corporation should have two networks, one commercial, which would carry entertainment programs, and one that was public, which would carry educational and cultural material. The public channel would broadcast the programs of the BBC plus a limited Irish element.

The secretary continued by stating that the public corporation he envisioned would lease time on the commercial network to a program contractor, much as the ITA did on Britain's commercial network. It was proposed that a contract with a commercial program company would last ten years, providing the company was willing to agree to conditions that the public corporation would require. This would include a commitment from the company that a certain percentage of its programs would have an Irish element and the agreement that the commercial company would help underwrite the cost of equipment and transmitters. O'Broin was confident that the British authorities would lend technical and logistical support to the public corporation. In fact, he expected that the British Post Office would assist the public corporation in its dealings with commercial program companies and hoped both the BBC and the ITA would also help get the

Irish service on the air. O'Broin did not see any difficulty in gaining permission from the BBC to obtain and broadcast its programs.

The Secretary of Posts and Telegraphs stated that he had gone over this proposal with Lemass, who had expressed satisfaction that the scheme would be accepted by the government. This would account for Lemass telling Blaney that he had spoken with O'Broin and was impressed by the secretary's ideas. O'Broin reported that after speaking with Lemass, he was left with the impression that the Tánaiste liked the proposals and would support them in the Cabinet. However, O'Broin admitted that Lemass was concerned about the ability of the Exchequer to finance the building of the public network, the one O'Broin hoped would relay the BBC. Lemass had told O'Broin that "he thought it might not be possible for the Exchequer to finance the second network."[36] However, this did not discourage the secretary. He wanted a commitment from the government that television would be under strict state control and contain two networks, one commercial and the other public.

While O'Broin was convinced that he had made progress with the Tánaiste, the Department of Finance remained a formidable source of opposition. Louis Fitzgerald at Finance wrote to O'Broin in August 1957, attaching a draft memo that contained his department's view on television. It stated that when Posts and Telegraphs made their submission to the government, Finance would send its own memo to the government expressing its opinion. Finance stated that it supported the O'Broin's desire to boost the Athlone signal, provided it could be done without cost falling on the Exchequer. Cost remained the paramount issue for Finance, which argued against building the expensive network of VHF transmitters that Posts and Telegraphs had proposed.

Television remained a key concern for the Department of Finance in spite of Whitaker's conciliatory tone at the interdepartmental meeting held July 27, 1957. Finance once again maintained that it was opposed to the introduction of this "luxury service," which, it feared, would be a financial drain on the nation. It also argued that "its initiation as a national service would encourage considerable expenditure by private individuals on television sets . . . and most of the programmes would necessarily carry appeals to spend on the advertisers' wares. A national television service would, therefore, be a disincentive to saving."[37]

This macro-view of the department would be expanded and employed by Finance over the next few years. The department may have sensed a shift in the Cabinet, believing that ministers might be more inclined to commit the state to some form of public service television. Finance, therefore, chose to emphasize the impact the service would have, not on the budget in one fiscal year, but on the national economy over several years. It also highlighted the difficulties the state was having in supporting important and very expensive social programs, arguing that:

It would be most unwise to undertake amenity expenditure for which there is no such pressing need. . . . State encouragement of, or assistance for, television would be altogether at variance with pronouncements emphasizing the need for saving to finance national development. . . . The Minister, therefore, considers that arrangements to provide a national television service should not be made until the demand for more essential amenities (particularly housing) has been largely satisfied.[38]

Finance argued that when the state was in a better position to afford television, it would support a service that included some form of public control. However any such service should, in the department's opinion, require no state funding.

The amended memo caused discord within the Television Committee itself. Maurice Gorham reviewed the revised document that O'Broin had written and raised a number of questions in criticism of the changes the latter had made. Gorham argued that the new proposal to have two stations, one that would rebroadcast the BBC and be a public service and one that would be modeled on the ITA, was a mistake. Gorham believed it would be difficult to get government approval for one station and that asking for two would make matters more difficult. He also questioned the political repercussions of relying so heavily on two British stations. Indeed, it is difficult to imagine how O'Broin expected to overcome objections of allowing an Irish service to be so overwhelmingly British. Gorham explained his thinking on the matter to O'Broin by stating, "I think if we had to choose either BBC or ITV as our main prop, we could more easily defend ITV, on grounds of being more popular in Britain (much more), and less British—official—propaganda."[39]

Gorham also pointed out that the European Broadcasting Union (EBU) had granted Ireland only one national wavelength for television broadcasting and that simply taking a second would create problems. He wondered how the secretary expected to gain the cooperation of the British if the Irish Government intended to ignore this international agreement. "But what chance would we have of getting a cheap-and-easy agreement with the BBC if we raised a howl from the BPO [British Post Office] and the EBU [European Broadcasting Union] for taking a set of second-programme wavelengths when we had asked only for and been allotted one?"[40]

Gorham's critique demonstrates that there was dissension within the Television Committee. O'Broin had taken his ideas to the Tánaiste and then simply redrafted the memorandum on his own, without asking for input from the Committee. He ignored the group with which he had been working, and the results were obvious. Gorham had a number of valid points that contested O'Broin's "new thinking." He was not afraid of challenging O'Broin and warned him that gaining the cooperation of the BBC would be difficult. Although Gorham's contribution to the Television Committee is difficult to measure, there is no doubt that he made a significant contribution to the committee's work. Gorham also exposed O'Broin's political naiveté in regard to a significant involvement of the BBC. This flaw in O'Broin's vision would create problems for the secretary that developed later.

On August 15, 1957, O'Broin wrote to his minister attaching a revised *Memorandum for the Government*, which was approved by Blaney and recirculated for comment to Finance, External Affairs, and Industry and Commerce.[41] All these departments indicated that they had no observations, with the exception of Finance, which stated that it would be submitting to the Cabinet a separate memo, which would accompany the formal Posts and Telegraphs memorandum. In the two months that had elapsed since the Television Committee had issued its original draft memorandum, it is clear that a more refined policy was beginning to emerge. However, there was still a great deal of work to be done before any sort of consensus could be established.

The formal *Memorandum for the Government* reviewed briefly the submissions that had been made to Posts and Telegraphs and examined the options it believed were available to the government. Citing the issue of national prestige, Posts and Telegraphs once again asked that the Michelson and McLendon proposals be rejected. A more detailed examination of the Copenhagen Plan was offered in an effort to address the sharp criticisms that Sean Lemass had made concerning the initial memo. The *Memorandum* also explained the general television policy that had developed under previous governments. This emphasized the importance of the July 1956 decision that the Inter-Party Government had made committing the state to public service television.

According to Posts and Telegraphs, the state had a number of options it could endorse. These ranged from establishing a pure public service to allowing a private company to build a station. These options were dismissed on economic and political grounds. The Cabinet was informed of Ireland's isolation compared to the rest of Europe. "Ireland is now practically the only country in Western Europe that has taken no step toward having a television service. (Iceland, Albania, and Greece do not appear to have television but they are hardly in Western Europe and are not the kind of countries we like to be compared with)."[42]

In the end the Cabinet was asked to approve O'Broin's most recent scheme. This envisioned the building of a two station network that would provide a commercial and a noncommercial channel. It was admitted that cost was the biggest challenge to this concept, but O'Broin was adamant in supporting the scheme, in spite of reservations expressed by both Lemass and Gorham. The Posts and Telegraphs submission to the Cabinet concluded by asking the government to promptly announce its acceptance that an Irish television station should be established as soon as possible and that any service should be controlled by a public statutory body that would oversee both television and radio.

The Cabinet met on September 17, 1957, and examined the submission by Posts and Telegraphs. Although the government was not able to address the entire memorandum, it came to a formal decision on part of the submission. The Cabinet considered the recommendations concerning the Michelson and McLendon proposals and agreed that these applications should be rejected.[43] It was also decided that the "experiment" of increasing the power of the Athlone transmitter should be allowed, with the stipulation that it would be done within the department's budget.

In October the government once again deliberated on the Posts and Telegraphs submission. This time the Cabinet indicated that it had studied the proposals raised in the memo and had come to a number of decisions. A formal notice from the Department of the Taoiseach announced that it was the government's position that Irish television should be "established as early as practicable; . . . under public control . . . [and], so far as possible, the service should be provided without cost to the Exchequer."[44] The Cabinet's decision concluded by announcing that a high-powered Cabinet Committee would be established to consider further details and report back to the government. This Cabinet Committee was to include the Tánaiste, Sean Lemass, and the Ministers for Posts and Telegraphs, Finance, and External Affairs.

Leon O'Broin and the Television Committee were wary of the decision announced by the Cabinet. It was understood that in mentioning "public control," the government had not endorsed a "public service." There was also the stipulation that stated that in establishing a television service, state funds should not be employed. However, the Cabinet's decision did not exclude the possibility of some sort of state support. The government ignored the more problematic and technical consideration of the actual structure of the service. This was left for the newly created Cabinet Committee to resolve.

O'Broin had dominated his department's thinking on television and had had some success influencing Lemass. The Department of Finance remained his most formidable opponent, although it appeared that Posts and Telegraphs was having some success in thwarting that department's determination to stop television. The government had committed itself to television, stating that a service should be established quickly under some form of public control. It also indicated that the service should not, "so far as possible," require support from the Exchequer. It was left to the Cabinet Committee to work out the details that would enable an Irish television service to be established. The efforts of this short-lived organization will be explored in the following chapter.

NOTES

1. Archives of RTE, Gorham Papers, no. 003. Confidential memorandum to Leon O'Broin, February 21, 1957.

2. Ibid. Memo prepared by Matthew Doherty, March 28, 1957.

3. Archives of RTE, 105/58, no. 5.

4. Archives of RTE, Papers of Maurice Gorham, no. 003, memo from Gorham to O'Broin, May 28, 1957.

5. Archives of RTE, 105/58, no. 5.

6. Archives of RTE, Papers of Maurice Gorham, no. 003, memo to O'Broin from Gorham, May 28, 1957.

7. Gordon McLendon Papers, Southwest Collection, Texas Tech University, Lubbock, Texas.

8. Archives of RTE, Papers of Maurice Gorham, no. 037, Memo from Maurice Gorham, July 5, 1957.

9. *Irish Times*, May 31, 1957.

10. Ibid.

11. *Irish Press*, June 6, 1957.

12. *Irish Radio and Electrical Journal*, 15, no. 173 (July 1957): p. 1.

13. Ibid., p. 8.

14. Ibid.

15. Ibid., *Irish Radio and Electrical Journal*, 15 (August 1957): p. 9.

16. Archives of the Department of Communications, Scotch House, TW894: 3, memo to Blaney from O'Broin, June 1957.

17. Ibid., draft memo to the Government from the Television Committee, June 26, 1957, p. 1.

18. Ibid., p. 10.

19. Ibid., pp. 11–12.

20. Ibid., letter from Lemass to Blaney, July 25, 1957.

21. Ibid.

22. Ibid.

23. Ibid.

24. Ibid.

25. Department of Finance, S104/1/50, memo to O'Broin, July 2, 1957.

26. Department of Communications, TW894:3, letter to O'Broin from Sean Murphy, Secretary of External Affairs, July 29, 1957.

27. Whitaker has explained that during his tenure, "We regarded TV as primarily for entertainment rather than education." Conversation and correspondence with Dr. T. K. Whitaker, Dublin, December 1990.

28. Department of Communications, TW894:3, minutes of the July 27, 1957 meeting.

29. Ibid., p. 3.

30. Tariff reductions had started in 1958 in anticipation of Ireland joining the Common Market. The tariffs had been in place since 1932 and were gradually eliminated under Lemass.

31. Ibid.

32. Ibid., p. 4.

33. Ibid., pp. 4–5.

34. Ibid., memo from Lemass to Blaney, August 1, 1957.

35. Ibid., memo from O'Broin to Sean O' Droma, July 31, 1957.

36. Ibid., p. 2.

37. Department of Finance, S104/1/50, memo from Fitzgerald to O'Broin, August 2, 1957.

38. Ibid., p. 2.

39. Department of Communications, TW894:3, memo from Gorham to O'Broin, August 10, 1957.

40. Ibid., p. 2.

41. Ibid., *Memorandum for the Government* from the Department of Posts and Telegraphs, August 15, 1957. The memo was altered to take into consideration some of Gorham's concerns.

42. Ibid., "TV Memo Supplementary Information. Comments on Finance Memorandum," p. 2.

43. Ibid., memo to the Department of Posts and Telegraphs from the Department of the Taoiseach, September 17, 1957.

44. State Paper Office, Department of the Taoiseach, S14996B, memo dated October 25, 1957.

CHAPTER 5

The Cabinet Committee

The Cabinet Committee that was formed in October 1957 had been established to determine the most effective means of bringing television to Ireland. The committee included the Tánaiste and Minister of Industry and Commerce, Sean Lemass; the Minister for Posts and Telegraphs, Neil Blaney, the Minister for Finance, Dr. James Ryan, and the Minister for External Affairs, Frank Aiken. This committee was established to examine television in light of the recent decisions that had been reached by the government. The new ministerial body was required to report to the Government after exploring how an Irish television service could be introduced, "as early as practicable, under public control . . . [and] . . . so far as possible, . . . without cost to the Exchequer."[1]

Sean Lemass dominated this short-lived committee. As the debate over television matured, one can see a confident Tánaiste asserting himself. Lemass was certainly not afraid to seize the initiative in this committee, nor was he hesitant to make important, unilateral policy decisions. The Television Committee at Posts and Telegraphs did not withdraw once the Cabinet Committee was formed. Rather, O'Broin and his associates continued to be involved in the development of the state's emerging television policy. Posts and Telegraphs worked with the Cabinet Committee and was responsible for preparing its final report, which contained the group's recommendations to the government. Posts and Telegraphs was also responsible for helping coordinate the work of the Cabinet Committee and providing it with technical and historical information.

The relationship between Posts and Telegraphs and the Cabinet Committee proved difficult, as the secretary and his associates were on the receiving end of policy decisions that they considered unacceptable. In the past the department had been proactive, as it was able to influence policy and debate on the subject of television. Indeed, it had experienced some success in trying to steer the government in the direction of a scheme it had developed. However, with the creation of the Cabinet Committee, the staff at Posts and Telegraphs found themselves reacting to the committee's proposals and declarations. This new relationship was difficult for O'Broin to accept. He was uncomfortable with the direction in which he believed Lemass and the Cabinet Committee were moving and frustrated by his inability to convince the ministers to change their approach to television.

The first task of the Cabinet Committee was to draft a public announcement that would be made by Neil Blaney, the Minister for Posts and Telegraphs. The Cabinet met in November 1957 and decided to allow Blaney to issue a public statement inviting proposals from companies interested in television broadcasting in Ireland. This statement had been carefully drafted by Sean Lemass and approved by the Cabinet Committee. It was an important announcement as it provided an indication of the type of proposal the government sought.

On November 11, 1957, Neil Blaney addressed the Association of Advertisers in Ireland and revealed the government's new position on television. After opening his speech with the now-familiar rhetoric about the power of the medium and the need to ensure that material it broadcast be of high quality, the minister told his audience that the government had decided to encourage the development of commercial television. He explained that the service would have to be commercial in character as the state simply could not afford to build and operate an expensive public service. The government was:

prepared to consider proposals from private interests for the provision of a transmission network that will ensure satisfactory reception in all parts of the country, as well as necessary studios and complementary indoor and outdoor equipment. The entire capital and maintenance costs will be met by the promoting group . . . in consideration of a license to operate commercial programmes for a term of years.[2]

Blaney revealed that his department had already received several very interesting proposals. He emphasized that it was anticipated that no cost would fall on the Exchequer. He continued by outlining the structure of the Irish service and defining its relationship with the state. "The television system will become state property and will be under the control of a

Television Authority. . . . The authority . . . will . . . make special arrangements regarding such matters as the presentation of news and the position of the Irish language. It will be a condition that part of the time will be made available for programmes of a public service character."[3] Blaney also addressed the issue of advertisements, indicating that the government had decided to discard the ban on foreign commercials (a policy that had been in force on Radio Eireann since 1934). He acknowledged that to succeed, commercial television would be heavily dependent on advertisements, and that limiting access of nonnative companies would be a mistake. The minister expressed confidence that Irish companies would still make "the maximum use of the new medium for advertising Irish goods to Irish people."[4]

The November 6, 1957 address marked a turning point in the painfully slow development of Irish television. The government made it clear that television in Ireland would be a service "largely commercial in character," with "private interests" responsible for building and running the service. The fact that the announcement was made at a convention of advertisers underscored the extent of the commercial commitment being made. The speech clearly reflected the desire of Sean Lemass to grant a license to a private company, which would have an exclusive right to broadcast in Ireland. The speech interpreted the government's decision of October 25, 1957 in a fairly strict sense. It discounted the role of an active and powerful television authority and stipulated that the state would not be involved in the building of transmitters or studios or the provision of additional equipment. It did indicate that the state would become the owner of the service, but it did not explain exactly how or when this would happen.

Blaney's speech was carried in the national press, which reported that the government had made a firm commitment to commercial television. The *Irish Press* reported that the announcement had created a great deal of interest among foreign companies interested in commercial television in Ireland. It reported that Blaney's speech marked an important change in the state's policy on television as proposals would now be welcome from companies all over the world. The *Irish Press* reported that the speech had prompted intense interest in Irish television from abroad: "the Department of Posts and Telegraphs was bombarded with queries as to how soon the Government wished to go ahead with its TV service. . . . So far the Minister has received and studied offers from Ireland, England, America, and France."[5]

One could reasonably speculate that either Blaney or one of the members of the Cabinet Committee leaked a few embellished details to the press to try and stir up additional interest inside the communications industry. Although proposals had been received from these countries, there is no evidence that the Post Office was suddenly inundated with new proposals or queries. O'Broin had observed that the government was using Blaney's announcement to "see what sort of fish are likely to enter the pool as well as the limits of concessions they are likely to make."[6]

The *Irish Independent* endorsed the minister's statement and applauded the government's decision: "The national finances are such that it is out of the question to introduce any scheme which will involve a charge on the revenue; television is and will be a luxury service and those who enjoy it will have to pay for it, without grant or subsidy."[7] It is important to note that the publication went so far as to employ the terminology used by Finance in describing television as a "luxury service." Opposition to the minister's announcement, which emphasized the commercial character of television in Ireland, would take time to mature. At this juncture, the three major political parties did not oppose the direction in which television was evolving.

The announcement took the communications industry in Ireland by surprise. An article that appeared in the *Irish Times* reported that the statement had been greeted with a great deal of optimism and happiness. One unnamed industry spokesman maintained that television would have a positive effect on the more remote parts of the country. He termed the decision a "godsend" to rural areas, suggesting that the introduction of television would "help to stem emigration."[8] How television would do this was not explained.

The announcement also created a good deal of confusion in the industry as, the *Irish Times* explained, "some got the impression that the Government wants a company to build a television studio, provide all the necessary equipment, put up the necessary television masts all over the country, and run the station till it becomes a success when it would become state property."[9] This was a fairly accurate summary of the state's new policy. The *Irish Times* reported that many in the television industry were not impressed by Blaney's speech. It reported that executives in the industry hoped the offer would include "some arrangement whereby an alternative frequency would be granted to the successful promoter when the Government took over the station. The promoting group could then continue with a different type of programme."[10] There was no scheme that envisioned any such agreement. However, the government had declared itself open to suggestions and proposals and very interested in trying to negotiate a deal.

It is clear that the proposals submitted by the McLendon Company and Charles Michelson had influenced Sean Lemass and the Cabinet Committee. These proposals had set high expectations, as they did not involve the spending of state funds. As Lemass and the Cabinet Committee examined the options open to the government, they realized that the two proposals remained attractive alternatives. It would be difficult, if not impossible, for an applicant that was not interested in building, or able to build, an international commercial radio network to match the offers of these wealthy and experienced entrepreneurs.

The new government policy, as articulated by the Minister of Posts and Telegraphs, was a blow to supporters of public service television, especially Leon O'Broin. If the government decision, announced in September 1957, that approved the rejection of the Michelson and McLendon proposals was seen as a partial victory by O'Broin, Blaney's announcement in November 1957 was clearly a defeat. In interpreting the September decision, the Cabinet Committee chose to emphasize the commercial makeup of an Irish television service. At this juncture, one can discern a growing sense of alienation overtaking Leon O'Broin. The secretary believed that all the efforts of the Television Committee to secure some form of public television for Ireland were in danger of failure.

Shortly after the announcement, Leon O'Broin was visited by E. A. Grace, the Secretary of Irish Cinemas Ltd., who informed the secretary that his company was interested in being considered for the television concession. O'Broin told Grace to submit a short proposal but to hold off from providing a more detailed plan until the public authority that had been mentioned in the minister's speech was established. O'Broin explained that the proposed television authority would collect more specific information once the entity was formed.

The concept of a state authority responsible for overseeing a television station was not a new one. It had been raised by the Television Committee and by private companies such as Michelson and Pye Ireland. However, Blaney's announcement indicated that a television authority would oversee television in the state and also perform a number of other important duties. Blaney had not indicated when this authority would be established and what role, if any, it would play in selecting a private, commercial-broadcasting company. The statement issued by the minister was purposely vague, as Lemass and his associates were unsure of the precise role the authority would play.

O'Broin wanted the new body to become involved quickly in television. He wrote to his minister the day after he had given his speech, inquiring about the authority and making specific recommendations. He believed that the authority should be established quickly and that it should be the entity to review proposals from companies interested in television broadcasting in Ireland. He argued that this organization should then make a recommendation to the government advising which proposal was the most appropriate.

O'Broin also asked his minister to try and get the Cabinet Committee to commit to the concept of a powerful authority that would be responsible for both television and radio. The secretary clearly was worried about the effect of television on the national radio service. He believed that steps had to be taken early to try and prevent the demise of Radio Eireann. With television seemingly on the horizon, O'Broin wanted assurances that the national radio service would not be ignored and allowed to wither on the vine. O'Broin also suggested that the new public authority could be known as Radio Teilefhís Éireann, or RTE.[11]

Sean Lemass strongly disagreed with O'Broin and believed that Posts and Telegraphs should remain actively involved in researching and interviewing various applicants. Lemass asserted that although the Cabinet Committee had not formally addressed who should review the applications and make the necessary recommendations, he was comfortable in making a unilateral decision on the matter. As Tánaiste and heir apparent to de Valera, Lemass did not fear being challenged. He wrote to Blaney instructing him how Posts and Telegraphs should assist the Cabinet Committee to complete its work. He stated that the Television Committee should review each proposal in a critical manner and submit a detailed report examining each submission. The Television Committee could then recommend the proposal that seemed most appropriate.

Lemass recognized that Posts and Telegraphs and Leon O'Broin had gained a good deal of experience in television and that it was logical that the department continue to work with the government in bringing the medium to Ireland. He was not about to allow this group to disengage from television at such a critical juncture. The Tánaiste requested that O'Broin draft clear guidelines to be given to applicants interested in Irish television broadcasting. These guidelines would have to be approved by the Cabinet Committee and would detail exactly what the government was looking for from commercial applicants. Lemass was hoping to receive additional input from O'Broin, and it is clear that in spite of differences concerning policy, O'Broin remained a valuable, though at times difficult, asset to the Tánaiste. Lemass told Blaney that he appreciated O'Broin's work and respected his opinion. "I personally should like to have his own view as to the decisions which he would recommend, but it might suffice if, when he has drawn up the agenda, he attended the next meeting of the Committee and gave his views there."12

It is unclear why O'Broin wanted to divorce himself and his department from television at this critical stage. Perhaps he and his associates had become tired of diverting so much energy and effort to the issue. After all O'Broin, Gorham, and their associates at Posts and Telegraphs and Radio Eireann had many other responsibilities to which to attend. O'Broin may have believed that he had been defeated and that a privately owned commercial service would soon be operating in Ireland. He certainly was uncomfortable with the idea of his department having to nominate a commercial company to establish an Irish television service. A more probable explanation was that the secretary, feeling upset that his suggestions were being ignored, simply wanted to send a strong message to Lemass. O'Broin was well aware that he and his department were the only people in government with detailed knowledge about the complexities of television. Consequently, he may have wanted to let Lemass and the Cabinet Committee know of his deep-rooted opposition toward the policy the Fianna Fail government had adopted.

While O'Broin would continue to play a role in the development of television in Ireland, his minister, Neil Blaney, would not. The secretary had initially thought that Blaney would be a successful Minister for Posts and Telegraphs. He recalled that Blaney had made a positive impression when dealing with issues concerning the Post Office, however, he also explained, Blaney had "got off on the wrong foot as regards broadcasting."13 In his autobiography, O'Broin recounted the problem that brought Blaney's career at Posts and Telegraphs to an abrupt end. The minister made a speech that was highly critical of the national radio service, exclaiming: "I cannot blame those who criticize Radio Eireann. . . . The very arguments being used in favour of more independence for Radio Eireann were the strongest arguments against it."14

O'Broin recalled that Maurice Gorham and the staff at Radio Eireann were incensed by the minister's remarks. "They were in fact quite outraged; and so worked up was a member of the repertory company that he openly insulted the Minister at a public dinner and had to be suspended."15 This created problems at Radio Eireann, as the entire staff resented the comments made by their minister. The Comhairle Radio Eireann, the council that had been established in 1951 by Erskine Childers, believed it had been insulted by a callous minister who was out of touch with broadcasting. Blaney had never approached either the council or Maurice Gorham to complain about the programs being broadcast by the Radio Eireann. The council demanded that Blaney disclaim the statement and also insisted he make a public statement expressing his support for Gorham and the Comhairle.

Maurice Gorham, the director of Radio Eireann and an active member of the Television Committee, wrote to the Secretary of the Posts and Telegraphs to indicate that he was considering resigning. Gorham stated that he would withhold his resignation until he had heard a disclaimer from Blaney, as there was some speculation that the minister may have been misquoted. The Director and the Comhairle attended a meeting arranged by O'Broin, which had been set up to clear the air. However Blaney canceled at the last minute, stating that he was ill and might not be available for a number of days. At this point the members of the Comhairle drafted a letter of resignation and threatened to resign unless Blaney withdrew or disclaimed his statement and pledged full confidence in the Director and the council.[16] Maurice Gorham described the events from his perspective, indicating that the episode caused a good deal of commotion at Radio Eireann. "Turmoil is not too strong a word. From the Council and the Director right through the programme staff, there was a surge of indignation. As one of the newspapers remarked, what was going on behind the scenes would make more exciting broadcasts than anything Radio Eireann could produce."[17]

The affair succeeded in undermining the confidence of the staff at Radio Eireann in their minister. It also alienated one of the most important figures on the Television Committee, Maurice Gorham. This latter consideration concerned O'Broin greatly. He told Blaney that Gorham was an indispensable asset to his department as an individual with a great deal of expertise concerning television:

I do not know whether I have made it sufficiently clear to you already that his knowledge of the subject is of the highest order—he is an ex-Director of BBC Television. . . . There is certainly nobody in this country who could replace him and we would be seriously handicapped if we had to try to deal with the subject in his absence."[18]

The entire episode poisoned the relationship between the minister and his staff, including the members of the Television Committee. Under the circumstances it is difficult to imagine how Maurice Gorham and other members of the Television Committee could continue to work with Blaney. Sean Lemass was aware that the Cabinet Committee, which he dominated, was dependent on the Television Committee for technical support and guidance. Neither Posts and Telegraphs, the Television Committee, or the Cabinet Committee were dependent on Neil Blaney, who was clearly expendable.

The Taoiseach, Eamon de Valera, removed Blaney from his position at Posts and Telegraphs and placed him at the Department of Local Government, where he became minister. De Valera would later state that the move had nothing to do with the controversy involving his young minister, although this is difficult to accept. Sean Ormonde was named as the new Minister for Posts and Telegraphs. This transfer was announced during the question period in the Dail by the Taoiseach on November 28, 1957.[19] Blaney was the object of some intense criticism and outright derision by opposition deputies, who questioned the wisdom of the speech he had given at the Fianna Fail party conference. However he refused to answer questions about the pending resignations of the Comhairle and rejected calls that he issue an apology for statements attributed to him at the Ard Fheis.*

Once Blaney was gone, the Comhairle reported that it regarded the matter as resolved and wrote to O'Broin stating that it was satisfied that the minister had moved on.[20] Eamon de Valera was not happy with the way in which the entire matter had been handled and was particularly upset with the Comhairle's assumption that the transfer of Blaney to Local Government was related to the critique he had made of Radio Eireann. De Valera called the Comhairle into his office at Leinster House in December 1957 and lectured the group on what he believed was its inappropriate, even arrogant, behavior. He reminded the council members that they had been appointed to serve Radio Eireann and that there was no guarantee they would be reappointed once their term expired.

De Valera was anxious to emphasize that the transfer of Blaney to the Department of Local Government had nothing to do with the statement the minister had made at the Fianna Fail Ard Fheis. Instead, he attributed the change in his Cabinet to the unfortunate death of a minister. The Taoiseach told the group that he had given specific advice to Blaney about his duties at the department. He explained, "When Mr. Blaney was being appointed Minister for Posts and Telegraphs, he had himself suggested to Mr. Blaney that it would be advisable to devote his particular attention, in the first instance, to the services of his Department other than Broadcasting."[21]

This is difficult to reconcile with the Taoiseach's statement at the same meeting when he expressed his own opinion concerning the importance of electronic media in the country. He maintained that both radio and television were important "from the national and cultural point of view. So great was the importance that such services could not be divorced from parliamentary control."[22] One can only wonder why de Valera would have counseled his

*Ard Fheis is the Irish term for national convention or conference.

minister to avoid paying much attention to broadcasting when he claimed to regard both radio and television as so important to the nation.

The transfer of Blaney allowed the Cabinet Committee and the Television Committee to continue work without the distraction of the outspoken, and now controversial, minister. The new minister had been a teacher who became principal at Kilmacthomas National School in Waterford before being elected to the Dail in 1947. He was not overly interested in interfering with the workings of Posts and Telegraphs or Radio Eireann. De Valera had chosen a replacement for Blaney who would not be controversial and who could get along with staff at the Post Office and Radio Eireann. Ormonde generally supported his secretary and deferred to him when television was at issue.

Meanwhile, the government continued to work to establish application guidelines for commercial companies interested in television broadcasting. O'Broin had, at the request of Sean Lemass, prepared an agenda for the initial meeting of the Cabinet Committee. The agenda contained a list of key issues that O'Broin believed had to be addressed in order for applicants to have an outline on which to base their proposals.

The first question brought up in the agenda concerned the commercial broadcasting proposals submitted by Michelson and McLendon. Although the government had decided to accept the advice of Posts and Telegraphs in September to reject these proposals, Blaney had never formally advised the two parties that their schemes had been officially declined. Therefore, as far as the companies were concerned, their two proposals were still under consideration by the state. Lemass had been advised by Blaney while he was still Minister for Posts and Telegraphs that the proposals of McLendon and Michelson should be reconsidered. He informed the Tánaiste that considerable political pressure had been brought to bear by supporters of the Michelson proposal and, to a lesser extent, adherents of the McLendon group. He advised Lemass:

We are under considerable pressure from the Hospitals Trust, Bord Failte, C.T.T. [the Export Board], and Aer Lingus in association, all of them being pushed by Mr. Michelson, while Mr. McLendon's Solicitor is active in pressing for a decision in favour of his client. The Michelson combination is particularly strong and Mr. Joseph McGrath has, personally, intervened in emphatic terms.[23]

Blaney had explained to Lemass that his department had simply advised these applicants that the government was not prepared to support the type of service that had been proposed.

Blaney had been under intense pressure from supporters of both the McLendon and the Michelson schemes. The reference to Joseph McGrath intervening on the part of Michelson illustrates that powerful Irish business interests supported the scheme submitted by the Paris-based Romanian expatriate. McGrath was a founding member of Cuman na Ngaedheal* and had been Minister for Industry and Commerce until he left politics in 1924. He had also been involved in founding Waterford Glass and the Irish Hospitals Sweepstakes. As the founder of the Irish Hospitals Sweepstakes, McGrath would have been very interested in advertising on a commercial radio station with an expanded range.

O'Broin's memo to the Cabinet Committee argued that the most important step that had to be taken was settling on an outline to which all applicants should conform. O'Broin indicated that once this was accomplished, the actual television authority should be established. He once again argued that it should be the new television authority that should decide which company should be allowed to establish a television station in the country. O'Broin underscored his point by maintaining that it would be inappropriate for individual ministers to interfere in awarding such an important government contract.

This is a revealing passage and illustrates another reason why O'Broin and the Television Committee may have wanted the television authority to be set up promptly. Mention had been made of the pressure that was being placed on Posts and Telegraphs from a number of semistate boards in support of the Michelson proposal. Individual members of the Dail, such as Erskine Childers, had also acted as agents of commercial applicants interested in bringing television to Ireland. It can be safely assumed that political pressures exerted on Posts and Telegraphs made O'Broin wary of being accused of favoritism or prejudice. The secretary addressed this issue in his autobiography when discussing the proposal made by Charles Michelson: "Directors of a number of semi-state bodies, led by an Irish industrialist, came to see me and urged that this particular application should be accepted. The industrialist went out of his way to tell me ever so bluntly that I, a Civil Servant, had nothing to lose unlike this promoter who was risking his own good money!"[24] The industrialist mentioned was undoubtedly Joseph McGrath.

O'Broin knew that if the proposed television authority chose the applicant that was to be granted the television concession, his department would

---

*Cuman na Ngaedheal was a political party founded in 1923 for supporters of the 1921 Anglo-Irish treaty.

free itself of the difficult task of having to recommend one company to the government. The department would also be free from pressures exerted by individual ministers and deputies, many of whom were lobbying fervently for their favorite proposal. O'Broin was also likely aware that no matter who was chosen, his department would be subject to charges of favoritism by disappointed applicants and their political allies.

O'Broin asked the Cabinet Committee to consider how much power the proposed television authority should have. The issue of ownership of the television infrastructure was also addressed. It was suggested that the successful applicant should own the studios and related equipment that would be housed in the physical plant, while the government should own the transmitters and transmitting stations. He also maintained that the new authority should exert strict control over programs that the service would broadcast. This would "uphold certain standards and ensure impartiality in regard to political and religious matters."[25] The memo also expressed concern about the need for government access to television. It stated that public service telecasts needed to be produced, as these programs would provide the state's only real opportunity to express itself on the new medium. O'Broin argued that the authority should have the power to produce material itself at its own expense. He maintained that these programs should address issues of culture that a commercial service would be reluctant to produce.

Posts and Telegraphs made specific recommendations about the commercial company that would be awarded the television contract. A key issue was finding a company that, though perhaps foreign, had a strong Irish element. Therefore, O'Broin stipulated that the company or companies should be registered in Ireland, have Irish representation in its organization, and employ Irish citizens. The memo maintained that the successful candidate should be granted a contract for ten years. It was also suggested that the contractor indicate the minimum number of programs that would be run during the week and that all applicants be asked what type of commitment they were prepared to make to programs of Irish interest, including news and Irish-language broadcasts. The issue of censorship was also addressed as the department admitted that previewing all programs would be a difficult task. It therefore argued that it was imperative that the proposed authority be vigilant and practice "post facto censure, reinforced by power to exact monetary penalties."[26] The issue of control was seen as critical, and O'Broin argued that the authority should have the teeth to enforce its policies. This would enable the service to ensure that only programs of a high moral standard would be broadcast. The Post Office also argued that the proposed authority should enjoy a significant degree of independence and be divorced of direct governmental involvement. O'Broin argued that there should be an independent statutory body that would control both television and radio.

Posts and Telegraphs had provided the Cabinet Committee with a substantial amount of information to consider. This included a list of the twelve companies that had made inquiries or sent proposals to the department. The entire package was sent to Sean Lemass and other members of the Cabinet Committee. It was intended to guide the members through their deliberations and to influence the decisions that would be made.

If O'Broin and the Television Committee were concerned with the direction that the Cabinet Committee was taking, a letter from the Department of Industry and Commerce, dated December 12, 1957, was cause for genuine alarm. Independent of the Cabinet Committee, Sean Lemass's department stated that it had reconsidered its position concerning the rejection of the McLendon and Michelson proposals. This signaled a new departure and an abrupt change, as Industry and Commerce decided "in favour of a combination of sound broadcasting and television on the basis which would meet the representations of Bord Failte Eireann, Aer Lingus, and Hospital Trust."[27] Lemass of course was the minister of the Department of Industry and Commerce as well as the Tánaiste. It is obvious that his department was clearly referring to the Michelson proposal, which was the only scheme that had succeeded in gaining the support of the semistate bodies mentioned in the letter.

Several days later, Lemass told the Minister for Posts and Telegraphs, Sean Ormonde, that the Cabinet Committee had made a number of decisions about the direction television should take. He sent the Cabinet Committee's conclusions to Ormonde and ordered Posts and Telegraphs to redraft them into a formal memo that would be submitted to the government for a decision. Posts and Telegraphs was instructed to review all the proposals that had been submitted and to report back to the Cabinet Committee recommending the one company that best conformed to the conditions outlined by Lemass and his associates.[28]

The conclusions of the Cabinet Committee categorically rejected many of the recommendations that Posts and Telegraphs had made. Lemass and his fellow ministers declined O'Broin's suggestion that the state own the television transmitters and stations. Instead, the Cabinet Committee expected that the contractor that was awarded a broadcasting license would build a national service and assume all capital costs for transmitters, buildings, and equipment. The entire system would eventually be purchased by the state after installment payments had been made to the contractor over an unspecified period of time.

O'Broin took little comfort in these decisions, as he feared the Cabinet Committee was moving in a direction that would endorse a scheme he strongly opposed. The pronouncement that upset O'Broin most was the Cabinet Committee's decision to consider once again the proposals of both Michelson and McLendon. O'Broin was disturbed that the Cabinet Committee had advocated the unusual step of reversing a government decision and saw this as evidence that pressure from the diverse parties supporting Michelson had succeeded in changing established government policy. The Department of Industry and Commerce had already exhibited support for the Michelson scheme. It is obvious that Lemass wanted both the McLendon and Michelson applications to be reexamined. O'Broin feared the influence of the future Taoiseach, believing he would be able to convince the Cabinet, and Eamon de Valera, that the Michelson scheme should be accepted.

The secretary also realized that the conditions outlined by the Cabinet Committee would favor the proposals of Michelson and McLendon. It is unlikely that applicants that were uninterested in international commercial radio would be able to match the elaborate offers these two groups had made. Companies such as Pye Ireland wanted to build a limited television service that would initially cater only to the Dublin metropolitan area. Pye and other applicants were not interested in international commercial broadcasting and therefore were unable to submit plans as extensive or generous as those proposed by Michelson and McLendon.

Leon O'Broin understood that he was being placed in a very difficult position. If his committee had to reconsider all the proposals on the lines stipulated by the Cabinet Committee, it would be difficult to ignore the attraction of either the McLendon or the Michelson proposals. O'Broin realized that the one proposal that had promised to conform to all these conditions had been made by Charles Michelson. None of the other applicants, with the possible exception of the McLendon Company, could hope to match the offer.

Sean Ormonde wrote to Lemass in January 1958 responding to the memo he had received from the Tánaiste, which had outlined the Cabinet Committee's decisions. Ormonde attached two memos from O'Broin and indicated that he supported the contents of both documents. The first memo was an emotional, personal minute that was highly critical of the decisions the Cabinet Committee had made. It was clearly intended for Lemass and contained a strong critique of the Cabinet Committee's decision. The fact that it was passed on to the Tánaiste illustrates the influence O'Broin held at his department and the support Ormonde was willing to provide his secretary. The second was a more formal submission that asked for clarification on a number of points that had been raised in the Cabinet Committee's report of December 17, 1957.

O'Broin's personal memo is interesting in several respects. It is clear he believed that the Cabinet Committee's decision to reverse established government policy concerning the Michelson and McLendon proposals signaled a disastrous shift that would have terrible consequences for the country. O'Broin expressed his disappointment with the Cabinet Committee, complaining that he was "profoundly unhappy" with the conclusion it had reached. He maintained that the decisions violated every feature of the policy that the Television Committee had developed since its inception in 1950. O'Broin predicted that if television was allowed to be organized along the lines that the Cabinet Committee had suggested, the government would experience "constant trouble."[29]

O'Broin reviewed the work with which his Television Committee had been engaged since its founding in 1950 and argued that the committee had always been concerned that such an important medium as television be under firm public control. It was clear that O'Broin was never comfortable with the thought of the private ownership of a national television service. He argued the Television Committee

realized that all the responsible elements in the community and particularly the Church, educationalists, cultural . . . organisations, and parents[,] . . . would be concerned that such an important service should be organized, controlled and operated . . . with the public interest constantly in mind. . . . from the outset we regarded it as unthinkable that its effective control should be in private hands.[30]

O'Broin once again referred to the schemes that the Television Committee had developed. "We wished for a service publicly-owned, controlled and operated, drawing its revenue from license fees and advertising programmes with an additional subsidy from the Exchequer, and if this were impossible because the Exchequer position put a subsidy out of the question, we felt it better to have no television at all."[31] The secretary argued that the state-owned commercial television service that he and his associates envisioned would be economical and, more important, would exercise control over the programs that would be broadcast. This would limit the amount of crass popular programs to be featured.

To emphasize this point, the secretary attached a resolution that had been submitted to the Taoiseach by the Irish Arts Council. The Arts Council had submitted a declaration to Eamon de Valera in December 1957 advising the

Taoiseach that it deplored the prospect of commercial television coming to Ireland, maintaining that it would be injurious to Irish culture. The council argued that

commercial interests tend unscrupulously to relate the cultural level of the majority of programmes to the tastes and standards of the most undeveloped mass-audiences. It follows that in commercial television not only does self interest, of its nature, override cultural values for the sake of appealing to mass-audiences but, in doing so, produces a proportionate and progressive vulgarization of public taste as a whole.[32]

O'Broin saw an ally in the Arts Council and did his best to exploit their resolution. He argued that other influential organizations would protest the decision to opt for a commercial service. However, at this time the Arts Council was the only group that came forward.

O'Broin next turned his attention to the proposals of McLendon and Michelson. He denounced the Cabinet Committee's desire to reconsider these proposals and hinted that political pressure was the only reason why these schemes were being reconsidered.

These applicants are all foreigners interested primarily in international commercial broadcasting for what they can get out of it. . . . But the fundamental objection to these applicants is that they are asking us to do something we cannot legally do. That should end the matter. We cannot consistently preach the rule of law in international affairs at the United Nations and in Áras an Uactarán* and then break the international radio conventions we have so solemnly signed.[33]

It is remarkable that O'Broin was not afraid to directly challenge Sean Lemass and lecture him in the responsibilities of the state. The Tánaiste respected the opinions and work of the secretary, but one cannot avoid thinking that Lemass was annoyed by the self-righteous tone of O'Broin's communication.

The second, more formal departmental memo from Posts and Telegraphs responded directly to the Cabinet Committee's report, which had instructed O'Broin to draft a formal *Memorandum for the Government*. Posts and Telegraphs informed the Cabinet Committee that since it had decided to reconsider the proposals of McLendon and Michelson, it should advise the government in this document how the required wavelength would be obtained. The Cabinet Committee was given a set of choices by a sarcastic

---

* Áras an Uactarán is the Irish term for House of the President.

Leon O'Broin, who made sure that the alternatives presented were as difficult as possible. The options open to the government ranged from simply appropriating a wavelength, which was described as a blatant violation of an international agreement, to withdrawing from the agreement and abandoning the policy of cooperating with the community of nations.

Sean Lemass responded to the Posts and Telegraphs memoranda quickly. He had hoped that the department would act on the Cabinet Committee's submission and prepare the memorandum he wanted to submit to the full Cabinet. In his response, one can sense a growing impatience with both O'Broin and Ormonde. The Tánaiste tersely stated that the Cabinet Committee had envisioned a commercial monopoly in their report and dismissed O'Broin's efforts to find an alternative. "It has been accepted that a T.V. service must be provided on a commercial basis and while, like Mr. O'Broin, most of us would prefer a public service if this were possible, it is, as you know, out of the question for financial reasons. The Government have decided to proceed on the basis of a commercial service and this question must be regarded as settled."[34]

Lemass stated that he wanted Posts and Telegraphs to comply with the wishes of the Cabinet Committee and draft a submission to the government that would embrace the report his committee had issued. In responding to O'Broin's polemic against McLendon and Michelson, the Tánaiste stated that the Cabinet Committee was aware of the complications that would be involved if one of these proposals was accepted. He maintained that although no decision had been reached, the Cabinet Committee "clearly understood" that accepting either of these proposals would require Ireland to withdraw from the Copenhagen Agreement.

Although O'Broin had tried to discredit both the conclusions of the Cabinet Committee and the proposals of Michelson and McLendon with dire predictions of international condemnation, Lemass was not impressed. The Tánaiste urged Sean Ormonde to quickly complete the task that he had been assigned. Lemass did indicate he would not be opposed to Posts and Telegraphs submitting separately its own observations; however, it is clear that Lemass was growing increasingly impatient with O'Broin.

Posts and Telegraphs complied with the wishes of Lemass and prepared a formal submission to the government that endorsed the report of the Cabinet Committee. Sean Ormonde accepted Lemass's offer to submit the views of his department with the formal submission for the government. The formal document set out the procedure that would allow for a selection of what was described as a "concessionaire." Once the government had set the conditions of the contract that would be employed, Posts and Telegraphs would be responsible for nominating the candidate that best conformed to the conditions outlined by the Cabinet Committee.

A separate memo that accompanied the formal submission to the government included the observations of Posts and Telegraphs along with the objections that had been raised by O'Broin. Once again, the secretary outlined the alternative first proposed in 1953 and developed in the *Supplemental Report of the Television Committee*, issued in 1956. Posts and Telegraphs again denounced the proposals of Michelson and McLendon and criticized the supporters of these plans. Charles Michelson was singled out as the most dangerous of these foreign applicants and described as a "person whose broadcasting projects in Europe have been shortlived and have given serious trouble to the Governments concerned."[35]

The reference to the troubles experienced by Michelson in Europe indicate the length to which O'Broin was prepared to go to try and discredit this Paris-based company. One could argue that the reference was unfair as it did not explain the context of the "difficulties" in which Michelson had been involved or the fact that he had been cleared of any wrongdoing by the French Government. It could be argued that Michelson was an intelligent capitalist who had taken advantage of unique situations in his dealings on the continent. The negative reference to Michelson illustrates that in spite of representations by staff on the Television Committee, the troubles of the Romanian expatriate impeded his efforts to win a broadcasting concession in Ireland.[36]

The *Memorandum of the Cabinet Committee*, which had been prepared by Posts and Telegraphs, and the separate "observations" of Posts and Telegraphs were submitted to the full Cabinet on January 10, 1958. The Cabinet Committee formally asked the government to approve of the recommendations it had made. However, the Cabinet did not take any immediate action on the report, although copies had been circulated to all its members.

On January 22, 1958, Sean Ormonde addressed the annual dinner of the Association of Advertisers, the same group Neil Blaney had addressed several months earlier. Those attending must have been disappointed as the new minister had little to say about television. He advised the group that detailed proposals received from commercial companies were being studied by his department. He also assured those assembled that the party that would be awarded a contract would produce programs of high quality and not broadcast material that would be "uniformly trivial and mediocre."[37] Doing so would alienate the Irish audience, many of whom could switch to British broadcasts.

The *Irish Times* applauded the minister's speech in an editorial carried the following day. It predicted that, based on government announcements, a commercial service would finally be established in the country. It also outlined the structure of a service that it saw as emerging in the "near future." This was a station "established on the lines of Independent Television in Britain, with a government appointed authority which will ensure the maintenance of certain standards in the programmes."[38]The *Irish Times* did not object to the arrangement but did warn of the dangers ahead. Ormonde was praised for stating that the service would have to broadcast programs of the highest standard or risk losing viewers. It was pointed out that "a commercial television service is primarily commercial and only secondarily a service. The 'more intelligent' British viewer always has the B.B.C. to return to when he tires of the 'admass' inanities of I.T.V. The Irish viewer—and this is what the Minister obviously fears—will also have the B.B.C."[39]

What is most significant is that the national papers did not object to the proposition that television would be a commercial service operated by a private company. In fact, the Irish national press supported the government's policy, and the state found surprisingly little opposition to its plans. One might argue that the press in many respects reflected the views of the tax-paying public, who would be concerned with the increase in taxes that would undoubtedly accompany a true noncommercial, "public" service.

The television industry was disappointed in the minister's speech, having hoped that Ormonde would use the opportunity to make a commitment to an Irish service. The voice of the industry, *Irish Radio and Electrical Journal,* reported that the association had hoped that Ormonde would make a "concrete statement" that would indicate when a television station would be built.[40] The *Journal* knew that the demand for its industry's products would increase dramatically with the opening of an Irish station.

The Arts Council had already voiced its opposition to the prospect of a commercial station coming to Ireland. A second group that came forward at this time was an organization that had more than philosophical differences with the government's decision to bring commercial television to Ireland. The Theatre and Cinema Association (Ireland) informed the Department of Posts and Telegraphs on January 21, 1958, that it had written to the Taoiseach expressing its concerns about the plan that the government had announced. The Association explained that its members were concerned about the challenge that television would present to the cinema business. It asked that before any final decision was made, "all ascertainable factors . . . be taken into account."[41]

The Association's submission was the second document sent to the government to articulate the opposition of a particular interest group. In the months that followed, a number of business, political, and cultural groups would follow suit. In reviewing the Association's statement, one is reminded of the opposition the newspaper industry mounted when radio in both Britain and Ireland began broadcasting in the 1920s. The attempt to delay the introduction of a native television station conducted by the Theatre and Cinema Association was a futile effort to halt the inevitable development of a new form of mass media in Ireland. Cinema owners were worried about their own livelihood, though they chose to emphasize the negative financial effect that they believed television would have on the country as a whole.

A meeting of the Cabinet had been scheduled for February 25, 1958, to consider the requests that had been outlined in the Cabinet Committee's report. Just prior to the meeting, the Minister of Health, Sean MacEntee, circulated a memo that abruptly halted the government's drive to accept an offer by a private company. MacEntee was troubled by the way in which critical decisions were being made about a medium as important as television. He saw in the past a lesson that might help guide his fellow ministers and referred to the experience gained in establishing Radio Eireann.

MacEntee pointed out that in 1923, early negotiations between private firms interested in radio and the Department of Posts and Telegraphs had caused a great deal of controversy, as they were conducted in a very secretive manner. In order to avoid similar complaints concerning the state's methods and motives, MacEntee suggested that the government follow the example set by its predecessor, which had established the Committee on Wireless Broadcasting to examine proposals regarding commercial radio. He strongly recommended that the Cabinet "set up a Commission with appropriate terms of reference to consider all the aspects of the proposal to establish a Television Service here."[42]

The suggestion of the Minister of Health was promptly accepted by the government. Sean Lemass had shown a desire to get a service on the air quickly and had illustrated a determination to take the necessary difficult decisions to achieve this end. However, once MacEntee's proposal had been circulated, it became difficult to justify opposition to the concept of an official commission that would review all proposals received by the state and provide a recommendation to the government. The decision to accept MacEntee's proposal suggests the influence of the Taoiseach, Eamon de Valera. His exhaustive, methodical style of management has been explored by a number of historians. This was in sharp contrast to the more determined

Lemass, who in a very short amount of time had immersed himself deeply in the government's evolving television policy.

The government announced on March 14, 1958, that a Television Commission would be established by the Minister for Posts and Telegraphs to examine all aspects of television broadcasting and to make recommendations to the government. The fact that Posts and Telegraphs would oversee the work of the commission was important, as it ensured that O'Broin would remain closely involved in the state's emerging television policy. O'Broin and his staff worked closely with the Television Commission and used every opportunity to try and influence the findings of this body.

Before the commission was actually established, several important issues had been decided. The first concerned the membership of the body, while the second addressed the "terms of reference" under which the commission would deliberate.

A long list of potential members was assembled, and pared down until the government had agreed on the acceptable individuals. The original list included literary figures, such as Sean O'Faoláin, Denis Johnston, and actor and writer Micheál Mac Liammóir, and politicians, such as Liam Cosgrave, Alexis Fitzgerald, Brendan Corish, Dr. Patrick Hillary, and Charles Haughey. Engineers and academics were also included, as were a number of Protestant and Catholic clerics. O'Broin submitted additional names to de Valera, who expressed an interest and was involved in deciding on the composition of the commission. After some discussion, the list was reduced and the more colorful writers and actors, who may have contributed a great deal to the commission, were omitted. Sitting members of the Oireachtas* were also excluded.

The members included Justice George D. Murnaghan, who was named Chairman of the Commission and who served as a judge on the High Court. A second lawyer, Thomas Finlay, had been a Fine Gael member of the Dail for Dublin South Central from 1954 through 1957. Members who were identified with the Irish language lobby included Donnchadha Ó Súilleabháin, Secretary of the Gaelic League; Pádraig Uas Ó Caoimh, General Secretary of the Gaelic Athletic Association; and Eoin Ó Haodha, a National School Teacher and farmer from Westport, County Mayo. One of the two women on the commission, Sighle Ní Chinnéide, was a historian at University College, Galway, and had published a number of books and articles in both Irish and English.

---

*Oireachtas is the Irish term for legislature or assembly.

The clergy was represented by the Very Reverend John Cannon McCarthy, who had held the Senior Chair of Moral Theology and Law at St. Patrick's College, Maynooth. McCarthy had contributed a number of articles to the *Irish Ecclesiastical Record* and the Catholic Truth Society, an organization that published pamphlets on moral and religious issues in Ireland. The Very Reverend Dr. Patrick J. McLaughlin, who had been Vice President of St. Patrick's College, Maynooth, was the second Catholic cleric on the commission. The Very Reverend Henry Robert McAdoo represented the Church of Ireland. He was at the time Dean of St. Finbar's Cathedral in Cork, and he later became the Anglican Archbishop of Dublin.

Business interests were represented by Commander George Crosbie, director of the *Cork Examiner*; Sir Richard Levinge, Assistant Managing Director of Arthur Guinness and Sons; and Edward B. McManus, Director of Messrs. Donnelly Ltd. Other members included Hugh De Lacy, a mechanical and electrical engineer who was employed as an instructor at the Institute of Science and Technology in Dublin, and a medical physician, Dr. T. J. O'Reilly, from the Dublin Rheumatism Clinic.

Also included were two writers of drama, Lord Longford, who was a substantial landlord and the Director of the Gate Theatre, and Dr. Roger J. McHugh, a playwright and Professor of English at University College, Dublin. Agricultural interests were represented by Michael Gibbons, a farmer, who represented County Kilkenny on the National Council of the National Farmers Association, and Eoin Ó Haodha. The commission was rounded out by a senior civil servant, Aindrias Ó Muimhneacháin, Chairman of the Oireachtas, and Mrs. James J. Stafford, who was described in the *Irish Press* as a journalist and contributor to radio in Ireland, England, and the United States. The last member of the commission was Terence Farrell, President of the Congress of Irish Unions and a veteran of the War of Independence.

The fact that the commission included several members of the clergy is a point that requires some comment. As has been noted, the Irish Catholic Church did not make a formal presentation to the Irish Government. One member of the commission has suggested that neither a formal nor informal submission was necessary, as all members would have been sensitive to the concerns of the hierarchy.[43]

The position of the hierarchy was articulated in journals such as the *Catholic Truth Quarterly*, which was published in Dublin. As has been noted, Reverend John Cannon McCarthy, a member of the Television Commission, was a frequent contributor to the journal. The Catholic Truth Society of Ireland was an organization whose management committee included John Cardinal D'Alton, the Archbishop of Armagh and Primate of All Ireland, as President. Other members included the Bishop of Galway, Reverend M. J. Browne, and the Bishop of Dromore, Reverend E. O'Doherty. The Society had been established in 1899 "to combat the pernicious influence of infidel and immoral publications by the circulation of good, cheap, and popular Catholic literature."[44]

An article that appeared in the *Catholic Truth Quarterly* in 1961 articulated the church's attitude toward the new medium. It warned that television could, in the wrong hands, be a powerful instrument for evil.

Where people had to go out of their homes to see movies, television can bring all this pagan propaganda into the family circle—with even more disastrous results. This is the big weapon of the anti-Christian forces today. More souls may be taken away from Christ through the gospel of pleasure they absorb through TV, than if the anti-Christ would start an open bloody persecution in our country.[45]

The faithful were warned not to use television as a baby-sitter since young people and adults could become addicted to watching mindless programs. The Catholic Truth Society recounted an incident that it believed illustrated just how dangerous the new medium could be: "A woman admitted the reason her baby was born in a taxi enroute to the hospital, instead of in the hospital, was because she just couldn't tear herself away from her favorite program."[46] The *Catholic Truth Quarterly* exhorted readers to carefully monitor what children watched and urged parents not to neglect spiritual discussions and the family rosary.[47] The Irish Government and the Television Commission were well aware of the concerns of the clergy and were not interested in alienating the Catholic Church by allowing objectionable material to be broadcast by a native service.

Although the Catholic hierarchy in Ireland did not make any overt submissions or suggestions to the Irish Government or the Television Commission, the church was still very interested in television. This is evident in examining the work of Father Agnellus Andrew, a Catholic priest who worked as Adviser for Roman Catholic Broadcasts in the Religious Broadcasting Department of the BBC. Father Andrew had lectured in Ireland on television on a number of occasions and had contributed an article to the *Irish Ecclesiastical Record* in 1955 that caught the attention of the Irish Bishops.

The article welcomed the introduction of television but warned of the dangers that would arise if the service was not closely monitored. Father Andrew reviewed the positive contribution television had already made in the United States and in Europe. "In America, Bishop Fulton Sheehan speaks each week to an audience of ten to fifteen millions over a coast-to-coast network, and each week some hundreds of Catholic programmes are televised. . . . In France . . . the Mass is televised each Sunday. . . . Regular Catholic transmissions have now begun in Holland, Germany, Italy, and other European countries."[48]

Father Andrew argued that television would have to be strictly monitored in order to ensure that objectionable material would not corrupt its audience. He expressed particular concern over the dangers to which children would be exposed. He warned parents to be vigilant in monitoring programs and even suggested that television sets be equipped with shutters that could be locked by parents to control access to this hazardous new medium. To emphasize his argument, he quoted Pope Pius XII, whom he described as being greatly interested in television:

The painful picture of the evil and disturbing power of the cinema is present before our minds. But it is impossible not to be horrified at the thought that through the medium of television it may be possible for that atmosphere poisoned by material-ism, fatuity and hedonism, which is too often breathed in so many cinemas, to penetrate within the very walls of the home.[49]

Father Andrew concluded by suggesting that Irish religious authorities prepare for television by following the examples of the American Catholic Church. He pointed to the establishment of departments of communication in American Catholic universities which were designed to provide highly specialized training to students. He also suggested that on the diocesan level, church authorities should organize television workshops for priests interested in religious television. He recommended that the Irish church form an advisory committee to make suggestions to an Irish television service.

It is not surprising to find that the Irish Bishops would turn to Father Agnellus Andrew for advice on television. In 1959 he advised his superiors at the Religious Broadcasting Department of the BBC that he had been approached for advice by the Irish Catholic Bishops, who were anxious to learn about religious broadcasting.[50] Father Andrew traveled to Dublin to attend a symposium on religious television at the invitation of the Irish Bench of Bishops. He described the conference as a private symposium "designed to create an informed opinion amongst some of the educated Dublin people so they may approach the question in a proper way."[51] The concerns expressed by the Catholic Church as television policy evolved will be examined in later chapters.

Returning to the establishment of the Television Commission, it is imperative to understand the orders under which the commission was established. The terms of reference agreed to by the government had profound implications for the commission and certainly limited the scope and effectiveness of its work.

Leon O'Broin tried unsuccessfully to influence the instructions that were to be given to the commission. He realized that the commission could reverse the general direction the government had taken if it had enough latitude in its warrant to explore all the possible alternatives open to the state. O'Broin did not want the commission to be restricted by language that would narrow the scope of its deliberations. His own proposal advocated that the commission should launch a wide-ranging investigation into all aspects of television. While recognizing the problem of cost involved in establishing a service, the secretary's proposed terms of references left it up to the commission to decide the best means for financing and building a quality service. O'Broin's recommendations were rejected by the Cabinet, which opted for terms outlined by Sean Lemass.[52]

Lemass's suggestion was both concise and direct and ultimately gained the support of Finance and the Taoiseach. Unlike the proposal put forth by O'Broin, the Tánaiste wanted the commission's work to be strictly defined where the question of financing television was concerned. The language he recommended relieved the commission of dealing with the controversial subject of financing a television station. He proposed that the Television Commission be created with instructions that would specify "that no charge should fall on the Exchequer, on capital or current account."[53]

This was the most critical qualification inserted into the commission's orders. This stipulation succeeded in limiting the ability of the Television Commission to conduct a thorough investigation and precluded it from submitting a truly comprehensive report to the government. It is clear that the Tánaiste was not interested in dredging up the subject of public service television or the model advocated by the Television Committee. He clearly believed that such a proposal was out of the question, given the financial difficulties the state was experiencing. Lemass contended that the commission should investigate all the proposals that had been received by Posts and Telegraphs and make a recommendation as to which scheme should be accepted by the government.

The final terms of reference were hammered out at Cabinet meetings with some input from the Taoiseach, Eamon de Valera. However, Sean Lemass proved to be the most influential person involved in drafting the orders given to the commission. The terms of reference conformed to the proposal that had been made by Lemass and clearly supported the thinking of the Tánaiste and the Department of Finance. The terms stipulated that the Television Commission would investigate the prospects for an Irish television service on the clear understanding that no cost was to fall on the Exchequer.[54] The terms also proved that the government did not want to ignore any proposals that had been submitted to it. It wanted the commission to evaluate closely all submissions received by the Post Office, including those made by Michelson and McLendon.

A formal announcement was made by the government in March 1958, and reports and editorials appeared in the national papers the following day. Again, the press indicated that it did not object to what was regarded as the inevitable commercial character of the expected service. The *Irish Times* maintained that it saw no alternative and even raised questions about the economic viability of a commercial service.[55] The *Irish Independent* referred once again to television as a "luxury service" and applauded the government's insistence that no charge should fall on the Exchequer.[56]

The national papers supported the decision to set up the Television Commission and provided short biographies of its members and the outlined terms of reference it was given. The *Irish Independent* offered the only real complaint about the composition of the commission, maintaining that it included no journalists or representatives of the literary profession.[57] It was not impressed with the inclusion of Mrs. James Stafford or contributors to clerical journals. However, the *Irish Press* described the body as being large and representative of the country.[58]

The small but vocal television industry in Ireland was not pleased with the creation of the commission. The *Irish Radio and Electrical Journal* believed the government had been close to a decision before it appointed the twenty-person board. It argued that:

The matter of television in the Republic was badly handled from the beginning. . . . [T]his Commission should be of no great surprise. It is a very obvious way open to any Government to remove from their own shoulders the responsibility of decision. We certainly do not wish to enter the arena of political belief but from the distance it seems a special 'solution' adopted by the De Valera Party.[59]

The voice of the small Irish communications industry also criticized the composition of the commission, stating that the television trade had been ignored.

Leon O'Broin has described how Posts and Telegraphs viewed the establishment of the commission and depicted the events that led up to its creation. He knew that intense lobbying was taking place behind the scenes, though he claimed to have been left in the dark about who might be awarded an exclusive contract to organize an Irish television service. In these circumstances, he explained, "We naturally feared that an unhappy choice would be made if an individual group was put into a monopoly position. However in March, 1958, the Government handed over all the applications to a Commission of twenty persons . . . among whom there was a fair amount of dead wood."[60]

Television was now in the hands of a commission that would deliberate until a final report was issued in May 1959. Posts and Telegraphs continued to be involved in the developing policy on television, as Leon O'Broin and his staff were responsible for providing secretarial and technical support for the commission.

In early 1958 television appeared imminent as the government had been very close to making a decision on the future of Irish television. Sean Lemass had become actively involved in deciding television policy and dominated the short-lived Cabinet Committee. He had quickly illustrated an inclination for private commercial television, much to the consternation of Leon O'Broin and the Television Committee. However, at the last minute, a commission was established, which delayed any decision for over a year. The Television Commission offered numerous interest groups the opportunity to articulate their hopes and concerns about television and its expected impact on Irish society. Companies interested in both radio and television broadcasting had the chance to testify before the twenty-member board. The deliberations of this commission provide insight into the thinking of a number of cultural and political groups and also illustrates how commercial concerns tried to influence both the commission and the government. The work of this body will be examined in the following chapters.

NOTES

1. State Paper Office, Department of the Taoiseach, S14996B, Cabinet Notes, October 25, 1957 meeting.

2. Department of Communications, TW894:3.

3. Ibid.

4. Ibid., p. 2.

5. *Irish Press*, November 8, 1957.

6. Department of Communications, TW894:3, memo from O'Broin to Blaney, November 8, 1957.

7. *Irish Independent*, November 9, 1957.

8. *Irish Times*, November 8, 1957.

9. Ibid.

10. Ibid.

11. Department of Communications, TW894:3, memo from O'Broin to Blaney, November 8, 1957. O'Broin's recommendation was accepted in 1961, when the new broadcasting authority designated the new combined service Radio Telefís Éireann.

12. Department of Communications, TW894:3, letter from Sean Lemass to Neil Blaney, November 9, 1957.

13. Leon O'Broin, *Just Like Yesterday* (Dublin: Gill and Macmillan, 1985), p. 207.

14. *Irish Independent*, November 21, 1957.

15. O'Broin, *Just Like Yesterday*, pp. 207–208.

16. State Paper Office, Department of the Taoiseach, "Special meeting of the Comhairle Radio Eireann," November 22, 1957, and letter of resignation from the Comhairle, November 23, 1957.

17. Maurice Gorham, *Forty Years of Irish Broadcasting* (Dublin: Talbot Press, 1967), p. 275.

18. State Paper Office, Department of the Taoiseach, S3532D, memo from O'Broin to Blaney, November 25, 1957.

19. *Dail Debates* (November 28, 1957): col. 1274.

20. State Paper Office, Department of the Taoiseach, S3532D, memo to O'Broin from C. J. Brennan, Chairman of Comhairle Radio Eireann, December 2, 1957.

21. Ibid., minutes of a meeting between the Taoiseach and the Comhairle Radio Eireann, December 9, 1957.

22. Ibid., pp. 2–3.

23. Department of Communications, TW894:3, memo from Blaney to Lemass, November 19, 1957.

24. Leon O'Broin, *Just Like Yesterday*, p. 209.

25. Department of Communications, TW894:3, "Notes on Proposed Questions for Cabinet Sub-Committee," November 19, 1957, p. 4.

26. Ibid., p. 8.

27. Ibid., letter to Leon O'Broin from the Department of Industry and Commerce, December 12, 1957.

28. Ibid., memo from Sean Lemass to Sean Ormonde, Minister of Posts and Telegraphs, December 17, 1957.

29. Ibid., memo from O'Broin to Ormonde, January 3, 1958.

30. Ibid., pp. 1–2.

31. Ibid.

32. Ibid., letter from the Arts Council to the Department of the Taoiseach, December 17, 1957.

33. Ibid., memo from O'Broin to Ormonde, January 3, 1958, p. 4.

34. Ibid., memo from Lemass to Ormonde, January 6, 1958.

35. Ibid., *Post Office Observations* [memo to the Government from Posts and Telegraphs] January 1958, p. 3.

36. This is a very generous interpretation of events. Michelson was motivated by self-interest and profit, and O'Broin, by a deep sense of patriotism. Although at times he could be arrogant and self-righteous, he was a dedicated civil servant intent on serving his country to the best of his ability.

37. State Paper Office, Department of the Taoiseach, S14996B.

38. *Irish Times*, January 23, 1958.

39. Ibid.

40. *Irish Radio and Electrical Journal*, 16 (February 1958): p. 12.

41. Department of Communications, TW894:3, letter from the Theatre and Cinema Association (Ireland) and Irish Cinemas Ltd. to Posts and Telegraphs, January 21, 1958.

42. Ibid., *Memorandum for the Government*, from the Department of Health, February 24, 1958.

43. A member of the Commission, the Most Reverend Henry Robert McAdoo, emphasized that all members of the Commission would share the hierarchy's concern that no immoral or offensive material be broadcast. Interview conducted by the author, Dalkey County, Dublin, December 12, 1990.

44. Terence Browne, *Ireland, A Social and Cultural History 1922 to the Present* (Ithaca, N.Y.: Cornell University Press, 1985), p. 55.

45. *Catholic Truth Quarterly*, 2, no. 10 (July–September 1961): 20.

46. Ibid., p. 21.

47. The *Irish Catholic*, a weekly published in Dublin, also warned of the dangers presented by television. See issues of February 5, 1958; February 26, 1959; May 21, 1959; June 4, 1959; and June 22, 1959.

48. Agnellus Andrew, "Television and Religion," *Irish Ecclesiastical Record*, 83 (1955): 15–17.

49. Ibid., p. 23.

50. BBC Written Archives at Caversham, E1/2096/2, memorandum from Father Agnellus Andrew to Head, Religious Broadcasting, September 15, 1959.

51. Ibid.

52. Department of Communications, TW894:3, memo from Moynihan to O'Broin, February 28, 1958.

53. State Paper Office, Department of the Taoiseach, S14996B, draft proposal by Sean Lemass, February 28, 1958.

54. Department of Finance, S104/1/50, memo from Moynihan Department of the Taoiseach to O'Broin, March 14, 1958.

55. *Irish Times*, March 3, 1958.

56. *Irish Independent*, March 3, 1958.

57. *Irish Independent*, March 27, 1958.

58. *Irish Press*, March 3, 1958.

59. *Irish Radio and Electrical Journal* 16 (April 1958): 5.

60. Leon O'Broin, *Just Like Yesterday*, p. 209. O'Broin had tried unsuccessfully to influence both the terms of reference and the membership of the Commission.

CHAPTER 6

British Influence in the Development of Irish Television

The Department of Posts and Telegraphs continued to be involved in television and worked closely with the new government commission. The department communicated with a number of European nations asking that they provide details about the structure of their television stations. Matthew Doherty wrote to television authorities in Denmark, France, West Germany, Holland, Italy, Sweden, Portugal, and Switzerland, asking that each service reply to detailed questions concerning costs, revenue, salaries, and programs. O'Broin also made direct inquiries to both the BBC and ITA. The research conducted by Posts and Telegraphs provided the commission with a considerable amount of information, which enabled its members to gain a thorough understanding of developments in television in the west of Europe. These administrations provided the department with a tremendous amount of data enabling Posts and Telegraphs to assemble an impressive file detailing the size, structure, and finances of these stations.

The Department of Posts and Telegraphs had maintained a close relationship with both the British Post Office and the British Broadcasting Corporation since the establishment of the Irish Free State. This relationship was nurtured during O'Broin's tenure at Posts and Telegraphs and became an important component in the development of Irish television. The Television Committee had consulted the BBC on a number of occasions while conducting its own research and preparing reports in 1953 and again in 1956.[1] Cyril Connor, the Head of External Services at the BBC had communicated with Maurice Gorham and spoken with the Director General of the BBC, Sir Ian Jacob, about Irish television on a regular basis. The BBC did not hesitate to contact Leon O'Broin when issues arose that caused the corporation concern. This is evident in an exchange that began in July 1957 and was initiated by Sir Ian Jacob, who served as the president of the European Broadcasting Union as well as Director General of the BBC.

Jacob wrote to O'Broin to express his concern over what he believed was a disturbing article carried in the *Belfast News Letter*. The paper featured a story detailing the proposal that the McLendon Investment Company had made to the Irish government. The Belfast paper reported this offer in a dramatic, if not sensational manner:

Powerful American radio and television interests are rushing eagerly to give free TV service, worth about £500,000 at a start, to the Eire Government—with many strings attached. The biggest string, which wraps itself right round Britain, would be that the Dublin Government would abandon the attitude towards commercial advertising radio that it has retained over many years by implied agreement with the British Broadcasting Corporation.[2]

The article continued by outlining the American proposal which, it claimed, would broadcast commercial programs into Britain twenty-four hours a day. It reported that the service would advertise mostly American goods to the British market. The Irish Government was described as very interested in the proposal, which promised to employ approximately 3,000 people and to be the start of an "invasion" of American investment in Ireland.

The Board of Management of the BBC met on July 22, 1957, to consider the situation. The Director General, Sir Ian Jacob, was clearly upset and very concerned about the press reports and the McLendon proposal in general. British broadcasters were initially confused about the reports that detailed the American proposal. Initially, there was genuine fear that American television programs would be broadcast from Ireland directly into Britain. The BBC had believed that Northern Ireland was the only section of the United Kingdom that might receive a dependable Dublin television signal. The Belfast report that Americans would build a transmitter capable of sending television signals deep into mainland Britain was cause for alarm.

The Director of Engineering at the BBC submitted a report that examined the prospect of a television station broadcasting from Ireland into Britain. The report maintained that the Stockholm Plan, which allocated the bands on which European states could broadcast television signals, permitted Ireland five stations. The five stations designated were Dublin, Kilkenny, Cork, Galway, and Ballyshannon, each of which could have a 50 kilowatt transmitter. It was pointed out that these stations would have a maximum range of fifty miles. The report maintained that for technical reasons, an Irish television station would not be able to reach Britain, and added: "The idea of beaming Irish Television to this Country does not make sense."[3] The Director of Engineering concluded in a paternalistic, if not disdainful, manner: "We actually looked after Ireland's TV interest at Stockholm because they knew nothing about it!"[4] The report of the Director of Engineering eased the concerns of the BBC, although the Irish were seen as being reckless in entertaining offers from wily American capitalists.

However the BBC realized that it was feasible to broadcast radio signals from Ireland into Britain if a high-power transmitter was utilized. As might be expected, the BBC and its Director General were appalled at the prospect of American commercial radio broadcasting into the heart of Albion. This message was conveyed in Jacob's July letter to the Irish Secretary for Posts and Telegraphs. He forwarded a copy of the article that had caused him so much concern and asked O'Broin to explain it:

I know you are finding it pretty difficult to determine what to do about television in the future, but the idea of the Americans moving into Ireland in a big way with the main object of broadcasting to the U.K. is not one that we will welcome. The Americanization of radio and television in Ireland would be a disaster. . . . The interlopers which exist already, like Luxembourg, Europe No.1 and so on, are . . . bad enough.[5]

O'Broin wrote back to Jacob and explained that a number of proposals had been received by his department and that all were under active consideration. He advised the British Director General that his government was well aware of international regulations concerning broadcasting and the allocation of wavelengths. In spite of this he revealed that it would eventually decide to broadcast directly into Britain. According to O'Broin, this was necessary to "keep in contact with the growing numbers of Irish men and women who go to work in Britain and who often have no other link with home. This need is recognised by the Government and the lack of means to meet it are clearly felt."[6] He pointed out that before this was done, his government would seek to revise the pertinent regulations that restricted the range of Irish broadcasts and promised Jacob that the BBC would be kept informed of any such effort.

This expressed desire to reach the Irish in Britain had been an issue that had recently entered into O'Broin's rhetoric whenever radio and television were being discussed. At this juncture, he certainly did not advise Jacob that he was adamantly opposed to McLendon's scheme. Although he shared a broad Reithian philosophy with the British director general, he chose to play his cards close to the vest. He hoped to exploit Jacob's fears to try and gain future concessions from the BBC. These concessions might emerge in the form of discounted, if not free, television programs for the modest Irish public service that he envisioned. The secretary concluded his letter by suggesting that a meeting be arranged to discuss television and implying that this would be in the interest of the BBC. He hinted that Jacob might be able to influence the debate on television taking place within the Irish government. "For financial reasons, there must be an outside element; if that is not British, it may well consist of American or other non-British commercial interests, primarily interested in exploiting Ireland's geographical position."[7]

The letter unsettled Jacob who promptly advised O'Broin that Hugh Carlton Greene, the Director of Administration at the BBC, would immediately travel to Dublin for a meeting.[8] Greene and Robert McCall, the Controller of BBC Northern Ireland, met with O'Broin in Dublin in August 1957. Greene asked the secretary outright if Ireland was seriously considering signing a contract with McLendon. O'Broin was purposely vague, though he explained that his government had received a number of interesting proposals which involved the building of powerful radio stations that would broadcast directly into Britain.

O'Broin carefully outlined some of the proposals his department had received. The secretary explained his country's efforts to attract foreign capital in an effort to maintain a certain level of anxiety among his guests:

In describing the general picture here I told them what efforts successive Irish Governments had been making to interest American capital in Ireland and said that our Department of Industry and Commerce would probably be inclined to look favourably on an American broadcasting proposition that was tied up, as I thought the McLendon proposal was, with possible developments in the tourist-hotel business and in other directions.[9]

The minister for industry and commerce was, of course, Sean Lemass. This was the first indication that Lemass was backing the American proposal. Earlier memoranda indicate that he was an active supporter of the Michelson proposal; however, there had been no clear indication that he was also interested in McLendon's scheme. Lemass certainly was looking for American capital to be invested in Ireland, and for this reason, the statement that his department supported McLendon makes sense.

O'Broin's guests responded by adopting a line that would be employed often by the BBC in regard to international commercial radio. Greene and McCall highlighted the difficulty in acquiring a wavelength and also lectured O'Broin about "the loss of sovereignty that would be involved in making an arrangement whereby the Americans could broadcast from . . . [Ireland]."[10] O'Broin knew that his guests were disturbed about the press reports and suspected that the British Cabinet was monitoring developments closely. He asked Greene if the BBC had been approached by government officials and asked to investigate the matter. Greene replied simply that the BBC was investigating the subject on its own. The secretary was skeptical, as he had recently been approached by the British trade representative in Dublin and asked detailed questions about Ireland's intentions concerning television.

Maurice Gorham, the Director of Radio Eireann, also met with Hugh Carleton Greene to discuss the future of television and radio in Ireland. Once again Greene asked about the proposal that had been made by the McLendon Company. Gorham followed the lead of O'Broin, and in spite of his own distaste for McLendon's scheme, the Director of Radio Eireann spoke favorably about the proposal and its chance for success. Gorham admitted to Greene that his government was interested in McLendon's scheme even though it involved broadcasting commercial radio programs into Britain: "I added that the prospect of American investment had particular appeal here. He began to talk about international agreements and I told him that when one talks in that style to commercial promoters they are apt to quote Luxembourg and the many American stations in Europe."[11]

Greene returned to London and completed a detailed, "strictly confidential" report for the British Director General and the British Home Secretary. The British Home Office was kept apprised of these developments and was satisfied to let the BBC take the lead in pressuring the Irish Government to resist being seduced by American capital. O'Broin was correct in believing the British Government, and not just the BBC, was concerned with the prospects of American capitalists coming to Ireland to build radio stations that would broadcast to Britain. Greene's "strictly confidential" report explained that he had been told by O'Broin that the Irish Government had been "swamped" with television proposals from American, British, and continental companies.

Greene's report provides insight into the political machinations taking place within the Irish government. He reported that he had been told there was "considerable pressure from some sections in the Government, led by Mr. Sean Lemass, . . . to accept an American offer. The inducement had been held out that the establishment of an American-financed television service would be the gateway to further American investment which Lemass believed must be obtained in some way or another for the development of the country."[12] O'Broin's sharing of confidential information concerning the political maneuvering inside the Irish Government is remarkable and proves that the secretary was very concerned that a foreign company might be granted a monopoly to operate a television station in Ireland.

O'Broin was correct to assume that the prospect of American commercial radio programs competing with the BBC would cause serious anxiety in London. There was also genuine concern that a new Irish radio station transmitting on an inappropriate wavelength would interfere with the BBC by disrupting its signal. Sir Ian Jacob was warned by his director of engineering that a radio station transmitting from Ireland could cause havoc in Britain and would be a clear violation of the Copenhagen Agreement. Jacob was told that Irish authorities should be advised that the BBC, "would . . . object most strongly if the pirating of a frequency for commercial radio came about."[13]

O'Broin traveled to Britain in the fall of 1957 on what he described as a fact-finding mission. While in London, he met with the Director General of the BBC, Sir Ian Jacob; William Alfred Wolverson, the director of the radio services department of the British Post Office; the Irish Ambassador to Britain, Con Cremin; and Sir Robert Fraser, the Director General of the Independent Television Authority. O'Broin visited the British capital in an unofficial capacity to try and sound out the BBC and the ITA about program costs. He was interested in determining whether the scheme he and his department had developed was feasible. To be a viable proposal, he needed a commitment from the BBC that it would provide its programs to an Irish public service either free or at a greatly reduced rate. He also needed an idea of the cost of commercial programs, which he realized would supplement an Irish public service. He still hoped that the government might decide to accept a version of the proposal that the Television Committee had been advocating.

O'Broin first met with Wolverson of the British Post Office, the department responsible for licensing and controlling both the commercial and public television services in the United Kingdom. The meeting between Wolverson and O'Broin proves that the two departments shared more than an official or professional relationship. O'Broin explained: "Wolverson displayed the traditional British Post Office cordiality towards me and quite unrestrained willingness to share information with us. We talked very frankly off the record about the B.B.C.'s prospects, both in sound and in television."[14]

It should be noted that the BBC charter was set to expire in 1962, and there had been a great deal of speculation about the future of both BBC radio and television. As the ITA had proven a considerable success, conjecture abounded suggesting that the monopoly that BBC radio enjoyed would be broken and that independent commercial radio stations would be allowed to develop and compete with the state-owned public service. This was an issue that had gained the attention of both Gordon McLendon and Charles Michelson, as both argued that commercial radio was inevitably coming to Britain. When discussing expenses Wolverson explained that he did not know what the BBC or independent companies would charge an Irish service for their programs. O'Broin brought the subject up several times in hope that Wolverson would indicate a willingness to provide discounted BBC programs to an Irish public service. However, he did not receive any satisfaction as Wolverson simply never picked up O'Broin's subtle suggestion.

While in London, O'Broin also met with the Irish Ambassador to the Court of St. James, Con Cremin. O'Broin revealed to the Ambassador that he had been trying to determine whether the British would be willing to offer programs of the BBC at reduced rates. He explained that the trump card he was trying to play was the prospect of an American company broadcasting commercial radio programs into Britain. Cremin told O'Broin that he believed the British would be forthcoming in offering programs of the BBC at a reduced rate. "The Commonwealth Relations Office, of which the former Ambassador to Dublin, Sir Gilbert Laithwaite, was now permanent head, . . . would . . . see the importance of keeping the Americans out and of maintaining their own influence in our island."[15]

Cremin had hit upon an important point. While warning the Irish about the dangers of Americanization, the British were keen to preserve their own hegemony in a region that they regarded as being within their sphere of influence. British authorities were concerned with the prospects of an American commercial service competing with the BBC and advertising American products to the British public. London also wished to preserve its own cultural and political influence within both Britain and Ireland. This influence was delivered in the form of BBC radio, which was popular throughout Ireland, and television, which was available to a considerable part of the Irish population. The state-owned and -operated electronic media formed a critical part of the vehicle that maintained this influence. Its disruption was anathema to British policy.

While in London, O'Broin also visited Sir Ian Jacob, the Director General of the BBC and acting President of the European Broadcasting Union. The Director General had written to O'Broin in July expressing his grave concern at the prospect of the Irish government agreeing to work with scheming American entrepreneurs. O'Broin recounted that Jacob wasted no time in telling him that he was still very concerned with the McLendon proposal and what he termed:

Americanization and [he] actually asked me would we go so far as to grab a wavelength to enable the Americans to broadcast from [*sic*] Dublin. I replied that we would behave with circumspection as we have always done, i.e. we would adhere to the international agreements we had signed; but I could see the possibility of an Irish Government becoming dissatisfied with our present restricted rights and deciding to go its own way.[16]

O'Broin explained to Jacob the difficult predicament in which he found himself. He revealed that he had outlined to his government an alternative to the proposals made by McLendon and others. He explained that the scheme he proposed entailed building a limited public service station that, he hoped, would broadcast a significant amount of BBC material. He hinted that his proposal was vulnerable due to the high cost of these programs. Jacob told O'Broin that the BBC would have no objection to an Irish service broadcasting its material. However, Jacob did not offer to help O'Broin's proposed Irish public service by providing programs at a discounted rate. The secretary may have been too proud to come out and directly ask the Director General for help, as this would have been quite awkward. He wisely realized that such a solicitation, if ever leaked, would create a great deal of difficulty for him and his vision of an Irish television service.

Jacob was oblivious to O'Broin's overture and responded by seeing an opportunity for the BBC to generate more income by selling its programs to an Irish service. In writing about his discussions with Jacob, O'Broin commented, "I did not ask for any special terms and the idea of offering such probably never crossed Jacob's mind."[17] O'Broin believed that Jacob was incognizant of his predicament and did not understand how difficult it would be for a limited public service to afford BBC programs at the standard rate.

The last meeting conducted by O'Broin was with the Director General of the Independent Television Authority, Robert Fraser, whom O'Broin believed to be Australian. Fraser told O'Broin that he had read the press accounts of the American proposals and did not hesitate to provide O'Broin with his advice. "He touched on the Americanization topic; he adored Americans but he thought it would be wiser for the Irish to do their own business, not leave it to outsiders. He had thought it would be equally mad, politically speaking, for us to give a monopoly of television to either the British or Americans."[18] O'Broin was impressed by Fraser's arguments. Indeed, many of the points made by the ITA's director general supported the secretary's own philosophy concerning television. This was especially true of his distaste for a private commercial monopoly being given a concession to operate a national service. Fraser advised O'Broin that since only one station would be broadcasting in Ireland, the station should avoid its programming being dominated by one company. He suggested that a state-run authority could be created and that it could choose material from competing program companies, thereby avoiding dependence on any one organization.

O'Broin's visit to Britain had not been especially productive, but it had been educational. Ironically he may have been most influenced by the Director General of the ITA, a service that he loathed for the "low-brow" programs it broadcast. One can discern the influence of Fraser in O'Broin's efforts to convince the Cabinet Committee in January 1958 to establish a strong authority that would hire competing program companies for an Irish television station.

While in London, O'Broin had failed to receive a commitment from the BBC to provide programs at a specially discounted rate. However, his talk with Jacob proved that the British were still very much concerned with the possibility that scheming American entrepreneurs might disrupt British airwaves and challenge BBC radio. Sir Ian Jacob remained very interested in developments in Ireland and maintained close contact with both Leon O'Broin and Maurice Gorham.

One year later, as the Television Commission deliberated, circumstances had changed and O'Broin was more forthright with the BBC. The secretary contacted Jacob and explained in more detail the precarious position in which he found himself. He portrayed himself as an active opponent of applicants interested in broadcasting commercial radio into Britain. O'Broin realized that his own agenda converged with that of the BBC, and he tried to exploit this mutual interest in order to defeat proposals that he feared might be accepted by the Television Commission. In July 1958, while the commission was in session, O'Broin wrote to Jacob addressing him in his capacity as president of the European Broadcasting Union. Jacob was asked to provide a legal opinion that would present the official position of the EBU regarding legal options open to Ireland as a signatory of the Copenhagen Agreement.

The Michelson group had submitted a legal brief to the Television Commission, which argued that the Copenhagen Plan allowed a country to gain a wavelength by simply notifying the international regulatory board of its desire to use a particular frequency. Michelson's lawyers had studied the treaty and argued that it contained loopholes that would permit a signatory to legally acquire a new wavelength. If this were proven true, O'Broin recognized that the Michelson and McLendon schemes would be much more appealing to the Television Commission and, ultimately, the Irish government. The secretary wrote to Jacob explaining this dilemma and included a copy of the brief that Michelson's lawyers had submitted.[19] The secretary asked Jacob, as the president of the European Broadcasting Union, to research the issue and provide him with the EBU's official opinion. O'Broin was clearly looking for a strong declaration from the European Broadcasting Union that would denounce the brief as erroneous. Such a judgement could be submitted to the commission as evidence to discredit both the Michelson and the McLendon proposals.

Jacob wasted no time in providing the answer for which O'Broin hoped. While in the past both Jacob and Greene had expressed concern about the advent of "Americanization" should the Irish accept a proposal of this sort, at this juncture, the rhetoric of the Director General—and president of the EBU—became more paternalistic. Jacob lectured the Irish Secretary of Posts and Telegraphs that it would be wrong to disregard the state's responsibilities. Reacting to the legal brief, Jacob wrote: "The document has no effect whatever on the moral obligations of a signatory of the Copenhagen Plan. It is for your government to decide for itself whether it will depart from its moral obligations, and I need hardly say that the existence of this document would have no effect on the view of the members of the E.B.U."[20]

O'Broin understood that this was the response he needed to help defeat the plans of Charles Michelson and Gordon McLendon. By submitting this letter to the Television Commission, he hoped to strengthen his argument that accepting either proposal would make Ireland an international outlaw. The secretary appreciated Jacob's letter for its candor but realized that the repeated reference to the Irish Government's "moral obligations," while perfectly reasonable to the imperious British Director General, was offensive, if not insulting, to the Irish Government. O'Broin telephoned the Director General's office and requested that the letter be rewritten. The BBC complied, deleting the word "moral," and forwarded the revised letter to the Television Commission as official evidence.[21]

The British director general had recognized that it was in the best interest of the BBC to quietly support the efforts of Leon O'Broin. Later in 1958, at the behest of O'Broin, Jacob ordered members of his staff to undertake highly confidential research to investigate the feasibility of establishing a link that would enable BBC television to be fed directly from Belfast to Dublin.[22] Engineers reported that the proposed Belfast-Dublin link would be inexpensive and easy to construct. When senior staff in London learned of the inquiry, they were greatly upset that they had not been informed or consulted about the overtures being made to the Irish government. The controller of Television Administration, S. G. Williams, complained to the Head of Overseas and Foreign Relations, Cyril Connor: "I am surprised that this correspondence has been going on for some time. . . . We would naturally be very much involved if . . . it were proposed to make wholesale 'offers' for Eire Television. . . . Surely something has gone wrong here?"[23] Williams was told that the research had been conducted in secret due to the sensitive nature of the subject. Both Jacob and O'Broin wanted to avoid the complex political problems that would have developed in Dublin, London, and Belfast should news of the inquiry leak to the press.[24]

The BBC cooperated with O'Broin out of pure self-interest. It was clearly understood that keeping American commercial radio out of Britain and Ireland was imperative if the dominance of the BBC was to be maintained. Jacob may have also come to understand that allowing BBC television programs to be transmitted into Ireland would not simply protect British influence in the region but enhance it. He therefore did not hesitate to try and influence the sensitive debate taking place within the Irish government. The BBC remained very interested in Irish developments and continued to provide support for O'Broin as the Irish Government continued to examine its options. The continued efforts of the British to influence the development of television in Ireland will be explored in later chapters.

NOTES

1. BBC Written Archives, E1/2,092/1. For instance, the BBC arranged a tour for Post Office engineers of the new television center the service had opened at Shepard's Bush in 1955. Members of the Television Commission received a similar tour in September 1958.

2. RTE Archives, 105/58, no. 012–A1, *Belfast News Letter*, July 1957. The BBC had not learned of the Michelson proposal and only became aware of the Pye and McLendon schemes through press reports. In May 1957, the Irish press had reported that McLendon had approached the Irish government but provided few details about its proposal.

3. BBC Written Archives, Caversham, E1/2,096/1, memo from the Director of Engineering, August 2, 1957.

4. Ibid. This "help" provided by British authorities limited the location and power of transmitters in the Republic while allowing Belfast a powerful transmitter capable of reaching deep into the Irish Republic.

5. Ibid., letter from Sir Ian Jacob to L. O'Broin, July 11, 1957.

6. Ibid., letter to Jacob from O'Broin, July 25, 1957.

7. Ibid., p. 2.

8. Hugh Carleton Greene became Director General of the BBC in the summer of 1959. He met with the Chairman of the BBC, Sir Arthur fforde, on July 11, 1959 and was told that 'the board of governors of the BBC had decided that they would like to appoint him to be the next Director General, provided he was not a Roman Catholic.' Greene's brother, the novelist Graham Greene, was a convert to Catholicism and this created some concern on the part of the board. Hugh Carleton Greene assured the chairman that he was not a Catholic and was appointed Director General. See Michael Tracey, *A Variety of Lives, A Biography of Hugh Greene* (London: The Bodly Head Ltd.), p. 180.

9. RTE Archives, 105/58, no. 012aA1. O'Broin wrote a detailed memo addressing his discussions with McCall and Greene.

10. Ibid., p. 2.

11. Ibid., memo by Maurice Gorham, August 17, 1958.

12. BBC Written Archives at Caversham, E/2,096/1. Memo from Hugh Carleton Greene to Sir Ian Jacob, August 20, 1957.

13. Ibid., memo, August 21, 1957.

14. RTE Archives, no. 012A(2). O'Broin kept detailed notes of these meetings. This particular memo is undated; however, the secretary traveled to London in September 1957.

15. Ibid., pp. 3–4.

16. Ibid., p. 4.

17. Ibid., p. 5.

18. Ibid., pp. 6–7.

19. Department of Communications, Comm. 3756, no. 17, letter from O'Broin to Jacob, July 8, 1958.

20. RTE Archives B1A, letter from Sir Ian Jacob, President of the European Broadcasting Union, July 15, 1958.

21. BBC Written Archives at Caversham, E1/2,096/1. Notation on redrafted letter from Jacob to O'Broin, July 17, 1958.

22. BBC Written Archives at Caversham, E1/2,096/1. Memo from E.L.E. Pawley to Cyril Connor, December 29, 1958.

23. Ibid., memo from S. G. Williams, Controller, Television Administration, to Cyril Connor, Head of Overseas and Foreign Relations, December 31, 1958.

24. Ibid., pp. 1–2.

CHAPTER 7

The Early Work of the Irish Television Commission

The first meeting of the Television Commission took place on April 9, 1958. Sean O'Droma, a senior civil servant who had worked as Secretary to the Television Committee, was named the Secretary of the Commission. He was later joined by an assistant, Paul Warren.[1] O'Droma and Warren provided both clerical and technical support to the commission. They also supplied important information which included research that had been compiled by the Television Committee over the previous five years. Leon O'Broin and Maurice Gorham remained available to give oral testimony concerning the specialized research that had been conducted by Posts and Telegraphs. As the one organization in government that had studied television in a comprehensive manner, the members of the Television Committee were an important source of information for the Television Commission. O'Broin, Gorham, and Matthew Doherty all testified before the commission, explaining their research and articulating their department's opinion concerning how television should be brought to Ireland. Posts and Telegraphs was also charged with conducting research for the commission and providing information of an economic and technical nature. As has been seen, this group had very strong ideas about television and was deeply troubled by the prospect of commercial television, operated by a private monopoly, gaining an exclusive concession to exploit the new medium in Ireland. The prejudice against this form of television found its way into the "official" work that was conducted for the commission.

The Department of Posts and Telegraphs prepared a document for the commission's initial meeting titled, *A Historical, Technical, and Legal*

Background of Television. The six-page memorandum was designed by the Post Office to educate members of the commission and bring them up to date on the status of television in the country. The document gave members a history of television, explaining how it had grown to become such a tremendously popular form of medium. It also offered a chronology explaining how government policy had developed as television had grown in popularity.

The memorandum focused on the evolution of government policy, first addressing a statement issued by the Minister for Posts and Telegraphs in 1956. Michael Keyes was quoted at length from a speech he had made in July of that year, when introducing the budget for Radio Eireann. This speech had clearly emphasized the need for the state to avoid accepting a privately owned commercial television service and asserted that the government wanted to set up a service based on public ownership and management.[2] This was contrasted to the announcement made by the Fianna Fail Minister, Neil Blaney, in November 1957, which proclaimed the government's acceptance that television would be largely commercial and dependent on private financing.

Posts and Telegraphs reported on the expansion of British television, noting that the BBC station in Belfast had increased its range. The report also addressed the proposals that had been received by the Department of Posts and Telegraphs. Twelve applicants were listed and a brief description of each of these proposals was provided. The omission of the McLendon and Michelson schemes was surprising, and revealing. These two companies, both of which had submitted detailed proposals, were relegated to a footnote, which did not even identify the parties by name.[3]

The acting Minister for Posts and Telegraphs, Kevin Boland,[4] opened the initial meeting of the Television Commission. Boland thanked the members for agreeing to serve on the commission and explained that the subject they were to investigate was a complicated one that would benefit from a detailed investigation. The acting minister referred the members to the terms of reference that had established the commission and cautioned the group to adhere strictly to them. The minister also explained the difficulties that confronted the country in trying to find a service that would be properly balanced and include high-quality programs:

What we would like is a television service, Irish in origin and character, that will enrich the lives of our people and bring them experiences which they could not get in any other way. We can imagine a service that would be a real boon to our people, especially those who are far from the big centres, and keep them vividly in touch with whatever is happening in our own country and the world at large."[5]

Boland stated that the government was committed to a national service and not interested in television that would be Irish in name only and would broadcast inferior, foreign programs. The issue of cost was raised as the minister warned that it was clear that the nation could not afford to finance Irish television. This meant that an Irish service would have to be largely commercial. Boland explained to the commission that the government had a good idea of what it wanted and what it did not want. The critical question concerned what the state could get.

The Chairman of the Commission, Justice George Murnaghan, thanked the minister and promised that the members were indeed prepared to undertake the task at hand. After the Acting Minister had left, the Chairman of the Commission spoke, outlining the preliminary information that he believed the Department of Posts and Telegraphs should gather for the members to review. Justice Murnaghan also made a point to emphasize to the commission the need for secrecy. The judge told the members that it was his firm opinion that all the proceedings of the commission should be held in private. He warned that it was imperative that members commit themselves to maintaining a strict confidentiality concerning all deliberations and submissions. "Many people would have an interest in getting any clue as to the probable outcome of the Commission's enquiry [and] . . . no information . . . should be disclosed in advance of the Report to the Minister."[6] Patricia Hughes, an assistant to Matthew Doherty, confirmed the degree of secrecy under which the commission and its support staff worked. "It was so hush-hush that I use to take my carbons home at night and burn them."[7]

The commission agreed to meet on Friday afternoons and that all business would be conducted on an informal basis. In a gesture to the members who were strong supporters of the language revival, the Chairman asked permission that the proceedings be conducted in English. The fact that the Chairman felt obliged to propose the meetings be held in English illustrates that he was acutely aware of the presence of members who were strong supporters of the Irish language. It is hard to imagine that any of the members seriously considered that the meetings would be conducted in Irish; however, the symbolic gesture was made in an effort to ensure that no member would be alienated at this early juncture. It was also decided that the meetings would be recorded for the convenience of the members.[8]

At this first meeting, a number of members expressed confusion about the terms of reference and asked for clarification. This illustrates the fact that from the start, members had difficulty in either accepting or under-standing the terms of reference that had been drafted by Sean Lemass. The point that had caused confusion was the section that addressed how the service would be financed. It was agreed that this issue would be considered at a later date.

Before the commission adjourned, one member, Dr. Roger J. McHugh, requested that more detailed information be provided on two applicant groups that had received only scant mention in the document distributed to the commission by Posts and Telegraphs. McHugh had seen the reference that mentioned two companies that were interested in radio and wanted additional information supplied to the commission. Although the two applicants were not mentioned by name in the report, it is clear that they were Charles Michelson and Gordon McLendon. Thus, the rather bizarre attempt of O'Broin and his department to bury these two proposals, was foiled at this first meeting of the commission. It is difficult to believe that O'Broin expected to get away with hiding these two proposals which had caused great interest and controversy within the government. The fact that O'Broin resorted to such dubious tactics reveals the depth of his opposition to the proposals.

The first task of the Television Commission was to obtain information concerning the financial and technical requirements that would be needed to set up a national television service. Once this information was available, members would be able to judge proposals made to the commission and ask questions in an intelligent manner. Posts and Telegraphs produced a lengthy memo on April 21, 1958, that answered many of the technical and financial questions that had been posed by the commission.

The memorandum detailed the technical requirements for an Irish serv-ice, addressing the need for transmitters, transmission links, and production resources. It also provided estimates of costs that would be incurred in building a national service. The commission was told that the best option for national coverage was to erect six high-power transmitters. Posts and Telegraphs were working on the assumption that an Irish service would eventually be a national one, and not the limited Dublin service that had been outlined by applicants such as Pye Ireland or the Television Commit-tee.[9] It was proposed that transmitters be erected in Dublin, Kilkenny, Cork, Galway, Sligo, and Cavan.

A technical issue explored in the report examined the "standard of definition" that should be adopted. This referred to the number of lines per frame in the television picture. It was pointed out that the United States had a standard of 525 lines, France and its dependencies used a standard of 819 lines, and Australia used 625 lines. Britain used 405 lines, and the report indicated that this was the definition that Ireland should also adopt. The more lines per picture or frame, the sharper and better defined the image tended to be. According to Posts and Telegraphs, the British had already decided the issue for Ireland. It was admitted that the British standard was not the most technically advanced and did not give the best picture. However, adopting a different standard would cause interference between Irish and British transmitters. It would also make the relaying or receiving of British programs through an Irish service very difficult.

The memorandum concluded by advising the commission that an Irish service would require the building of a station that would depend mostly on programs "relayed" from Britain. However, it also maintained that an Irish station would need the proper facilities to enable it to broadcast programs produced in Ireland. It was implied that locally produced programs would only augment material that would be mostly British in origin.

Arrangements were made for members of the Television Committee to give oral evidence to the commission. Although this organization had ceased to function as an official committee with the establishment of the Television Commission, the core of senior civil servants and engineers who had formed the group remained involved in television. Leon O'Broin, as the secretary of the Department of Posts and Telegraphs, continued to be actively involved and in fact testified before the commission on several occasions. His influence remained considerable as the commission deliberated in 1958 and 1959. Maurice Gorham also continued to be a key figure at this stage. As the director of Radio Eireann, Gorham had a direct interest in how television would be introduced into the country, as he realized it could adversely affect the radio service. Matthew Doherty, an administration officer at Radio Eireann worked with the commission, compiling evidence for its members. He also worked closely with O'Broin and Gorham in trying to influence the commission's final report. John O'Keefe, the Engineer in Chief at Radio Eireann, continued to provide specialized information to the commission. He also reviewed the technical feasibility of proposals that had been submitted to both Posts and Telegraphs and the commission.

Gorham, O'Keefe, and Doherty all testified before the commission in May 1958. One of the first issues that was addressed considered the range of an Irish service. Gorham told the commission that the memo his department had prepared tried to consider a number of options that might be employed. It had therefore set out the cost of building a station that would start as a Dublin metropolitan service and expand to cater to Dublin and the more populated regions of the country before finally becoming national. It should be noted that a national service was defined as one that would cover the twenty-six counties of the Irish Republic, and *not* the six counties of Northern Ireland.

The commission had been informed by Posts and Telegraphs that the Irish Republic was limited in the number, location, and power of television transmitters it could build. This was due to the fact that Ireland was a signatory to the Stockholm Plan, which governed the allocation of television transmitters in Europe.[10] By international law, these transmitters were to be limited to 50 kilowatts. Posts and Telegraphs advised the Television Commission that the Belfast transmitter had a longer range than transmitters allowed to the Irish Republic under the Stockholm Plan.[11]

This is significant for a number of reasons. While the BBC and later ITA programs could be received in a considerable part of the Republic, the Stockholm Plan precluded a powerful Irish station from broadcasting directly into Northern Ireland. While the cultural and commercial imperialism of British television had established itself inside the Irish Republic, there would be no reciprocation by Dublin.[12] A later submission from Posts and Telegraphs indicated that even if a small transmitter was added in Cavan, and the power of the Sligo area transmitter was increased to 100 kilowats, the network of six transmitters was not intended to broadcast into Northern Ireland. John O'Keefe, the Engineer in Chief at Radio Eireann, had written to the commission and explained that six transmitters, conforming to the Stockholm Plan, could be expected to reach most of the population in the twenty-six counties of the Irish Republic.

The power of the proposed transmitters ranged from 100 kilowatts for Sligo, to 50 kilowatts for Dublin, Kilkenny, Cork, and Galway.[13] A small (1 kilowatt) transmitter proposed for Cavan further illustrates that Northern Ireland was not to be a target of an Irish television service. It is obvious that the Department of Posts and Telegraphs assumed, and the Television Commission accepted, that an Irish television service would be one designed for the twenty-six county Irish Republic.

The Television Commission touched on the issue of coverage to Northern Ireland briefly when the Engineer in Chief of Radio Eireann gave oral evidence. Under questioning, O'Keefe admitted that an Irish service using the transmitters his department recommended would cover parts of Counties Down, Fermanagh, and Tyrone. It is important to understand that at this juncture, the issue of broadcasting specifically into Northern Ireland was not developed. Instead, the testimony turned to questions about the wisdom of adopting the British standard of 405 line transmission, and the advantages and disadvantages were debated. The Chairman later led the conversation back to Northern Ireland, noting that from "a political point of view, . . . you would want to broadcast to the North."[14] This point was raised as an aside and not pursued by members of the commission or those testifying on behalf of Posts and Telegraphs.

Dr. McHugh, a member of the commission, dismissed the value of broadcasting into Northern Ireland, ignoring the nationalist minority that made up at least one-third of the population of the province, and a significant majority in Counties Fermanagh, Tyrone, and Down. He maintained, "Culturally, there will not be much chance of the Six Counties being interested in Irish television, the same applies to parts of England."[15] McHugh had brought up the question of coverage of Northern Ireland during a discussion that considered the desire to attract advertisers who would be interested in reaching the widest possible audience. However, his remark concerning the lack of interest in Northern Ireland demonstrates enormous insensitivity to nationalists living in a province whose administration actively suppressed its nationalist culture. What is equally remarkable is that the statement did not produce any protest among the other members of the commission.

McHugh was interested in the commercial prospects of a service that could extend beyond the twenty-six county Irish Republic. He asked the Engineer in Chief for calculations that would detail the added expense of a service that could be received in Northern Ireland and in western parts of Britain. O'Kccfc explained that it was not possible for an Irish television service to reach the west coast of Britain. When pressed by McHugh about Northern Ireland he made it obvious that an Irish service, if desired, could cover the North. O'Keefe explained that a transmitter installed in Dundalk "would give reasonable coverage for the Six Counties."[16] O'Keefe had told the commission that it would be possible to erect a transmission network that would cover all thirty-two counties which, according to the Irish Constitution, defined the nation. Ignoring the "Six Counties" did not conform to the antipartition rhetoric of the de Valera Government. However, it was clear that where television was concerned, the border defined the nation.

The Department of Posts and Telegraphs provided additional information concerning the number of television receivers in Ireland in 1958. The Television Committee had been trying to get an accurate idea of the number of television sets in the country for quite some time. The committee had requested an informal poll in the Dublin area to determine the number of sets first in 1955. The census was carried out by mail carriers, all of whom were asked to count the number of television aerials attached to homes on their route.

In the city center and the postal districts of Ballsbridge, Ballinteer, Churchtown, Crumlin, Dundrum, Fairview, James Street, Phibsboro, Rathfarnham, Rathmines, and Whitehall, a total of 1,098 aerials were counted. A national survey revealed that in 1955, towns and counties along the border and down the eastern seaboard as far as Wicklow had the most television sets. Monahan had 130 sets and Dundalk had 200; reception was described as "good most of the time." In the west, Westport had 1 set and reception was described as "good only under most favorable weather conditions." Mallow had 1 set, and reception was described as "poor or bad most of the time."[17] When the Post Office made additional inquiries into the number of television sets in May 1957, the number of receivers had grown, and in some areas the growth was dramatic. While the number of receivers in Lifford had increased from 100 in 1955 to 121 in 1957, the increase in Letterkenny was more substantial, rising from 30 to 121 over the same period.[18]

By 1958, O'Droma was able to report to the Television Commission that the number of receivers in the country was estimated at 20,000 sets. The Central Statistics Office in Dublin had submitted a similar estimate of 21,000 to 22,000 sets. The figures illustrate that while the public had demonstrated an appetite for television, the number of receivers in the country in 1958 remained fairly small.

The Television Commission had also requested that the Department of Posts and Telegraphs provide the written results and reports of the four Listener Surveys that had been conducted by Radio Eireann in March and September 1953, and again in 1954 and 1955. These surveys were the only measure of the popularity of Radio Eireann and its programs and the only poll conducted that provided information on the preferences of listeners. The commission was curious to determine the listening habits of the public, even if the medium that was surveyed was radio and not television. A review of the results would afford the commission a sense of what types of programs were popular and what programs were not, as well as a general understanding of when peak audiences could be expected.

Posts and Telegraphs and Radio Eireann forcefully resisted sending the survey results to the commission. Both argued that the complete results of the survey could not be given out for a number of less-than-convincing reasons. Maurice Gorham had received a request from the commission in May 1958 asking that these reports be made available. He wrote to O'Broin stating that it had been Radio Eireann's policy in the past not to release the Listener Surveys to the public, and that the same policy should be applied to the commission. Gorham suggested that the commission be sent a press release from June 1955, which provided a bland summary of the Listener

Survey. The press release did not provide the detailed tables and charts that the commission was interested in examining.

O'Broin wrote to Justice Murnaghan, the Chairman of the Commission, in July 1958 indicating the department's reluctance to supply the actual survey results:

I greatly regret that this is a type of confidential information which Radio Eireann . . . does not feel itself free to make . . . available to any third party. . . . {T]he complete figures have not been made public because it was not felt right to direct public attention to the comparative success or failure of individual programmes and performers.[19]

A summary of results was sent to the commission, but this did little to satisfy its members. O'Broin argued that the information that had been forwarded would simply have to suffice. Later, as a compromise, he suggested that the Director of Broadcasting, Maurice Gorham, might be able to address the commission and make reference to the report without making individual comparisons between programs.

The question of releasing the Listener Surveys had been a controversial one for some time. The real reason why both Posts and Telegraphs and Radio Eireann did not want the polls released had more to do with the miserable showing that Irish-language broadcasts were producing. This is evident in the manner in which the results of the surveys had been handled since they were first developed. A Radio Eireann survey carried out in March 1953 had polled 7,315 listeners and reported that the Irish-language broadcasts were decidedly unpopular.[20]

The *Irish Times*, in an editorial of November 12, 1953, criticized the government for the manner in which it had handled requests that the results be published. The then minister for Posts and Telegraphs, Erskine Childers, had been asked about releasing the results of the survey but had refused for what he described as "obvious" reasons. "What are these obvious reasons? . . . As it is, everybody is free to speculate on these "obvious" reasons for the Department's silence, and inevitably the worst possible construction will be put on it. Already the rumour goes round that the findings have been so sweepingly condemnatory of Radio Eireann's programmes that the authorities simply dare not publish them."[21]

The reasons why Childers refused to release the results were summarized in a minute of a Cabinet meeting that took place on September 25, 1953. It had been decided not to publish the survey "in the light of the very poor showing of programmes in the Irish language."[22] The government clearly feared that releasing the controversial poll would damage the credibility of

Radio Eireann. The results were certainly an embarrassment. However, one could argue that they reveal more about the quality of the Irish-language broadcasts than the fact that the broadcasts were in Irish.

Five years later, the department again refused to issue the full results of the Radio Eireann surveys. However, in 1958, it was not a member of the Dail asking for the release of the surveys, nor was a demand made to release the material to the general public. The government-appointed Television Commission, which conducted all its business in strict secrecy, was told that it could not have access to material that was pertinent to their investigation. The extraordinary refusal by O'Broin to release the surveys suggests once again that the genuine reason was fear that the members would see just how poorly Irish-language radio had been received by the listening public.[23] The secretary realized that the commission might conclude that any similar effort on the part of a television service would produce the same results. While the secretary opposed broadcasting a substantial amount of Irish-language material in a state-owned television service, he realized that a limited number of these programs would have their place.

In the end, a compromise was worked out, as Maurice Gorham forwarded copies of the full reports of the Listener Surveys to the Secretary of the Commission. However, even at this juncture the Director of Radio Eireann tried to place conditions on who should be able to examine the surveys. Gorham asked that Murnaghan not show the reports to any of the other members of the commission and asked that the surveys be returned after the Chairman had examined them.

The "language question" was an issue that created a great deal of difficulty for the government in its efforts to set up a television service. Idealists argued forcefully that the new technology should be exploited to revive the native language. They were opposed by self-described "pragmatists," who argued that what the country needed was a popular commercial service that would attract advertisers and revenue for the station. The contentious issue of the Irish language and its role in television will be considered in detail in later chapters.

Meanwhile, a notice that the Television Commission had published in the national newspapers and broadcast on Radio Eireann produced a sizable response. The notice had asked interested parties to forward submissions to the Secretary of the Commission.

One organization that contacted the commission was the Irish Association of Advertising Agencies. This group submitted a memorandum outlining its concerns regarding an Irish television service. It referred to Radio Eireann's history of broadcasting what it considered unpopular programs and warned that an Irish television service should learn a lesson from the experience of the radio station. It explained that the key to a successful television service would be reaching a large audience with popular programs. If this was not done, viewers would switch to the British alternative and the Irish service would lose viewers and eventually, advertisers. The Advertising Association concluded that "from a practical point of view, the positioning of minority-interest programmes must be most carefully considered. The artificial insertion of such programmes into peak viewing times can do nothing to further the interests involved; rather it will wreck the pattern of viewing for the remainder of the evening."[24]

The term *minority interest programs* was a code used to describe Irish-language programs. The Advertising Association did not feel comfortable in addressing the issue directly by naming the "minority interest" that it regarded as the major threat, but the implication was clear. It anticipated that commercial television would be regarded with a great deal of suspicion by a number of social and cultural groups and warned the commission not to make too many concessions to these "minority interests." Advocates of the Irish language had powerful enemies in the country who considered many supporters of the language fanatics who had to be kept in check.

The Joint Committee of Gaelic Bodies, representative of Connradh na Gaeilge, Comhdháil Náisiúnta na Gaeilge and An Comhchaidreamh, submitted a detailed memorandum to the Television Commission. The memorandum was the first comprehensive effort of the language lobby to examine the impact television would have on the state's effort to revive the Irish language. The language lobby would constitute an articulate, highly motivated force that tried to shape the direction of Irish television in order to force the government to ensure that steps were taken, not just for the preservation of the language, but for its revival. The Joint Committee initiated what has proved to be a long and difficult struggle to have the language question addressed.

Connradh na Gaedhilge (perhaps better known under its Anglicized name, the Gaelic League), described itself as an organization devoted to the restoration of the Irish language as the vernacular of the entire country. It was estimated that in 1958, the organization had approximately 4,000 branches in the thirty-two counties. The group taught classes in Irish and generally tried to foster an appreciation of the Irish language through plays, literature, and lectures.

Comhdháil Náisiúnta na Gaeilge, the National Congress of the Irish Language, was a government-funded organization created to coordinate the work of the various Irish-language groups. The organization made submissions to the government and individual ministers on issues that interested supporters of the language revival. An Comhchaidreamh described itself as an inter-university group that catered to graduates and students of Irish universities. The organization published a monthly journal, *Comhair*, and also contained another group that it had established, Gael-Linn. Gael-Linn had become well known for publishing a weekly racing form, a pool on Irish games that awarded prizes. The money raised by selling racing forms was used to fund a number of projects, including the making of short films in Irish. These films were distributed to cinemas throughout the country and shown free of charge, usually prior to a feature film. The group was also involved in small-scale employment projects in the Connemara Gaeltacht, where it had built a small factory to process fish and vegetables. Gael-Linn was an innovative organization that later became involved in the debate on television when it submitted a formal proposal of its own to the Television Commission.

The Joint Committee of Gaelic Bodies submitted a memorandum that expressed grave concern over the manner in which the government would act to bring television to Ireland. It regarded television as an important medium that could be exploited to further the aims of the language lobby. The Joint Committee argued that television was much more powerful than any other medium and that it was the responsibility of the state to see that it was closely supervised. It maintained that the government should act decisively to protect a frail Irish national character, which had been "greatly weakened by the effects of a long foreign domination."[25]

The committee also attacked the terms of reference that set up the Television Commission as being grossly inadequate for handling an issue of such importance. In an insightful passage, the Joint Committee pointed out the difficulty the commission would have in functioning as an effective investigative body. It argued that the strict terms of reference had weakened the ability of the commission to deliberate and decide on the best alternative for the country. The Joint Committee regarded a privately owned commercial entity as incompatible with what it described as the national interest. This was true, it believed, even if the service was monitored and supervised by the state. The committee argued that business interests would have priorities that would diverge from those of the nation, especially where programming was concerned.

The Joint Committee maintained that the effort to revive the national language could either be greatly assisted by television or destroyed by a service that ignored the unique culture of the Irish people. A national television service that failed to protect the Irish language would accelerate its collapse and "ensure the failure of the revival."[26] Accordingly, the Joint Committee argued that if the state was unwilling to assume complete control of a national television service, it preferred that no service be established.

The Joint Committee advocated the creation of a service that would be financed by the state and run by a government-appointed television authority. When addressing the specific question of the place for the Irish language in a state-owned service, the committee had strong ideas. It argued that the state had accepted that the preservation of the national language was a national priority. Since the government was committed to the language, the committee asserted that television should be used in the interest of the language revival. It was therefore only natural that a state-owned and -operated service should develop programs that would increasingly employ the Irish language in all types of programs. The Joint Committee argued that the television service should be staffed by Irish speakers. It admitted that initially, exceptions might have to be made in order to recruit qualified technicians. However, the committee was serious in recommending that only Irish speakers should be hired on a permanent basis.

The Joint Committee warned of the influence of foreign programs that would be broadcast on an Irish service. It called for the strict censorship of all material it regarded as unsuitable. The desire to censor foreign material went beyond the call that individual programs be "adjusted." This can be seen in the committee's demand that an Irish service adopt a 625-line standard for television transmissions. The 625-line standard of definition was employed throughout much of continental Europe, while the British had relied on a 405-line standard. While the 625-line standard offered a better picture than the 405-line standard employed in Britain, the reasons why the Joint Committee supported the European standard were not related strictly to a technical preference. At first the committee argued that the 625-line standard should be adopted as it would be better suited to the inevitable development of color television. However, the real reason the Joint Committee wanted to employ the 625-line standard was to reduce the influence of Britain in Ireland. The committee fully realized that a television receiver operating on the 625-line system would not be able to receive a signal from a service, such as the BBC broadcasting on the 405-line standard.

The advocates of the language revival assured the Television Commission that there would be widespread public support for their position. Notions of large-scale opposition to a service that would emphasize the Irish language were dismissed. In fact, the committee predicted that the general public would welcome the "wide use" of Irish on television.

The position of the language lobby was developed further when the Joint Committee of Gaelic Bodies testified before the Television Commission in July 1958. Tomás Ó Muircheartaigh testified on behalf of the Gaelic League, Earnest Blythe represented the Comhdháil Náisiúnta na Gaelige, and Tomás Ó Floinn represented An Comhchaidreamh. After introductions and brief opening statements, the three men answered a number of questions concerning the memorandum that had been submitted to the commission.

The Television Commission first asked the group for their opinion concerning the percentage of Irish-produced programs that should be featured on an Irish service and then moved on to ask about the proportion of programs that would be broadcast in the Irish language. Ó Floinn indicated that his group believed 50 percent of all programs featured should be produced in Ireland, broadcasting in both Irish and English. Earnest Blythe argued that a more realistic number was 25 percent, noting that a native service would find it difficult to provide quality programs even at this level.

The Chairman of the Commission expressed an interest in Irish-language programs targeted to children, though he was skeptical that such programs would hold a young audience. Blythe agreed that programs in Irish would be difficult for children, who generally had very little knowledge of the language. Murnaghan asked if the committee would be receptive to programs that were popular among children, such as the "Lone Ranger," dubbed in Irish. While Blythe appeared receptive to the idea and flexible about the amount of Irish-language programs that might be broadcast for children, Tomás Ó Floinn had other ideas:

Being realistic, and speaking of programmes for children alone, they should all be in Irish. Why not? Our system of education presupposes that the children learn Irish and that the children know Irish. . . . I would not be entirely in agreement with Mr. Blythe on that particular point, this giving them the Lone Ranger through the medium of Irish.[27]

The testimony given to the commission illustrates that the Joint Committee of Gaelic Bodies had considerable internal differences. Blythe's more moderate opinions were in sharp contrast with the dogmatic approach of Ó Floinn. Ó Floinn argued that it was his group's opinion that the government was not responsible for simply providing entertainment to the public. The idea of the Lone Ranger conversing with Tonto in Irish did not sit well with him. Instead, he argued that the government needed to commit itself to an active role in producing Irish-language programs that would be instructive and informative.

The Chairman of the Commission took issue with what he regarded an impractical approach advocated by Ó Floinn. Murnaghan believed Ó Floinn was being unrealistic, "The difficulty comes . . . when you speak of a type of nationalism that is sometimes alleged in . . . this country, I am afraid . . . to put on programmes that the majority of children won't look at. I think you have got to be realistic, and that we can be realists."[28] Blythe agreed, as he was less concerned with bestowing on children the duty of reviving Irish. "I don't think, while we have to lay more emphasis on the national language because of the weakness in the country as a result of history—we, at the same time, don't want to go totalitarian on Irish, don't want to cut our children off from things the children of other countries have."[29]

During the course of the Joint Committee's testimony, a member of the commission asked if Gael-Linn would be able to produce Irish-language television programs. Members of the commission had discussed among themselves a strategy where a private company, granted a monopoly license to broadcast in Ireland, would be required to produce a certain amount of material in Irish. The Joint Committee, and Gael-Linn in particular, were told that under such an arrangement, the broadcasting company would need input from an organization capable of producing quality Irish-language material. The commission believed that Gael-Linn could provide an important component to this type of commercial scheme.

Earnest Blythe was not impressed with this approach and argued that the state would have to accept responsibility for funding the production of Irish-language programs. He believed that Gael-Linn would be "foolish" to try and produce programs on its own. Blythe told the commission that it would be impossible to get sponsors to purchase time during Irish broadcasts. "Even the Irish papers with great difficulty scramble [to gather] some advertisements. The ordinary advertiser does not give a damn about the comparatively small group that either reads or listens to Irish. The Irish programme will have to be subsidised; it won't pay for itself out of advertisements."[30]

In spite of the opposition of Blythe, Ó Floinn was enthusiastic about the concept of Gael-Linn working as a program contractor for a commercial Irish service. The Chairman of the Commission and other members encouraged Gael-Linn to start thinking in these terms. Murnaghan provided an early indication of the direction in which the commission was headed. He theorized that if the government were to accept the recommendation that any service have a certain percentage of Irish-language programs, "immediately the question arises: where are you going to get Irish programmes. If the situation is that there is an organization like Gael-Linn, who are in a position to do it, you are first in the field. You may have no opposition."[31] The commission was impressed by the testimony of the Joint Committee of Gaelic Bodies and intrigued by the idea of Gael-Linn contributing to a privately owned commercial service.

A number of other groups also gave testimony to the commission. The Irish advertising industry, represented by W. P. O'Donoghue, the Managing Director of Marketing and Research Limited, gave evidence in May 1958. O'Donoghue had provided a written submission that addressed his concerns as a businessman who had been involved in producing sponsored programs for Radio Eireann. O'Donoghue advised the commission that he belonged to organizations that had a number of concerns about the introduction of an Irish television service. (He was a member of the Market Research Society and the Sales Managers' Association.)

O'Donoghue's primary concern was the announcement that Neil Blaney had made at the Advertising Association's Annual meeting, revising Radio Eireann's established advertising policy. Blaney had stated that commercial television in Ireland would not maintain the restrictions that Radio Eireann had employed. These regulations had prohibited the advertisement of foreign products on the Irish radio service. O'Donoghue was anxious about the financial impact such unrestricted access would create for Irish businesses, which would no longer be protected from foreign competition. He articulated the fears of Irish companies and their advertising agents, who were concerned that foreign competition would make it impossible for Irish companies to advertise on an Irish television service.[32]

Irish advertising agents wanted to exploit what was still a relatively protected domestic market with an Irish television service that would restrict foreign advertisers. O'Donoghue believed that Irish firms needed protection from British companies that would initially flock to an Irish commercial service, only to abandon it once the new ITA station was opened in Belfast. O'Donoghue warned that unless protection was provided to Irish advertising agents and their clients, the Irish service would be threatened with collapse. He reasoned that the British commercial service broadcasting from Belfast would offer better programs and be more attractive to viewers.

O'Donoghue made it clear to the commission that he was expressing the fears of an industry that would face stiff competition once the protectionist policies that had insulated Irish companies were abandoned. It is clear that Irish advertising companies feared competition from British advertising firms promoting British products. Much to the dismay of Irish advertising agents like O'Donoghue, the protectionist policies that had benefited Irish companies were being slowly dismantled. This phenomenon became government policy under the direction of Sean Lemass, especially in the 1960s. One can sense in O'Donoghue's testimony a fear of the future and of the technology that would transform the advertising trade. The introduction of television would contribute to the opening of Irish markets, exposing protected companies to real competition.

The commission listened to O'Donoghue and realized that it had yet another plea to consider when drafting its report to the government. The commission was interested in O'Donoghue's testimony but, as in the case of the Cinema Association, did not make any commitments addressing his concerns. It became evident that television would have a detrimental effect on a number of industries in the country.

Another witness who testified to the effect of advertising on a television service was M. J. O'Connor. O'Connor appeared before the commission on behalf of the Trade and Periodical Branch of the National Union of Journalists (NUJ) and also offered testimony of a strictly personal nature. He indicated that the NUJ would welcome the introduction of commercial television. Although he admitted that there were only about sixty journalists in the branch of the NUJ that he represented, he argued that journalists would appreciate the employment opportunity that television would offer.[33]

What is more interesting is the testimony O'Connor offered examining the effect of a national television service on provincial newspapers. He pointed out that since the conclusion of World War II, the cost for the production of newspapers had risen almost tenfold. He told the commission that newsprint, which had cost £10 a ton prior to the war, cost £63 a ton in 1958. O'Connor maintained that provincial papers operated on very slim profit margins and complained that these newspapers would lose a critical source of revenue to a commercial television service. He advised the commission that he had every reason to believe that large companies that helped support these papers through their advertisements would find television a much more attractive medium to exploit.

O'Connor's testimony is remarkable because of the concern he expressed for the survival of an important component in the life of rural Ireland. The provincial press had played an important role in rural areas, providing local and regional news that the national dailies could not supply. O'Connor argued that the loss of these papers would create a void that could not be easily filled by the national press or other forms of media, such as radio and television. The witness warned of the detrimental effect that television could have on Irish society and pointed to the difficulties being experienced by provincial papers in Britain in order to bolster his argument.

The commission continued to interview parties interested in television and in how the new medium might best be introduced to Ireland. Some of the most interesting evidence was given by parties interested in building and operating a television service. Charles Michelson and his associates testified before the commission and explained in detail a proposal that created a tremendous amount of interest and controversy. His testimony and that of his supporters will be examined in the following chapter.

NOTES

1. Paul Warren granted a number of interviews with the author in Dalkey, County Dublin, the fall of 1990. He also shared his private papers recollecting his years at the Department of Posts and Telegraphs.

2. *Dail Debates* (July 19, 1956): col. 1546.

3. Department of Communications, TW3756, Comhad 8, agenda of the first meeting of the Television Commission, March 31, 1958.

4. Early in 1958 Sean Ormonde became ill and Kevin Boland became acting minister. Ormonde returned but resigned due to ill health in June 1959. He was replaced by Michael Hilliard.

5. Department of Communications, TW3756, speech of Kevin Boland to the Television Commission, April 9, 1958, p. 2.

6. Ibid., transcript of the first meeting of the Television Commission, April 9, 1958, p. 5.

7. *Access*, RTE's Free Press, 4, no. 17 (December 16, 1982).

8. Department of Communications, TW3756, transcript of the first meeting of the Television Commission, April 9, 1958. The Commission offered several witnesses the option of testifying off the record. Although some testimony may have been given without a stenographer present, the lion's share was recorded.

9. Department of Communications, TW3756, Comhad no. 10, memo from Posts and Telegraphs to the Television Commission, April 21, 1958, p. 2. The memo examined the cost for a service that would be a Dublin metropolitan service, suggesting that this might be built before the entire country was included.

10. Archives of RTE, Survey of Developments in Television Affecting Ireland, March 1957.

11. Department of Communications, TW3756, Comhad 8, *Television Commission. Historical, Technical, and Legal Background*, p. 9.

12. The Commission was told that according to a survey conducted by Posts and Telegraphs "about 40% of the total population of the Twenty Six Counties" was able to receive the Belfast transmissions. R.T.E. Archives, Doc. Gen. 1, *Survey of Developments in Television Affecting Ireland March 1957*, par. 8.

13. The 100-kilowatt (kw) Sligo station exceeded the 50-kw station that had been allowed in the Stockholm Plan and indicates that it was believed a change

could be requested. However this was not intended to increase the range of an Irish service inside Northern Ireland.

14. Department of Communications, TW3756, Comhad 17, minutes of the Television Commission, May 2, 1958, p. 4.

15. Ibid., p. 25.

16. Ibid.

17. Department of Communications, TW9821, "Television Reception in the Provinces," 1955.

18., Ibid., memo from Sean O'Droma, May 22, 1957.

19. Archives of RTE, 105/58, 4A;15, memo from O'Broin to Murnaghan, July 1958.

20. State Paper Office, Department of the Taoiseach, S15580, Ministers' notes on Radio Eireann Listener Research Report, p. 6.

21. *Irish Times*, November 12, 1953.

22. State Paper Office, Department of the Taoiseach, S15580, Cabinet Minute, Department of Taoiseach, September 25, 1953.

23. The June 1955 Listener Survey determined that Irish language broadcasts remained unpopular. The news in Irish, Nuacht, received 4 percent of the audience, while other Irish programs such as Amhrain polled 1 percent and An Tathair Damien polled 5 percent.

24. Department of Communications, TW3756, Comhad no. 17.

25. Ibid., "Memorandum to the Television Commission from a joint committee representative of Connradh na Gaelige, Comhdháil Náisiúnta na Gaeilge and An Comchaidreamh," p. 2.

26. Ibid., p. 4.

27. Department of Communications, TW3756, no. 17. Testimony given to the Television Commission, July 25, 1958, pp. 9–10.

28. Ibid.

29. Ibid., p. 11.

30. Ibid., pp. 13–14.

31. Ibid., p. 15.

32. Ibid., Testimony of W. P. O'Donoghue, May 23, 1958, p. 29.

33. Ibid., Testimony of M. J. O'Connor given to the Television Commission July 4, 1958, p. 2.

CHAPTER 8

Charles Michelson, the Vatican, and the Development of Irish Television

The most controversial proposal that had been made to the Irish Government was that of Charles Michelson. This submission created a crisis for O'Broin and his associates, who came to abhor everything for which it stood. The scheme generated a great deal of interest both inside and outside Ireland. Michelson proved to be an astute entrepreneur who was clever enough to cultivate and exploit a number of powerful sources within the country. He also demonstrated an impressive ability to gather support from powerful European interests who lobbied on his behalf. The Television Commission received evidence and heard testimony from many of these supporters, who strongly supported the scheme he submitted. Michelson asked for, and was granted, the opportunity to testify before the commission on behalf of his proposal. Michelson's proposal created an unusual alliance of supporters who lobbied the government and the Television Commission on his behalf. The proposal and the reaction it produced provides fascinating insight into the working of the government.

Before Michelson testified, the commission received a number of documents submitted as evidence that supported the Romanian expatriate's scheme. Aer Lingus, the Hospitals Trust, the tourist board, Bord Fáilte, and the Irish Export Board, Córas Tráchtála Teoranta, all presented evidence to the commission. Bord Fáilte, Hospitals Trust, and Córas Tráchtála appeared before the commission to offer oral evidence on behalf of Michelson.

Aer Lingus submitted a memorandum to the commission welcoming the government's decision to consider the establishment of an Irish television service. The national airline stated that all organizations in the country that were responsible for the development of tourism were interested in promoting Ireland to the outside world. In its submission, Aer Lingus asserted that as tourism was the second largest of all Irish industries, it made sound financial sense to promote it aggressively in the international marketplace. The memo complained that Ireland was unable to promote itself as a tourist destination in foreign markets and that this was impeding the growth of the industry and depriving the country of a valuable source of income. Aer Lingus argued that little was known about Ireland abroad and that this situation had to be corrected. "One of the reasons for this widespread ignorance about Ireland arises from the absence here of the great modern devices of long range sound broadcasting, television and a fully developed film industry . . . [which] makes the publicity task of Aer Lingus . . . infinitely more difficult."[1]

The key phrase employed in this statement, "long range sound broadcasting," particularly interested the national airline. Aer Lingus advised the commission that it recognized the financial difficulties that confronted the state in the attempt to bring television to Ireland but maintained that it had found a solution. In these difficult circumstances, the best option was to grant a contract to a company that could exploit radio commercially by broadcasting overseas. Aer Lingus was most interested in advertising on a radio service that would reach both Britain and the continent. This was the only reason why the company had gone to the trouble of submitting evidence to the commission. Aer Lingus did not identify the company that it supported; however, it soon became clear to the commission that the national airline supported the scheme of Charles Michelson.

Aer Lingus concluded its written evidence by stressing its support for Irish television, which it regarded as a defining feature of an independent developed nation:

Any country without it will not be regarded as a modern progressive nation, and, indeed will come under the direct influence of those neighboring countries that can reach Ireland. . . . With television this country can have a voice and a recognisable presence in the European community; without it Ireland will become an obscure island as far away from Europe, despite all its other modern developments, as was Hibernia to the Romans.[2]

Aer Lingus yearned for an international radio station that would allow it access to listeners abroad. The Michelson plan promised to make special arrangements that would enable Ireland's national airline free access to a radio service that would broadcast into Britain, Europe, and eventually America.

Bord Fáilte Eireann was more direct in its submission. It told the commission that it had followed recent developments concerning television with great interest, and like Aer Lingus, it argued that the Irish tourist industry needed to market itself overseas. Although at this juncture a specific proposal was not identified, Bord Fáilte was clearly most impressed with the Michelson scheme. It advised the commission that it supported building a commercial radio station that would reach an audience in Britain and on the continent, concluding, "We have carefully examined aspects of this scheme, and we are convinced that this type of scheme offers highly significant possibilities for the promotion of Irish tourism in overseas markets."[3] The Irish Tourist Board maintained that it was sympathetic to the financial position of the government and acutely aware of its inability to fund a sustained advertising campaign in Britain, Europe, and the United States. Bord Fáilte argued that exploiting an international radio service would allow the state to circumvent this difficult problem and permit Ireland to compete in an expanding and very competitive industry.

In June 1958, Mr. O'Driscoll and Mr. Sheridan, representing Bord Fáilte, appeared before the commission to offer evidence in support of its written submission. Their evidence illustrates how the Michelson Company had lobbied semistate bodies in a successful effort to gain their support. In his testimony Driscoll reiterated many of the points that had been highlighted in Bord Fáilte's written evidence. He also stressed that advertising overseas had become exceedingly expensive, while budget restrictions limited his organizations' ability to market Ireland abroad.

The Chairman of the Commission, George Murnaghan, asked if he was correct in assuming that the scheme that Bord Fáilte supported was the same one that had been advocated by Hospitals Trust and the Irish Export Board. O'Driscoll admitted that these firms had agreed with Bord Fáilte in recognizing Charles Michelson as the entrepreneur who had made the most attractive offer. On further questioning from Murnaghan, O'Driscoll revealed that he and these semistate bodies had been approached by groups other than Michelson. He stated that the McLendon Company had solicited Bord Fáilte, as had Associated Rediffusion. According to O'Driscoll, the McLendon Company had approached his organization to discuss the possibility of establishing a commercial radio service that would broadcast internationally. O'Driscoll told the commission that the McLendon Group had kept a lobbyist in Dublin—an American identified as a Ronald J. Kahn—for several months. Kahn had lobbied a number of organizations, including semistate bodies, to promote his company's proposal.

O'Driscoll explained to the commission the attraction in the offers made by McLendon and Michelson. "The McLendon group offered us so many dollars worth of free time on their radio network in the U.S.A., as well as anything that would be going here. . . . Michelson . . . would be prepared . . . to give what we call institutional advertising; that is advertising without reference to a particular brand."[4] Although O'Driscoll testified that Bord Fáilte was not tied to any one applicant, it is clear that the group was most impressed with Michelson's proposal.

O'Driscoll stated that Charles Michelson had been introduced to Bord Fáilte through the Department of External Affairs, after he had made inquiries at the Irish Embassy in Paris. He also explained that Aer Lingus, the Export Board, Hospitals Trust, and Bord Fáilte had worked together in scrutinizing the plan he had proposed. "Finally we got together—the four of us—the group responsible for doing this promotional work abroad, and we exchanged views. We had Michelson in on one occasion and [the] four Companies represented put him through a pretty severe grilling one whole afternoon. At the end our conclusion was that this, certainly, was something well worth looking at."[5]

The Television Commission then focused on what might be referred to as the character issue. Under questioning, O'Driscoll admitted that the investigation that he and his associates conducted was not extensive and that no thorough background check had been conducted on Michelson. The four companies were aware that Michelson had been involved with Radio Monte Carlo and Europe Number One, and O'Driscoll emphasized that Michelson had never tried to hide the fact that he had been associated with these commercial stations. The group clearly did not know that Michelson had experienced significant trouble in his continental business ventures. As far as O'Driscoll and his associates were concerned, Michelson's integrity was never an issue. All four companies were reported to be initially skeptical of the proposal, however, this suspicion disappeared after Michelson had been interviewed and his proposal analyzed.

O'Driscoll also explained that the group of semistate bodies that supported Michelson was satisfied that the proposal was financially feasible. He maintained that the McLendon Company's proposal was very similar to Michelson's and proved that commercial sound broadcasting was lucrative. O'Driscoll admitted that the comparison the group had made between the McLendon and Michelson schemes was not exhaustive. He also informed the commission that he believed McLendon's interest in Ireland to be waning.[6]

O'Driscoll was asked about the issue of wavelengths and whether the group of semistate bodies was convinced that Michelson could set up such a service and conform to international regulations governing the allocation of radio frequencies. He replied that the group was satisfied that the service could be legally established. He stated that his group had asked Michelson this question directly and that the entrepreneur had produced an opinion from a highly respected legal source arguing that Ireland could legally gain the needed wavelength.

Córas Tráchtála Teoranta, the Irish Export Board, also submitted evidence to the commission and testified before it in support of the Michelson proposal. In written evidence forwarded in May 1958, M. J. Killeen stated that Córas Tráchtála would be very interested in a scheme that would bring commercial international radio to Ireland.[7] Killeen and a Mr. Walsh of Córas Tráchtála testified before the commission and declared the support of the Export Board for the Michelson scheme. Walsh explained to the commission the importance of advertising and publicity for encouraging exports. He admitted that his organization was not so much interested in television as it was in international commercial radio. Like Aer Lingus and Bord Fáilte, Córas Tráchtála was primarily interested in advertising on an international radio station. It recognized that Michelson's proposal provided a unique opportunity to reach and exploit a potentially lucrative market. Walsh argued that access to this market would greatly increase Irish exports, which would benefit the Irish economy.[8]

Walsh testified that the Export Board could not afford to advertise Irish products on American or European radio stations. He told the commission that Michelson had offered to provide inexpensive airtime to Córas Tráchtála on the proposed station. Walsh claimed to have studied the documents and considered the question of wavelength acquisition. He told the commission that he was convinced that an international Irish service could legally broadcast programs while conforming to the conventions governing European wavelengths. On the question of the integrity of Michelson, Walsh advised the commission that Aer Lingus, Bord Fáilte, Hospitals Trust, and the Export Board had all pooled their resources and evaluated Michelson and his scheme. At the conclusion of this investigation, each one of these organizations expressed satisfaction with the integrity of both the applicant and his proposal.

Walsh mentioned the involvement of the Hospitals Trust, stating that this group had been involved with the Córas Tráchtála, Bord Fáilte, and Aer Lingus in supporting the Michelson scheme. Irish Hospitals Trust had operated the Irish Sweepstakes since 1930, selling tickets throughout the world to raise money for medical facilities in Ireland. The Trust was also interested in gaining access to international radio in order to advertise its lottery tickets. Along with Aer Lingus, Bord Fáilte and Córas Tráchtála, the Hospitals Trust recognized an opportunity in the Michelson proposal. It forwarded evidence to the commission that argued for the importance of international radio and the need for the Irish Sweepstakes to expand its market.

Documents submitted as evidence by Hospitals Trust contended that the Copenhagen Convention, the regulatory roadblock that had prevented the Irish Government from broadcasting from a high-power transmitter, had been ignored by a number of European nations since its inception. These countries included the German Federal Republic, Sweden, and, of course, Monaco and Luxembourg.[9] Hospitals Trust considered the Copenhagen Plan an obsolete agreement that had been ignored by much of Europe and accepted Michelson's opinion that it could be legally circumvented.

The most surprising Michelson supporter was undoubtedly the Roman Catholic Church. In July 1958, Monsignor George Roche and Monsignor Andrea Deskur, the Assistant Secretary of the Pontifical Commission on Cinema, Radio, and Television, went to Dublin to visit the Minister for Health, Sean MacEntee. The minister's brother-in-law, Father Michael Browne, had provided the emissaries from the Vatican with a letter of introduction to MacEntee, who was a member of the Irish Cabinet. MacEntee later reported to the Taoiseach, Eamon de Valera, and explained that the clerics had come to express the strong interest of Pope Pius XII in Irish television and radio. Roche explained that he had recently been involved in a discussion with the Pontiff when the subject of Irish radio and television came up. Monsignor Roche mentioned to the Pontiff that the Irish Government was considering establishing a television service.

The Holy Father had at once expressed great interest in the matter and subsequently had arranged that Monsignor Roche should come to Dublin, accompanied by Monsignor Deskur. . . . Having put their submission to the Television Commission, Monsignor Roche stated that they had been charged to express informally the great personal interest which His Holiness had in the matter, because of the great service which he believed a television service under the auspices of an Irish Government could render in combatting irreligion and materialism.[10]

The Monsignori told MacEntee that Pope Pius XII believed:

practically all broadcasting and television systems everywhere were under the control of groups who, at best, were not greatly concerned about moral issues, or as in the case of communist controlled stations, were actively hostile to Christianity and the Catholic church in particular. It was because of this situation that the Holy Father had been particularly struck by the potentialities of an Irish television service. He emphasised the fact that the influence of radio and television as a media of mass communication had been particularly bad in traditionally Catholic countries in South America and Europe, because of programmes which in their treatment of moral and religious issues had been highly objectionable. He then went on to say that His Holiness felt that, by reason of its geographical situation, the Irish television installation could be of great service to the Christian religion provided that a transmitter be installed which would be sufficiently powerful to transmit its programmes to trans-oceanic territories. He trusted, therefore, that when the type, power and site of the television transmitter was being determined this consideration would be given great weight by those responsible. In this connection Monsignor Deskur emphasised how advantageously Ireland was situated for the purpose of radio transmission.[11]

Although the Vatican appeared confused over the range of an Irish television service, the Church demonstrated that it was aware of the potential power of radio transmissions that could be broadcast from Ireland. The Roman Catholic Church was yet another party interested in exploiting what had become Ireland's precious natural resource: its geographic position in relation to Britain and continental Europe. The Monsignori were offered an appointment with the Taoiseach but declined, fearing that on such short notice, they be would imposing. They thanked MacEntee for the offer but advised the Minister of Health that they would be satisfied if MacEntee conveyed their concerns directly to de Valera.

Before departing, the Monsignori made a formal request concerning the report of the Television Commission. They asked that the Pontifical Commission on Radio and Television be provided with a copy of the commission's report before a final decision on television was made by the government. The Vatican wanted the opportunity to review the report of the commission and perhaps make suggestions to the Irish Government before a final decision was made.

Eamon de Valera reviewed the memo from his Minister of Health and agreed that an advance copy of the report should be made available to the Vatican. It was agreed that special arrangements would be employed to forward the document to Rome. The use of official diplomatic channels was avoided as the emissaries from the Vatican feared that going through the Department of External Affairs at Iveagh House would jeopardize the secrecy of their mission. There was concern that the involvement of the Papacy might be leaked to the press and that this would embarrass both the

Irish Government and the Vatican. It is clear that from the outset of this dialogue, the Vatican was obsessed with secrecy and anxious to avoid word getting out of its interest in Irish radio and television. The fact that the Vatican avoided official channels in contacting the government through the Minister for Health is indicative of this concern.

It is interesting to note that the visitors from Rome appeared before the Television Commission during their visit to Dublin. Although no records have been found to prove that the two clerics actually testified before the commission, there is a possibility that the Monsignori testified informally and "off the record" to a select number of commission members.[12]

One month later, in August 1958, the Irish Ambassador at the Vatican was approached by Monsignor George Roche. Roche gave the ambassador a complete copy of the Michelson proposal and advised him that the Vatican supported Michelson's candidacy. Roche asked the ambassador not to report to the secretary of his department until the Monsignor had a chance to speak with him once again about the Michelson proposal and the Vatican's support of it. The ambassador was told later by Roche that he had two reasons for wanting the Vatican's interest in Michelson's plan kept secret. The first was that it wanted Michelson's plan to be considered as an ordinary, commercial proposal. The second reason sounds more plausible: "He feared that in a large office like Iveagh House the proposals might fall to be dealt with by someone whose prejudices would cause him to look with suspicion on an activity backed by the Church and so create difficulties not justified by the intrinsic nature of the scheme."[13]

The ambassador reported to his government that the Vatican strongly supported the Michelson proposal.

I learned from Monsignor Roche that the Church is deeply and actively interested in this scheme as an anti-communist weapon. You will see that the proposals are not confined to television but include sound broadcasting on both short and medium waves. No doubt existed, the Monsignor assured me, about the availability of the necessary funds or the technical experience. If the scheme was adopted Ireland would become a center from which would radiate programmes conforming to the ideals of Christendom and western civilization and competing with communist propaganda. . . . He used very great caution in his exposition but left no doubt that an interest is being taken in the scheme at the very highest level.[14]

While Michelson had shown himself adept at assembling backers for his scheme, the "blessing" of the Vatican was certainly the most remarkable.

The Michelson group testified before the commission on July 18, 1958. The commission had already received a copy of the company's proposal and heard testimony in support of this scheme. The party that accompanied Charles Michelson to the hearings included twelve individuals from very diverse backgrounds. The group included Professor Henri Rolin, a lawyer who had represented the interests of Michelson since 1939 and who had provided a detailed opinion concerning the legality of opening an international radio station based in Ireland. Also present were two engineers, Louis Kahn and Yvon Delbord, and Richard Cronan, an American attorney who also represented Michelson. Other members of the party included a member of the French Parliament, Hubert Lefevre-Pontalis; the well-known Irish actress Siobhan McKenna; the writer and dramatist Denis Johnston; and the entrepreneur Charles Michelson, himself.

Monsignori George Roche and Andrea Deskur were also with the Michelson group. When the party was introduced, the commission was told that the Monsignori wished to testify and make a statement. The Chairman of the Commission, George Murnaghan, asked in what capacity the Monsignori were attending. Speaking as Michelson's attorney, Richard Cronan advised the commission: "They are very interested in television in this application and television for Ireland generally. I was going to ask your permission to have them read a brief statement, or to present a number of statements, and further to ask your permission that they be allowed here during the hearing."[15]

As the Monsignori were not a formal part of the Michelson group, the chairman ruled that they could not remain while Michelson and his associates were outlining their proposal. Instead, it was suggested that the two clerics return after the Michelson group had given their evidence. The two men retired from the hearing, and if they did return to give evidence, their testimony was not recorded. It is doubtful that they returned to testify before the commission that evening, and no evidence has been found to suggest that the two men ever gave formal testimony. No record of written or oral evidence submitted by the clerics has been found by this writer, although there is some indication that some form of submission was made. Siobhan McKenna and Denis Johnston also retired but returned later that evening to testify before the commission.

Michelson testified before the commission at length, explaining that he and his associates were willing to build and operate a television network in Ireland in exchange for an exclusive license to broadcast international radio programs from the country. Two television stations were proposed. One, a commercial service designed to develop a large national audience, would broadcast primarily entertainment programs. The second would be a public service station, which would broadcast cultural and educational programs, including material in Irish. It was explained that the company was willing to work out a profit-sharing scheme that would allow the state to purchase the television network after a number of years. The Michelson group maintained that it would be years before the television enterprise would become profitable and stated that the proposed commercial radio station would enable the television enterprise to run at a loss, as it would generate revenue to cover the expected deficit. Michelson emphasized throughout his testimony that the proposal was flexible and could be shaped to address the concerns of the Irish Government. He also told the commission that his proposal would benefit domestic Irish radio, as he was prepared to give Radio Eireann an outright grant of £90,000 a year to improve its program. This grant would allow Radio Eireann to abolish commercial advertisements from the national radio station.

In his proposal Michelson had indicated that the television service could be received as far away as the west coast of Britain. Testimony revealed that this was based, not on any scientific tests conducted by Michelson's engineers, but on experience gained by Michelson on his extensive travels in Ireland. He noted that when traveling in Wicklow, he had seen homes with television aerials. After speaking with residents he learned that the signals from a BBC transmitter in Manchester were being received along the coast on a regular basis. He therefore reasoned that if signals from the British mainland were being received in Ireland, Irish signals would be picked up in Britain. Michelson's contention that an Irish television service could reach Britain had caught the attention of the four semistate bodies that had endorsed his proposal, as well as the Vatican. One can only question Michelson's motive in allowing this aspect of his scheme to be circulated as fact.

Michelson also addressed the commission's concerns about his past business dealings on the continent, which was a subject that deeply interested the skeptical chairman, George Murnaghan. It should be noted that Michelson chose to bring up the subject himself and was not afraid to speak for himself in spite of the attorneys present to represent his interests. He realized that he had to convince the commission that he was an honest businessman and therefore personally explained the problems he had encountered on the continent. Though Michelson was prepared to confront the controversies that had stalked him from Algiers to Monaco and France, the commission was more interested in his involvement with Europe Number One. Michelson maintained that he had built a successful commercial radio service in the Saar, during the postwar period when France administered the territory. He claimed that the station had antagonized

Radio Luxembourg, a popular station with powerful friends in the French Government. He told the commission that he had been granted a contract by the Saar administration in 1952 to build the commercial radio service and that the contract had stipulated that the government would receive 50 percent of all profits made by the station. He further indicated that he was well aware that in proceeding with the building of the station, he would create a number of powerful enemies.

Michelson, a Romanian expatriate living in Paris, then explained why he had been treated so poorly by the French authorities. He told the commission that those who had opposed his plans to build Europe Number One were unique people.

These people, these powerful people abroad have power on the continent. . . . They got a lot of political support. You asked me my citizenship at the start, Mr. Chairman. . . . I am stateless. Stateless means: a poor fellow that you can shift as you want. I was stateless sticking to the letter, making money. . . . [T]hen, one day . . . I was requested very kindly to leave for Corsica. Why Corsica? Because Corsica on the French geographic map is the furthest Department from Paris. . . . I found my way back in such a way that the Minister of Home Affairs said that I was entitled to go free because it was bad information he made it on . . . every measure taken against me was without a hearing, and every measure was withdrawn.[16]

Michelson explained that he had been a victim of an unfair campaign to slander him, launched by jealous rivals intent on discrediting his work and destroying his radio station. He provided the commission with documents from the French Government that had cleared his name and dismissed all charges against him. He hoped that these documents and his testimony would allow the commission to put aside these concerns. Murnaghan, a Justice on the Irish High Court, was not overly impressed. He suggested that Michelson's success in court had more to do with the high caliber of his legal team than his innocence.

Michelson was queried as to why he had left Europe Number One if the station had been the financial success that he claimed. "Because I was slandered to death. . . . At the time the Board of Directors—they said to me that I was going out under political pressure, outside pressure. . . . I went out to save their business and to save my skin."[17] He maintained that he was forced to sell his shares in Europe Number One in March 1955 and that the radio station that he had created continued to enjoy a great deal of popularity in Europe.

The testimony of the witness moved on to what was the most difficult issue in both the Michelson and the McLendon proposals. This concerned the question of wavelength allocation and how these groups planned legally to operate a commercial, high-power station that would broadcast directly into Britain. The witness was evasive when asked specifically about the origin of the wavelength he would use. In spite of Murnaghan's continued efforts, Michelson refused to provide a satisfactory answer to the commission. Michelson finally admitted that his company was interested in safeguarding the details of its business proposal for fear that another applicant might be influenced by the work his company had completed. He told the commission that without a commitment from the government, he was not prepared to divulge his plan for gaining the critical wavelength. He assured the commission that his company had developed a plan that would allow it to legally operate an international radio service.

Murnaghan advised Michelson that his stance would hurt his company's prospects. He explained that as he understood the proposal, Michelson planned to broadcast on a wavelength that might cause interference with another nation's radio service. If this was the case, the chairman emphasized that the government would have to know the identity of any nation that might be affected in order to initiate negotiations with that country.

Later in its testimony, the company advised the commission of the strategy it would adopt in gaining a wavelength, but it refused to reveal which particular wavelength it would target. Professor Henri Rolin, the law professor who had written a legal opinion for Michelson, argued that the Copenhagen Plan was a flawed treaty. He maintained that it was being ignored by signatories and nonsignatories alike. Rolin advised the commission that several nations that had signed the agreement had broken it by simply informing the European Broadcasting Union of their intentions to use a particular wavelength. Once this notification was given, the countries simply negotiated with the states that were affected until an agreement was reached.

The commission also considered the report of the 1949 British Beveridge Commission, which had investigated the then current and future state of broadcasting in the United Kingdom. Murnaghan brought up the report as it addressed the issue of foreign commercial broadcasts transmitting into Britain from abroad. The chairman read into the record the part of the Beveridge Report that addressed these foreign broadcasts. When the findings of the commission were presented to the British Government, Radio Luxembourg was the only foreign commercial radio station broadcasting into Britain. However, the Beveridge Commission had been warned about "the possibility of a full scale attack by commercial advertising from the

United States . . . [that] might . . . come at any moment through use of stations in neighboring countries."[18]

By highlighting the concerns of the British authorities, the chairman suggested that a plan such as that proposed by Michelson would antagonize Ireland's powerful neighbor. Murnaghan read another paragraph that considered the options open to the British if commercial broadcasts became a problem:

In the last resort, if we do not want either political propaganda or commercial broadcasts from abroad we may be driven to jamming, as Soviet Russia has jammed much or most of the information about the world outside which the British and American broadcasting authorities have endeavored to supply to the Russian people. Those who think that commercial broadcasts are as objectionable as gambling forecasts or political propaganda, however dishonest, must contemplate jamming.[19]

The chairman abruptly stopped reading from the report at this juncture. Murnaghan clearly implied that the radio station Michelson proposed would fail as the British authorities were prepared to jam its broadcasts. However, Michelson proved that he was well aware of the contents of the Beveridge Commission's report. He asked Murnaghan to continue reading where the chairman had stopped. Murnaghan obliged and reluctantly read further from the report of the Beveridge Commission. "Those who feel that advertisement by radio, even if we do not want it to dominate radio and even if we do not want it from the BBC, is not in itself as bad as other things that can happen in the world today, may be prepared to make a bargain."[20] Michelson seized on the word "bargain," arguing that the British would be willing to come to terms with the commercial radio service that he proposed. He dismissed the possibility of the British jamming commercial broadcasts as impractical.

Michelson complained that one had to keep in mind that the British were heavily involved in international broadcasting themselves, to such an extent that the foreign service of the BBC broadcast in forty-two different languages. Nonetheless, Murnaghan was concerned with how the British government might react to a powerful commercial radio station broadcasting from Ireland. He speculated that the British might retaliate by pronouncing: "We won't take in Irish cattle."[21] The fear of British economic retribution was quite real. Murnaghan was simply articulating a concern that, at least in the official mind, had to be taken into consideration.

Michelson and his associates proved that they had prepared a thorough proposal. Indeed, Michelson had demonstrated an impressive ability to recognize some of the more complex issues in Irish society. When questioned about how such subjects as religion and the national language would be handled by the television service, he skillfully explained that his company would look to the government for guidance on these issues and allow the state to decide policy. It was made clear that the state would have full control over the content of the public service channel and it would be up to the government or an appointed state body to decide how sensitive issues would be addressed. The commercial entertainment channel would also be under government supervision and care would be taken to ensure that the programs broadcast would not insult, subvert, or offend Irish sensibilities.

Michelson was careful in addressing the subject of the Irish-language, being aware that it was a complex and difficult one. He was intelligent enough to evade questions concerning the amount of Irish-language broadcasts that should be shown on the public station. This did not stop Michelson from supporting efforts to subsidize television in the Gaeltacht. Michelson advised the commission that he was prepared to provide sets to every Irish-speaking community at cost and to allow the sets to be paid for over a period of five years.[22]

Michelson admitted having met with representatives of Bord Fáilte and the Irish Export Board, but he told the commission that he had learned most about Ireland from spending over nine months traveling throughout the country. The session concluded with Michelson promising the commission that he would foreword additional information that would provide technical and financial data.

Once Michelson had given his testimony, the transcribed evidence was sent to the Department of Posts and Telegraphs for analysis and comment. As might be expected, O'Broin and his associates were not impressed with the testimony offered by Michelson and his supporters.[23] The department questioned the veracity of their claims, especially when the question of wavelength acquisition was discussed. O'Broin concluded his review by reporting that his department had communicated with the appropriate authorities and determined that the Copenhagen Plan was not the flawed document derided by Michelson's attorneys. Posts and Telegraphs explained that the only way Ireland could gain a wavelength was to withdraw from the agreement after providing a one-year notice. This was an option that the department found most distressing.

Leon O'Broin appeared before the commission on October 31, 1958, and testified about his own personal views on television. The secretary outlined once again the scheme that he believed would best address the nation's need for a television service. The proposal he outlined was more refined than the crude service that had first been mentioned in the 1953 report of the Television Committee. He first asserted that an Irish service would have to be operated by a public authority. O'Broin told the commission that it was imperative that this authority have a great deal of independence and be free of civil service control. He referred to Radio Eireann as a service that had been greatly hampered by its close relationship to the state and called for a "maximum measure of separation" for television.[24]

O'Broin warned the commission that handing over a medium such as television to commercial interests would be a terrible mistake, as private investors would not promote Irish culture. "Their concern is to make money by attracting and holding large audiences; by giving them standardised entertainment of a certain elemental character. What we should aim at, I believe, is the opposite, the maximum of diversity with adequate representation for minority interests."[25] O'Broin believed that a decision by the commission to recommend a commercial service would have devastating consequences. He foresaw an endless stream of mindless programs that would damage the national culture. He complained that British commercial television produced material that was unsuitable for the Irish people and that ITA programs were broadcast to "keep the viewer at a high pitch of excitement" in order to ensure that they did not change the channel. Thrillers, slapstick comedy, and game shows were featured to try to keep the audience entertained. The result was a crass service that, unlike the BBC, had little cultural value. "They cannot afford to be subtle or to pay attention to minorities. . . . Under such a set-up there is little or no room for programmes in a second language, for good music or for many other features one finds done so well and at such lengths and at all sorts of hours by the B.B.C."[26]

O'Broin dismissed the argument that the country had to accept commercial television as a compromise that would allow the government to escape assuming a heavy financial burden. He cited the statement issued by the Irish Arts Council, which condemned the concept of Irish commercial television, predicting it would cater "to the tastes and standards of the most underdeveloped mass audiences, which will over-ride cultural values, and, in doing so, would produce a proportionate and progressive vulgarisation of public taste as a whole."[27]

O'Broin addressed the proposals of Michelson and McLendon and pleaded that both be rejected. The secretary employed the same arguments that he had used in the past to try and to convince the government that these proposals should be dismissed. He defined the schemes as "morally, legally, and technically . . . completely unsound."[28] The secretary acknowledged that the Michelson plan had been backed by a number of influential groups interested in gaining access to a powerful international radio station. He criticized supporters of these plans for being shortsighted in not examining the content of the material that would be broadcast on these radio stations.

The secretary advised the members of the commission that they had a difficult choice to make, which he defined in very stark terms. They could choose between a commercial service that would corrupt the nation's unique culture and the continued status quo, whereby Ireland would simply go without television. This was an option that the secretary maintained was not so unappealing. "I personally would not find that a frightening prospect, especially if it were a question of choosing between it and commercial television. . . . I do not agree with the commonly voiced opinion that we must have television and that we can't afford not to have it. Television is not essential to our national life. We can afford not to have it."[29] This contention contradicted earlier statements that had argued that Ireland must protect its political and cultural integrity by establishing a television service. The argument was tactical and intended to make his own proposal, which he subsequently outlined, appear more attractive.

The secretary explained that he and his department had put together a scheme that would allow the nation's unique culture to be protected while the difficult question of cost would be handled in a responsible manner. However, before offering a brief description of his proposal, the secretary returned to the strict terms of reference that had established the Television Commission. These instructions were described as the key obstacle impeding the commission's effort to consider more appealing options. According to O'Broin, the commission was doomed to failure unless a way was found to overcome this formidable obstacle. As a solution he suggested that the commission interpret the terms of reference in a very broad manner. "It may well be that the condition of no charge on the Exchequer could mean no *ultimate* charge[;] . . . that is, that the cost of establishing and operating a service, if met initially by the Exchequer, could be ultimately repaid by installment."[30]

O'Broin advised the commission that if this interpretation was accepted, the state could finance and build the necessary facilities to house an Irish television station. The scheme he envisioned would begin by serving the Dublin metropolitan area and expand to the rest of the country over an unspecified period of time. An Irish television authority would be created to provide programs of Irish origin and a limited number of popular programs, which would have mass appeal. To help finance the service, O'Broin admitted that the Irish authority would have to sell time to commercial advertisers. He considered this a small price to pay for having control of such an important medium as television. To O'Broin it was imperative that the control of television be kept out of the hands of foreign capitalists, who were interested only in maximizing profits and showed little inclination to provide programs that would serve the public.

The secretary testified that the source of the noncommercial programs for the station he envisioned would be the British Broadcasting Corporation. The television authority he described would choose very selectively from the best of the programs that were shown on the independent network in Britain, however, the main source would be the BBC. O'Broin explained to the commission that the plan would work only if an agreement could be arranged that would allow the Irish service to receive BBC programs at a significantly discounted rate. Under questioning he agreed that this was the most critical part of his plan, as he knew that the programs, if made available only at the market rate, would make the scheme unworkable. After some discussion, it was agreed that O'Broin should speak with the BBC on an informal basis to try and determine if it would be willing to agree to special terms.

There were some misgivings about O'Broin's scheme among members of the commission. Their concerns focused on BBC programs that would be regarded as containing a strong or offensive British bias. O'Broin argued that selectivity would be crucial and that an Irish authority would choose only the programs that it deemed acceptable to Irish sensibilities. This prompted one member to retort, "It might be like selecting England's old clothes?"[31] O'Broin disagreed with the remark but admitted that he was not sure whether broadcasting British material would cause political problems.

Before concluding his testimony, the secretary was asked if he had made this proposal to the government. He declined to answer the question, knowing that doing so could complicate matters for himself and his proposal. The commission was impressed with the evidence given by O'Broin and invited the secretary and other members of his department back to explain details of their scheme and comment on other proposals that were under review.

At the end of 1958, the commission issued an *Interim Report* to the Government, which included both a minority and majority opinion.[32] This document and subsequent developments including the final report issued by the commission will be considered in the following chapter.

NOTES

1. Department of Communications, TW3756, Comhad no. 17. Evidence submitted by Aer Lingus to the Television Commission, 1958, pp. 1–2.

2. Ibid., p. 4.

3. Ibid., evidence submitted by Bord Fáilte Eireann, 1958.

4. Ibid., testimony of O'Driscoll and Sheridan for Bord Fáilte, June 27, 1958, p. 5.

5. Ibid., p. 6.

6. Ibid., p. 9. This is an interesting revelation. If McLendon lost interest, Michelson would have been the only company actively seeking a license to establish a radio service in exchange for setting up a television network.

7. Ibid., evidence submitted by Córas Tráchtála Teoranta, 1958.

8. Ibid., testimony of Walsh and Killeen, June 27, 1958, p. 2.

9. Ibid., evidence submitted by the Hospital's Trust, 1958, p. 6.

10. State Paper Office, Department of the Taoiseach, S14996B, memorandum from Sean MacEntee to Eamon de Valera, July 21, 1958.

11. Ibid., pp. 1–2.

12. See RTE Archive file 105/58, no. 5, confidential minute of Maurice Gorham, reviewing the testimony of the Michelson Company. The memo of August 16, 1958, p. 2., refers to "the evidence of the Monsignori." The Most Rev. Dr. Henry Robert McAdoo, a member of the commission who was interviewed by the author, in Dalkey, County Dublin, December 12, 1990. He did not remember any such testimony or evidence and was not aware of the interest of the Vatican.

13. State Paper Office, Department of the Taoiseach, S14996B, letter from the Irish Ambassador at the Vatican to the Secretary, Department of External Affairs, September, 11, 1958.

14. Ibid.

15. Archives of RTE 105/58, no. 5, oral evidence provided to the Commission by the Michelson Group, July, 18, 1958, p. 1.

16. Ibid., p. 46.

17. Ibid., p. 49.

18. Ibid., p. 73.

19. Ibid.

20. Ibid., p. 74.

21. Ibid., p. 79.

22. Ibid., p. 102. O'Broin commented sarcastically on this commitment: "When he discovered . . . that we had a language problem, he promptly said that all Gaeltacht families would be given a free television set." *Just Like Yesterday, An Autobiography* (Dublin: Gill and Macmillan, 1985), p. 209.

23. RTE Archives, 105/58, no. 5, memorandum of the Department of Posts and Telegraphs, September 8, 1958, p. 6.

24. RTE Archives, 105/58, no. 14. Testimony of Leon O'Broin, October 31, 1958, p. 2.

25. Ibid., p. 4.

26. Ibid., p. 5.

27. Ibid., p. 8.

28. Ibid., p. 9.

29. Ibid., p. 10.

30. Ibid. (italics added).

31. Ibid., p. 24.

32. Department of Communications TW3756, Comhad no. 3, *Interim Report of the Television Commission*, 1958.

CHAPTER 9

The Reports of the Television Commission

On December 23, 1958, the Television Commission submitted a brief *Interim Report* to the Minister for Posts and Telegraphs that expressed both a majority and a minority opinion. In writing to Sean Ormonde, the Chairman of the Commission, George Murnaghan, advised the minister of the general thrust of the report. He explained that the majority of those on the commission wanted the government to take the steps necessary to ensure that time would not be lost in building the infrastructure required to start a television service. The dissenting minority agreed that time should not be wasted in this regard but were concerned with other issues they believed were not being addressed by the majority. Murnaghan advised Ormonde that he need only concern himself with the opinion of the majority and dismissed the minority's contention that the commission was deadlocked.

The commission had hoped to issue a unanimous provisional report that would simply advise the government of the need to prepare the way for the introduction of television. However, a minority disagreed and issued its own, separate report. The main report advised the government that certain steps should be taken promptly to ensure that no matter who would operate a television service, it could be on the air quickly. It was the opinion of the majority that the state should help build the physical structure of a television network.

The commission reported a great urgency, which compelled it to recommend that the government take concrete steps to ensure that a service would be established with minimum delay. It is obvious that the commission was most concerned with the breadth and influence of British broadcasts. It warned the government that the range of British transmitters would increase with the opening of the ITA service that was scheduled to begin broadcasting from Belfast in 1960. The report noted that there were over 20,000 television sets in the country and argued that experience had shown that the "viewing habits" of an audience formed quickly. It therefore concluded that "it would be unfortunate if a growing number of viewers had formed the habit of viewing not only the B.B.C. programmes, but also an alternative pro- gramme emanating from outside the Republic before a television service was established here."[1]

The commission expressed tremendous apprehension over what it con- sidered a relentless invasion by an insidious British culture. This anxiety was used to advocate the taking of decisive government action to curtail what was described as an intolerable situation. The commission urged the government to take a number of steps to ensure that when a final decision was made concerning the nature and structure of a television service, the necessary facilities would be in place to enable the station to get on the air quickly. It estimated that unless the state acted quickly and started building the critical infrastructure for Irish television, its introduction would be delayed by as much as eighteen months. The commission also maintained that in building a television service, it was imperative that the initial transmitter be situated in a location that would serve the largest possible area. The Dublin metropolitan region was therefore viewed as the natural home for the first Irish television transmitter.

When considering the question of cost, the report implied that the commission was reinterpreting the terms of reference, perhaps under the influence of Leon O'Broin, who had suggested that they be understood as indicating that no *ultimate* charge should fall on the Exchequer. "The cost involved will necessarily fall in the first instance on moneys to be found by the Government, but since these will be recouped as part of the arrangement for the establishment of a television service, this will entail no permanent charge on the Exchequer."[2] The *Interim Report* did not concede that the terms of reference had been reinterpreted, nor did it acknowledge that their recommendation violated the key order in the charter that had created the Television Commission. The report was written carefully and did not commit the commission to any one type of television service. It simply assumed that whoever ran the service would be able, and willing, to reimburse the state for the costs of constructing a transmitter. The ambigu- ous language was intentional, as the commission had not decided on the type of structure it would endorse.

The *Minority Report* objected to the majority opinion for a number of reasons. However, the primary objection to the *Majority Report* concerned the viability of a service set up within the terms of reference furnished to the commission. While the majority had expressed themselves as satisfied that a service could, in fact, be established within the confines of the terms of reference, the minority were very skeptical.

The *Minority Report* was strongly influenced by the testimony provided by Charles Michelson and his associates in this regard. Michelson had testified that a commercial television service dependent on advertising and license revenue alone would not be a viable enterprise. The minority were convinced that commercial television would not generate the revenue needed to sustain a desirable service. Accepting the arguments that had been made by Michelson, the minority maintained that advertisements and licence fees would not produce enough revenue to fund a service that could be truly Irish in character and compete with BBC and ITA programs.

The authors of this report were impressed with the scheme submitted by Charles Michelson and wished to pursue his proposal further. However, this was impossible given the split that had developed within the commission. The minority advised Sean Ormonde and the government that it believed that the work of the commission was being obstructed by certain members of the commission who were hostile to one particular applicant. They maintained that these members had created an impasse that restricted the work of the commission. The minority believed that the Michelson group was not being treated fairly by the commission. They argued that the investment of £6,000,000 and the building of international broadcasting stations were impressive proposals that required careful and serious consideration as they had "far-reaching importance to Ireland's political and economic future."[3]

As has been seen, Michelson had refused to provide specific information to the commission to explain which particular wavelength would be acquired. This had created a stalemate, which was a serious problem in the eyes of the minority. The minority agreed with Michelson that he should not be required to disclose technical "research and discovery . . . immediately and unconditionally to the Commission."[4] It is clear that Charles Michelson had caused a good deal of dissension within the ranks of the commission as the minority forcefully expressed support for the proposal and voiced concern about the manner in which his application was being handled.

One can sense that a certain degree of frustration troubled the Chairman of the commission, who clearly was not impressed with Michelson or his supporters on the commission. In forwarding the *Interim Report* to Sean Ormonde, George Murnaghan denied that the commission had reached an impasse. "As Chairman of the Commission, I have to say that no such 'deadlock' exists."[5] Murnaghan advised Ormonde that in spite of the dissenting view expressed in the *Minority Report*, all members of the commission agreed it was urgent that preliminary steps be taken to expedite the opening of an Irish television service.

The report was not published, nor was it made available to members of the Dail. Sean Ormonde was questioned about the document in the Dail in January 1959, several weeks after it had been forwarded to the government. He advised deputies that he had no intention of sharing the confidential report with them or the general public.[6]

In November 1958, the *Irish Radio and Electrical Journal* had reported that the commission had reached an impasse in their deliberations. The television industry's publication expressed concern over rumors that the commission was badly divided on key issues. The journal complained about the secrecy under which the commission labored and appeared anxious about reports of a split among the ranks, reporting, "the Commission has become 'broken' into two camps. . . . One favours the objective considera-tion of the fundamental issue—'whether we are to have a national television service'—while the second belief is that it must come within the Commis-sion members' scope to lay down, in effect, the 'hows' and 'whys' down to the last full stop."[7] It attributed the confusion and discord that troubled the commission to the terms of reference, which it deemed inadequate.

The journal called for the government to step in and set the commission back on track. It believed that the commission had a simple task that was being complicated by members who insisted on obtaining detailed answers to questions that were beyond its scope. The journal argued that it believed a commercial service should be accepted as the only viable alternative available and criticized opponents who continued to advocate some form of a public service. "The Commission would do well to be realistic. The Government has apparently accepted the principle of commercial televi-sion. The commission should do likewise!"[8]

The *Interim Report of the Television Commission* was reviewed by Posts and Telegraphs, which prepared a formal *Memorandum for the Government* on January 1, 1959. The memorandum was sent by Leon O'Broin to Sean Ormonde, who approved of its contents and recommendations. Following established procedure, a copy was sent to the Department of Finance for review and comment. Posts and Telegraphs supported the request that had been made by the Television Commission in the *Interim Report*. This is not surprising, as O'Broin had advocated that the state at the very least own the transmitters and other equipment essential to operate and maintain a television service. To O'Broin, acquiring a site for the initial transmitter would be the first step in any effort to secure a network of state-owned transmitters. Posts and Telegraphs realized that its message was having an impact on the commission and reported, "Evidently the majority of the Commission consider that the Commission's terms of reference do not exclude a *temporary* (as distinct from *permanent*) charge on the Exchequer."[9]

Posts and Telegraphs reported that it had already found a location for a Dublin transmitter, noting that it was the same site that had been identified by a number of the commercial applicants. The site was described as being on the top of a mountain at a height of over 2,000 feet. The cost for purchasing the site and building a road to the top of the mountain was estimated to be £23,000. O'Broin assured the government that it need not worry about the cost required to build the Dublin transmitter, maintaining that the "loan would be readily recoverable from prospective television licence revenue."[10]

It is clear that O'Broin hoped the government would approve the commission's request, as he believed it represented a step in the right direction. He realized that a variation on his own scheme might once again become a viable option. O'Broin understood that the commission had, with his vigorous support, maneuvered to force the state to make a financial commitment to television. The proverbial foot was in the door. Once the government had agreed to build a significant part of the technical infrastructure, he hoped it would be easier to convince it to maintain ownership of the transmitters.

The Department of Finance was not impressed with Commission's *Interim Report* or the Post Office *Memorandum for the Government* that supported it. This is evident in a series of internal memos written by Louis Fitzgerald to the Secretary of the Department of Finance, T. K. Whitaker. Finance was concerned with the request that public funds be used to acquire a site and build the necessary services for a transmitter, even if these funds were defined as "recoverable." Fitzgerald and Whitaker believed that the recommendations contained in the report violated the strict terms of reference that had been given to the commission. The Department of Finance understood that if the government made a commitment to financing a television station, precious revenue would be drained from the treasury. It is not surprising, therefore, that Fitzgerald and his department saw the *Minority Report* as the most sensible component of the commission's

Interim Report, concluding, "Of the two reports on T.V. it seems to me that on the whole the minority one is more sensible."[11]

Fitzgerald argued that deciding important questions before the commission issued a final report would be a mistake, as it would force the state to commit public funds to television. "Quite clearly if the Government authorises expenditure on the acquisition of a site etc., there is no turning back."[12] Fitzgerald realized that if the request of the commission was accepted the state would become an important player in the building of an Irish television service. His statement that there would be "no turning back" illustrates that Finance realized that if the government supported the commission in this regard, the chances of the state keeping clear of this expensive medium were at risk.

Finance was highly critical of the rationale employed by the commission and endorsed by Posts and Telegraphs, which maintained that the recommendations of the report were urgent and required immediate action. "The reason which impels the Commission to ask for this blank cheque is unconvincing. No time must avoidably be lost in getting T.V. going for fear the viewers should have formed the habit of looking at B.B.C. or I.T.V. . . . This argument . . . ignores in a virtually Marxist way the element of individual choice."[13] Finance argued that viewers would not ignore British programs once a native service was operating concluding, "Anyone who believes this will believe anything."[14] The department had not tempered its hostility toward state involvement in television and, as the language in the memo suggests, did not want the government to issue a "blank check" to the "Marxist" thinking Post Office or Television Commission. Finance believed that the commission was reacting to a false sense of urgency orchestrated by Leon O'Broin.

Fitzgerald suggested that his minister advise the Cabinet that no financial commitment should be made by the state until the Television Commission had issued a final report. He argued that the commission should adhere strictly to the terms of reference and believed that if it did so, public funds would not be at risk. Finance had succeeded in convincing the Cabinet and Sean Lemass, of the need to impose strict terms of reference, under which the commission deliberated. The department had every intention of holding the commission to these terms. Fitzgerald suggested his minister advise the government that the commission should support "some particular organisation . . . prepared to finance at their own expense a T.V. system."[15] Whitaker fully supported his assistant, advising the Minister of Finance, Dr. James Ryan that the department should oppose the request of the Television Commission. Television had been seen as a "luxury service" by

Finance for quite some time. This remained the opinion of Whitaker who told Ryan, "Expenditure on T.V. must rank very low on any sensibly constructed list of objects of state policy."[16]

In spite of the protests made by Finance, the government accepted the request of the Television Commission. The Cabinet met on January 20, 1959, and later advised the Department of Posts and Telegraphs that it had decided that a site for a Dublin transmitter should be acquired and developed and that all costs should be recouped from the organization that would operate an Irish service. On January 28, 1959, Posts and Telegraphs formally advised the Television Commission that the government had accepted, in principle, their request as outlined in the *Interim Report*. The commission was also advised that the government favored building the transmitter at Kippure Mountain in County Wicklow. Posts and Telegraphs had made experimental broadcasts from Kippure and measured the signal strength, determining that it was the best site for both VHF radio and television transmissions.

A short time later, Sean O'Droma, the Secretary to the Commission, advised the Post Office that six applicant groups had been approached and advised of the preference of Posts and Telegraphs. He advised Posts and Telegraphs that of the six applicants, only one had proposed an alternative site. The dissenting voice among the applicants was Pye Ireland Limited. Pye submitted a report to the Television Commission which argued that a transmitter should be built on the north side of the Dublin harbor at Howth. Pye believed that building a transmitter at the top of Kippure Mountain would be a difficult and expensive undertaking. While Pye maintained that either site would provide satisfactory range, it favored Howth as the less expensive, more accessible site. It argued that to build a transmitting station at Kippure, as opposed to Howth, an additional £165,000 would be required and construction would take an added twelve months.[17] Pye also expressed confidence that a transmitter located on the hill at Howth, with a mast of 750 feet, would not pose a threat to aviation if it were properly secured with warning lights.

The dispute that developed over the question of a transmitter site is important, as it may have discredited Pye, the Irish subsidiary of the English-based communications corporation. There was no question that building a transmitter on the top of Kippure Mountain would be an expensive task. Pye was concerned that if it were awarded the television contract, it would have to reimburse the government costs of building the facility. It became apparent that the site proposed by Pye would provide less coverage, and in spite of assurances to the contrary, it would indeed pose a threat to aviation. Industry and Commerce, the department that was responsible for ensuring aviation safety in the state, advised Posts and Telegraphs that the Howth site was not acceptable. Even with a flashing beacon fixed to the 750-foot mast, it regarded the Howth site as an unnecessary hazard, given the high volume of air traffic in the area. Consequently, it dismissed Pye's position as unacceptable.

However, Pye Ireland unwisely went to the trouble of submitting an eight-page document reiterating its support for the Howth site, which only succeeded in further alienating government officials. It is clear that the Pye Company was interested in finding the easiest and least expensive path to build a television service. In a report to the Cabinet, Posts and Telegraphs challenged the veracity of Pye's position, maintaining that it was imprudent. The department alleged that Pye had misrepresented the costs of both sites in an effort to present Howth as the only sensible alternative. The government was told that the estimates Posts and Telegraphs had employed for developing the Kippure site were correct, while those used by Pye had been intentionally inflated and were "grossly inaccurate."[18]

Pye had been one of the early applicants for a television broadcasting concession in Ireland. The rather transparent effort to convince the government to opt for the cheaper, and more hazardous, Howth site was a concern for the Irish government. This may have hurt the credibility of the Pye proposal. It proved that finding a responsible commercial company would be more difficult than originally thought. After some delay, the government decided that in spite of objections from the Pye Company, the Kippure site would be developed.

The government had decided that in spite of objections raised by the Department of Finance, the state would become directly involved in financing television. This was a significant step, especially in light of the success Finance had enjoyed in maintaining its influence in the Cabinet when the subject of television was an issue. The decision represented a major victory for Leon O'Broin, who had succeeded in convincing the Television Commission and the government to become actively involved in financing a television service. While the government and the Television Commission believed that a private company would assume control and ownership of the transmitter site, Finance wisely feared that O'Broin had succeeded in making progress toward a state-owned service. Once the government made a commitment in this regard, it would be very difficult for the state to surrender the infrastructure of such a powerful medium.

Eamon de Valera was concerned that the decision taken by the government might be exploited or misinterpreted, and he did not want the decision announced until he was comfortable that the time was right. An indication of his difficulty with the decision can be seen in an order he issued to the Cabinet, which was recorded by his secretary. "The Taoiseach directed yesterday that no notification of this decision should be issued for the present. . . . Mr. O'Broin will take the necessary preliminary steps with a view to the acquisition of the site and will provide a statement for publication at the appropriate time."[19] The decision was not formally announced by the government until a press release was issued on March 24, 1959. Arrangements were made for the Commission of Public Works to acquire the property necessary to build a road to the top of Kippure.[20]

Meanwhile, the Irish television industry expressed its concern at what was perceived to be the Television Commission's lack of progress and the mystery surrounding its deliberations. The *Irish Radio and Electrical Journal* criticized the failure of the commission to communicate in an open manner with the press. This lack of communication was criticized as causing harmful confusion in the trade and leaving the press to speculate and employ what the *Irish Radio and Electrical Journal* called "scare" headlines.[21]

Irish retailers were upset for a number of reasons, including the inability of the commission to announce what "standard of definition" would be employed by an Irish service. Rumors had circulated in the press that a 625-line standard would be adopted which would make many television sets obsolete. The *Journal* complained that these rumors had hurt sales, as consumers were unwilling to purchase sets that would receive British broadcasts on the 405-line standard but not broadcasts from an Irish service using the (incompatible) 625-line standard.

While the government arranged to prepare the site that would house a transmitter at Kippure, the Television Commission continued its work. A large number of groups and individuals continued to testify before the commission. This included the Comhairle Radio Eireann, representatives of workers who staffed Radio Eireann, and applicants for the television concession, including American businessman Gordon McLendon and Canadian entrepreneur Roy Thomson. The willingness of the commission to hear testimony from a large number of groups helped to inform members of the positions held by a number of parties variously interested in the economic, social, and cultural implications of an Irish television service.

The April 1959 edition of the *Irish Radio and Electrical Journal* reported that the commission would present its final report on May 7. The *Journal* reported that the commission would provide the government with a shortlist of companies that they favored. It also maintained that a proposal submitted by Gael-Linn and backed by the National Broadcasting Company in the

United States had become quite popular and gained a good deal of public support.[22]

One month later, the *Journal* addressed the Gael-Linn proposal and the popular support it had attracted. It warned: "sectional pressure groups should be ignored. . . . The Government will be well advised to examine the question objectively without regard to political leanings and sectional pressure groups."[23] The *Journal*'s allusion to "sectional pressure groups" was a clear reference to Gael-Linn, an organization devoted to the propagation of the Irish language. The television industry feared that if Gael-Linn was granted a concession to operate a television service, the result would be disastrous, as Gael-Linn would use the medium to pursue its own, narrow political and cultural agenda. This would alienate a majority of viewers, who were primarily interested in popular entertainment programs. In such circumstances the public would not purchase television sets and the station would be a financial failure.

The final *Report of the Television Commission* was forwarded to the government on May 8, 1959. Again, the commission's report included a *Majority Report* and a *Minority Report*, as well as a number of reservations. After negotiations had been completed between the government and the commission, it was agreed that revisions should be made in the report, which could then be published. A separate, confidential supplement was made available to the Cabinet. This supplement was classified as secret and was not made available to the public or members of the Dail. This addendum provided a review of each proposal that had been made to the commission.

George Murnaghan, the Chairman of the Commission, reviewed the report with the Minister for Posts and Telegraphs, Sean Ormonde, and agreed to make omissions that would facilitate the government's desire to publish the report. The identities of the applicants were kept secret, as were many of the details of their proposals. Dr. Roger McHugh, a member of the commission who acted as spokesman for the minority, also agreed to revisions in the *Minority Report*. Sean Lemass was very interested in the reports of the commission and became personally involved in seeing that all but the most confidential passages were published. It is important to note that the government felt obliged to publish most of the commission's report. As has been seen, public pressure had intensified, as had criticism of the secrecy that surrounded the deliberations of the commission and government handling of the television question in general. Ignoring demands that the report be published would have created serious difficulties for the government.

The published *Report of the Television Commission* was a seventy-page document divided into twelve chapters. It included a nine-page *Minority Report* signed by four of the nineteen members of the Television Commission.[24] The document reiterated many points that had been brought up by witnesses who had testified before the Commission or submitted evidence to it. The commission indicated that it believed television was no longer a "luxury service," as the Department of Finance had repeatedly defined it. Indeed, the commission recognized that "television . . . is coming to be regarded as a prime necessity in the modern home."[25]

The commission reported that, if operated in a responsible manner, television could be an asset to the nation. The educational possibilities of the medium were emphasized, as was the fact that through television, refined entertainment could be brought into Irish homes. In a reference that may have been intended to address the concerns of the Catholic hierarchy, the commission cautioned that television would have a negative effect on children, and on society in general, if steps were not taken to ensure the suitability of the material that would be broadcast.[26] Parental supervision was emphasized as an important tool for limiting the influence of the new medium in the home.

The commission addressed what it defined as the "special problems" of television in Ireland. It referred to the established television stations in Britain, noting that the BBC and the ITA had created significant challenges. The commission maintained that the fact that Ireland did not have a native service but did receive British programs was a national disgrace. It argued that this problem made it "imperative that Ireland should have a television service of its own, and without delay. The alternative is a progressively increasing number of Irish viewers taking the B.B.C. programme and in the near future the additional I.T.A. programme."[27] While the commission recognized that the British produced high-quality television, it stated that these programs were geared toward a British audience and espoused British values. The report maintained that the material being broadcast into Ireland was not necessarily appropriate or desirable for Irish viewers. In considering these factors, the commission admitted that it initially had harbored strong reservations about the viability of an Irish service being set up under the strict terms of reference written by the government. However, this had changed due to the "optimism, based on what appeared to be sound economic considerations, of many of the proposers who appeared before the commission in support of their respective proposals to provide a television system for Ireland on a commercial basis."[28]

This decision prompted a minority of the Television Commission to dissent and to support a position that was articulated in a separate minority report. The commission reviewed the finances of a hypothetical commercial service and presented estimates of expenditures and revenue. It determined that by the third year of operation, when a service would afford national coverage, the balance sheets of a privately owned commercial service would show £650,000 for expenses and income from advertisements and license fees of £680,000. The consensus among members was that a commercial television service that adhered to the terms of reference was, in fact, feasible.

The entire debate concerning the merits of public television compared with a private commercial system was examined in detail. The protests that had been received by the Arts Council and articulated by Leon O'Broin were addressed, though neither the Arts Council nor O'Broin were identified. Three possible alternatives were outlined in the commission's report. The first was a public service, which was out of the question, as it did not conform to the commission's terms of reference. (The commission did indicate a preference for such a structure in a different economic climate.) The second option that was outlined clearly referred to the proposal that had been developed and supported by O'Broin and Posts and Telegraphs. The commission maintained that this proposal, which called for a state-owned commercial service, had been examined in detail but was determined to be unacceptable.

The commission concluded that commercial television operated by a private monopoly was therefore the only viable alternative:

If . . . Ireland is to have a television service, and under the existing circumstances the commission does not accept that Ireland can afford to be without its own television service, it follows that a service must for the present be provided by private enterprise, notwithstanding the considerable difficulties that are attendant on the establishment of a commercial service by private enterprise.[29]

The commission clearly favored a public service but recognized that, given the terms of reference under which the Television Commission had been established and the economic climate of the country, it was in no position to endorse such a structure.

The report issued by the commission outlined how a commercial service based on private ownership should be structured. It argued that the key to ensuring government control was the creation of a public authority that would oversee the operation of commercial television. It agreed with testimony that had been given by the Posts and Telegraphs, which had outlined the powers that a public authority should possess. The commission recommended that the authority have its powers and responsibilities defined by statute. It suggested the authority should supervise programs to ensure that they were not offensive or substandard, handle the finances involved in monitoring a television service, hire and fire staff at the authority, and enforce the conditions of the contract between the private company and the government.

The commission suggested that the authority should include nine members, who would be appointed by the Taoiseach on the advice of the government, for a term of three years. The state would reserve the right to dismiss any member of the authority as was deemed necessary. The report maintained that at some point, the television service should become the property of the state. At that time the proposed authority would become the body that would assume control and ownership of the service. The report explained that all the applicants had accepted that there must be advisory committees to assist the successful company in the handling of sensitive program material. The commission stated that the authority should appoint committees to work with the private entity running the service to deal with issues such as religion, language, and programs for children and farmers. When considering news broadcasts, the commission cautioned that all care should be taken to ensure that the dissemination of news was conducted in a balanced manner.

The commission also considered how a commercial station might include in its broadcasts material that would celebrate Irish culture. The commission recognized the difficulties a commercial service would experience in producing appropriate cultural programs. However, it still believed that an Irish service had to express the unique character of the Irish nation. The commission recommended that the privately owned commercial service develop programs that would address "a variety of factors [such as] . . . religious beliefs, traditions, language, customs, habits, games, music, songs, folklore, and history."[30]

The report recommended that television be employed in a positive manner to promote the Irish language and that the television authority have a clear understanding of its national importance. The commission championed what it considered an "enlightened approach," a reference that appeared to dismiss the dogmatic policy that had been advocated by more passionate supporters of the language revival. In this respect the commission suggested that Irish be slowly introduced into program material and that children's programs be intelligently employed to nurture a love of the Irish language. "The Commission considers that at the start it is preferable that little would be done well rather than much done badly, and that there should be a gradual and natural increase in the use of the language in its programmes."[31] Rather than explore specifics, the commission suggested that the television authority should consult with an advisory group that could make suggestions about cultural programming. The commission made a gesture to the Irish-language movement but still avoided a very contentious subject in recommending that the issue be delegated to a committee or advisory group.

The commission laid out terms on which, it believed, the government should base negotiations. These included the stipulation that the contract entered into with a private company would not exceed a period of ten years. The successful applicant was expected to have a Dublin service up and running within fifteen months of signing a contract and to deliver a truly national service within three to five years. The commission recommended that the transmission system and studios built by the private company be vested in the television authority either during the course of the contract or at the end of the contract period.

There were reservations to the report. The first reservation was signed by six members of the commission who, while accepting the general thesis of the report, objected to the conclusion stipulating that television in Ireland would have to be commercial. The dissenters who signed this reservation believed that the state should own and operate the television service, and they rejected the premise that television in Ireland should be run by a privately owned commercial company. They argued that the state should grant to a television authority £1,000,000 to build the necessary transmitting stations. This group was influenced by the arguments articulated by Posts and Telegraphs and by the plan for a state-owned commercial service proposed by O'Broin.

A second reservation was signed by two members of the commission who objected to the decision arrived at in the report to adopt a "line standard" that would match that employed by the British. The two members argued that accepting the 405-line standard used by the British was short-sighted, as the 625-line standard used throughout most of Europe was more modern and would not quickly become obsolete. The signatories were not bothered by the fact that adopting a 625-line standard might not be suitable for the reception of British broadcasts. The "cultural nationalists" who signed this reservation were more interested in keeping British television out of Ireland than in simply adopting a standard of definition that took advantage of the most recent technical developments in the medium.[32]

The *Report of the Television Commission* included a *Minority Report* signed by four members who rejected the conclusions of the majority. The *Minority Report* objected to the portion of the report that considered the financing necessary to operate a successful commercial television service. The *Minority Report* acknowledged that an Irish service could not be a public service under the terms of reference issued by the government, under which the commission had deliberated. The members who signed the *Minority Report* were concerned that a commercial service, as outlined by the majority, could not compete successfully with the BBC and ITA.

It is clear that the minority had accepted the argument made by Charles Michelson and his associates, who had maintained that commercial television alone would not be a viable business enterprise. Although all references to Michelson and other applicants had been deleted in the published report, they were spelled out in the unpublished supplement that was circulated in secret to the Cabinet. In order to establish a successful commercial service, the minority supported the concept of what it termed international commercial sound broadcasting ("ICSB"). In the unpublished supplemental report, the minority referred to the McLendon and Michelson proposals and endorsed the strategy these applicants had articulated. The minority were most impressed by the Michelson scheme and by the testimony given by representatives of Aer Lingus, Bord Fáilte, Córas Tráchtála Teoranta, and Hospitals Trust, all of whom supported the Paris-based entrepreneur.

The minority clearly believed that the revenue generated by the proposed international radio service would ensure the establishment of two successful networks, one, a commercial channel, and the second, a cultural alternative. It firmly believed that if the government adopted a service based on the recommendations of the majority, the station that would emerge would be a weak organization dominated by British commercial programs. This, it was argued, would erode the already fragile state of Ireland's unique culture. In the eyes of the minority, the proposal put forward by Michelson was simply too attractive to ignore.

The unpublished, confidential reports of the Television Commission are revealing as they explain the commission's position on the various applicants. In the secret *Majority Supplement*, the commission addressed each proposal and developed a shortlist that contained what it considered to be the best proposals. The government was advised that it should enter into serious negotiations with the companies on the list and accept the applicant that was most willing to modify its proposal to conform to the desires of the state. It also contended that it had no preference for any one of the three organizations it identified as most attractive.

The first proposal that was addressed was that of Gael-Linn. Gael-Linn had testified before the commission as a member of a combined group that represented a coalition of Irish-language organizations. It later submitted a proposal to the commission asking that it be granted the right to operate a national television service. Gael-Linn had proposed establishing a national commercial service, which would be available throughout the country in four to five years. The service would be financed by selling time for commercial advertisements and a license fee of £3 per receiver. Gael-Linn asked that it be granted an exclusive twenty-year contract and proposed that the infrastructure for the television network be turned over to the state after a fifteen-year period.

Gael-Linn had advised the commission that an initial £1.5 million for capital costs would be required for the service. It proposed to raise this money from its own resources, as well as foreign sources who had expressed an interest in backing the enterprise. The group advised the commission that it had received inquiries from two foreign corporations interested in supporting Irish television.

Gael-Linn submitted a more detailed, revised proposal after the commission had completed interviewing the applicants and reviewing the original proposals. This document was an impressive fifty-page proposal that outlined the group's plan, advising the government how it would finance and operate a national television service if it was rewarded a concession by the state. This second proposal was not considered by the commission, as it was submitted too late. The commission made note of this in the introduction to the *Supplemental Report*, indicating that it regretted being unable to consider the revised Gael-Linn submission. The original submission that had been made to the commission was effective enough to impress the members, even though it had also been submitted late and was viewed as containing serious flaws. The commission advised the government that the application deserved serious consideration: "Gael-Linn is the only wholly Irish group amongst the proposers[, which]is in its favour."[33]

While the commission recommended that Gael-Linn receive consideration, it is obvious it had strong reservations. The first difficulty was the manner in which the group had proposed to finance the service. In the opinion of the commission, the financial plan of Gael-Linn was overly optimistic and displayed a certain degree of naiveté. The commission indicated that the group had submitted unrealistic estimates, which might create problems for the state should the proposal be accepted. Another disconcerting aspect of the proposal concerned the political and cultural agenda being pursued by the organization. The commission concluded that a service run by Gael-Linn would dedicate itself to the narrow goal of reviving the Irish language. This could be a problem according to the commission, as its "enthusiasm" for the language revival might "lead it into the error of a possible concentration on that subject to the detriment of what should be the primary object, namely the provision of an adequate television service."[34]

The commission was also critical of the request made by Gael-Linn to be granted a twenty-year license, as it had recommended limiting the term of a license to ten years. In concluding its review, the commission admitted that Gael-Linn had no experience in television and would be dependent on technical aid from foreign sources. The review of the proposal offered by the commission was hardly an endorsement, and one might wonder why members included the Gael-Linn proposal on a shortlist.

It is obvious that although the commission was not comfortable in endorsing a service that would be operated solely by Gael-Linn, it appreciated that the group was the only applicant that it believed capable of contributing an Irish element to a commercial service. The commission indicated a willingness to support a modified proposal that would allow Gael-Linn to be part of a larger, more comprehensive scheme. The commission envisioned an arrangement whereby Gael-Linn would provide Irish-language programs to a privately owned station, thus ensuring that a "cultural" component would be featured in a commercial service. It is obvious that in exploiting the "enthusiasm" of Gael-Linn, the commission hoped to temper a commercial service that it feared could degenerate into what O'Broin had described as a mere extension of the ITA. Unfortunately for the commission, Gael-Linn had not approached any of the other applicants to try and work out an arrangement of the type suggested. In spite of efforts made by the commission to entice the group into being the "Irish component" of a commercial service, Gael-Linn was much more interested in operating television itself.

The second applicant that the commission put on the shortlist was the Television Corporation of Ireland Ltd., a scheme referred to earlier as the Pye project. The commission reported that this group had testified before it on three occasions, offering three different versions of the same proposal. The first meeting occurred in June 1958, and the group failed to impress the commission, which described the proposal as unappealing. A revised scheme was later sent to the commission, and the organization again appeared to offer testimony. Again the commission was disappointed, describing the revised proposal as unacceptable. A third proposal was more interesting in the eyes of the commission, as the Pye group had reconstituted itself as the Television Corporation of Ireland Ltd. and offered a more attractive application. This last effort was made by a group that now included the Pye Company, Associated Television Ltd. and Columbia Broadcasting Systems, Inc. (CBS).

Associated Television Ltd. (ATV) was a British program company that provided material to the ITA and CBS was a giant American television firm with tremendous resources and considerable experience in television broadcasting. This newly organized company had appeared before the commission in November 1958 and succeeded in impressing the members for a number of reasons. This time, the applicant finally indicated a willingness to establish and operate a national service that would cover the country in three to four years. A twenty-one-year exclusive license was sought, and the group promised that the company would remain under 75 percent Irish control. It promised to provide funds that would allow the television authority to broadcast programs in Irish.

The applicant was seen as experienced and well financed, and therefore the commission recommended that the proposal receive additional consideration. However, the commission had a number of concerns about the scheme. While the company could rely on its association with ATV and CBS to provide diversified programs, the commission feared that it might become too dependent on British and American material. Pointing out that the station would be dependent on income from advertisements, the commission feared the plan "might involve the risk of a degree of subservience to the dictates of advertisers."[35]

The final proposal to make the commission's shortlist was that of Roy H. Thomson. This was a surprise, as Thomson's proposal did not appear to generate much interest from within the Television Commission or the Department of Posts and Telegraphs. The applicant was described as having been involved in television, radio, and newspapers in Canada. Thomson was also identified as being the ITA program contractor for Scotland.

Thomson had testified before the commission in December 1958 and proposed building a metropolitan Dublin station. He advised the commission that he would later build one in Cork, with a final station situated in Donegal. Initially, Thomson had not been interested in building a service that would eventually be turned over to the state. However, he later modified his views and forwarded to the commission a revised proposal, in January 1959. The commission noted that Thomson proposed the station be transferred to the Irish government after a period of ten years, on the condition that he be named as the station's exclusive program contractor. Thomson was viewed as an experienced applicant who should receive serious consideration from the government. His experience as a program contractor in Scotland and the fact that he appeared well financed had clearly impressed the commission.

While the aspects of the Thomson proposal that were described as "positive" raised a number of serious questions concerning the problem of foreign control, the "drawbacks" listed suggest that to put this group on the shortlist was, at best, a generous interpretation of its scheme. It also demonstrates that the proposal was poorly developed and, in many respects, incoherent. It is difficult to understand why this proposal was attractive to the commission. The terms outlined by Thomson failed to conform to the guidelines that had been set out in the commission's report. Thomson had not even developed the scheme to the extent that the commission could analyze it in a critical manner. Although Thomson had been put on the shortlist, he was clearly not an ideal candidate. The commission admitted:

One of the serious drawbacks to this proposal is that the Proposer himself proposes to retain control, and in this way would keep control of the Irish television service outside the state. This proposal is difficult to evaluate in the absence of final and definitive proposals. . . . The estimate of capital expenditure given . . . to the Commission was £600,000. The Commission doubts that an adequate service can be established on the basis of this proposed expenditure.[36]

The evaluation of the Thomson scheme was a confused and contradictory effort. Why would the commission even consider a scheme that violated several of the most important guidelines that it had drafted? Why consider a plan that would not turn control of programming over to the state at the end of a ten-year contract? Moreover, why would it seriously consider negotiating with a company that planned to invest such a small amount of capital that there were grave concerns whether the service would be a viable one?

The commission admitted that of the three proposals on the shortlist, none of the schemes should be accepted without further negotiation. The commission was not overly enthusiastic about the Gael-Linn proposal, the revised Pye scheme, or the Thomson plan. However, it reported to the government that these three proposals represented the best of a large group that had expressed interest in Irish television.

The commission evaluated eight other proposals that had been received by the government and recommended that all eight be declined. The Michelson proposal was rejected by the majority, who pointed out that the organization was not interested in television unless it was granted permission to establish an international, commercial radio station. Reference was made to the manifold difficulties in obtaining a wavelength for such a service. The commission concluded "that the part of this proposal which dealt with commercial radio was undesirable. . . . In view of this decision and because the Proposer made it quite clear that commercial radio was an essential element in this proposal the commission considers it unnecessary to make any recommendation on that part of the proposal that deals with television."[37]

The McLendon Investment Corporation was also rejected for reasons that had been outlined in the dismissal of the Michelson proposal. Even after the McLendon Company had revised its proposal in August 1958 and agreed to operate a service with the help of the Radio Corporation of America, the commission believed that the conditions that were requested were unsatisfactory. Other applications that were rejected included an application submitted by the Associated British Picture Corporation Ltd. (ABC). The commission had heard evidence from this organization in January 1959. The group did not, in the opinion of the commission, warrant additional consideration. Rediffusion Ireland Ltd., which was acting in collaboration with Associated Rediffusion, was also rejected. The British firm was identified as one of a number of program contractors based in London. This applicant had become upset with the terms outlined by the commission after a number of representatives had testified in November 1958.

The last group to be considered was a consortium of Irish, American, and British firms, including Sir Basil Goulding, Lord Pakenham, and Irish Cinemas Ltd., the Irish subsidiary of the Rank Group. This company had testified before the commission in May 1958 and at that time had indicated that they also had the support of the American based National Broadcasting Company. This organization was prepared to set up a national service, but the terms that were outlined were not deemed attractive to the commission, which advised the government to reject the scheme.

The commission also reviewed the proposal that had been presented by Leon O'Broin and his associates at Posts and Telegraphs. Although this was not a formal proposal and fell outside the terms of reference outlined by the government, the commission believed it had an obligation to address this scheme. It reported that investigations had been carried out by Posts and Telegraphs, which had approached the BBC about supplying program material at a discounted rate. The British were reported to be receptive to O'Broin's overtures and were willing to provide material to a state-owned Irish service.

The commission explained that if the government was prepared to borrow the capital necessary to build a television station, a state-owned service could be established that would depend on inexpensive BBC programs. After considering the proposal articulated by O'Broin, it was decided that his scheme should be rejected. The commission explained that because it was anxious to have public television in Ireland, it had "considered this proposal very carefully, but . . . decided that the obtaining of programme material from the B.B.C. on the terms suggested was a very unsatisfactory basis for a national television service for Ireland, inasmuch as it made the latter service dependent on the good graces of the B.B.C., and for this reason alone had to turn down these suggestions."[38] The commission made it clear that a national Irish television service could not afford to be a public service if it would be subservient or dependent on the British. The political and cultural price for this form of public service station was regarded as simply too high.

The *Confidential Supplement of the Television Commission* also included a report written by the minority. This attacked the conclusions of the majority and argued that the much-discussed, controversial Michelson scheme deserved more serious attention. The members who signed the *Minority Report* included in the supplement a large amount of material that had been submitted by this Paris-based entrepreneur in an effort to prove that his was a viable scheme that would address Irish concerns. The minority used the unpublished *Supplemental Report* to try to prove that the Michelson plan was a scheme that required serious consideration from the government.

The Television Commission submitted its report to the government in May of 1959. The document was a confusing, contradictory report that failed to reach any real consensus or present a coherent recommendation to the government. Parts of the document were well researched and provided a great deal of information concerning how television might contribute to Irish society. However, in the final analysis the report was a disappointing effort. The fact that the commission believed the government should enter into serious negotiations with the three organizations on the shortlist demonstrates that the commission was, in many respects, a failure.

The failure of the commission can be traced directly to the terms of reference, which limited the scope and depth of its investigation. The Department of Finance and the Tanaiste, Sean Lemass, were responsible for the restrictive terms of reference which seriously impaired the effectiveness of the commission. The fear of spending or losing public funds on an enterprise cynically described as a "luxury service" was indicative of the deeply conservative fiscal policy endorsed by all Irish governments since the foundation of the state. It also demonstrated that the economic crisis that haunted the nation throughout the 1950s deeply affected crucial policy decisions.

It would be a mistake to dismiss the Television Commission and its report as a completely wasted effort. The government had the opportunity to examine in detail the thorny problem of how television might best be introduced to Ireland. Many qualified witnesses and organizations expressed concerns and gave advice to the commission. This enabled the government to be much better informed and better prepared when the television service was finally established. Many of the suggestions made by the commission would be employed when the service was organized.

The commission had completed its work, and the government of Eamon de Valera could no longer justify a policy of procrastination. It was time for a definitive decision to be made. The reaction and consequences of the commission's report will be addressed in the next chapter.

NOTES

1. Department of Communications, TW3756, Comhad no. 3, *Interim Report of the Television Commission*, 1958, pp. 1–2.
2. Ibid.
3. Ibid., p. 5.
4. Ibid., pp. 5–6.
5. Ibid., Appendix B of the *Interim Report*, letter to Sean Ormonde from Chairman George Murnaghan, December 23, 1958.
6. *Dail Debates*, 172 (January 14, 1959): col. 475.
7. *Irish Radio and Electrical Journal* 16 (November 1958): 11.
8. Ibid.
9. Department of Communications, TW3756, Comhad no. 3, *Memorandum for the Government: Interim Report of the Television Commission*, January 1, 1959.
10. Ibid.
11. Department of Finance, S/101/1/59 memo to T. K. Whitaker from Louis Fitzgerald, December 31, 1958.
12. Ibid.
13. Ibid.
14. Ibid.
15. Ibid.
16. Ibid., memo to James Ryan, January, 1, 1959.
17. Department of Communications, TW3756, Comhad no. 3, *Considerations Governing the Choice of a Suitable Television Transmitting Station Site For Dublin,* by Pye, Ireland Ltd., February 26, 1959.

18. Ibid., *Memorandum for the Government*, from the Department of Posts and Telegraphs, March 6, 1959.

19. State Paper Office, Department of the Taoiseach, S14996C, handwritten memo from the Taoiseach's secretary, March 14, 1959.

20. Department of Finance, S38/1/59, letter from the Commission of Public Works to the Department of Finance, April 3, 1959. The site was purchased from the Powerscourt Estate for £500.

21. *Irish Radio and Electrical Journal* 17 (March 1959): 16.

22. Ibid., 17 (April 1959): 3.

23. Ibid., 17 (May 1959): 10.

24. The Earl of Longford resigned on October 27, 1958.

25. *Report of the Television Commission* (Dublin Stationery Office, 1959), p. 11.

26. See Joseph Foyle, "The Mass Media Apostolate," *Capuchin Annual* (1965): 356–364. Foyle maintains that the Irish Catholic Church had not created an organization capable of reviewing television until the service was broadcasting. The Catholic Television Committee was then established, with the Most Rev. Dr. T. Morris, Archbishop of Cashel and Emly, as chairman.

27. *Report of the Television Commission* (Dublin Stationery Office, 1959), p. 13.

28. Ibid., p. 15.

29. Ibid., p. 23.

30. Ibid., p. 38.

31. Ibid., p. 40.

32. Ibid., p. 56. The last reservation was signed by three members who accepted the report but were concerned with the loss of revenue that would accompany the introduction of commercial television. The group argued that to defray these losses, the Exchequer should keep the license fees collected from the public.

33. Archives of R.T.E., 105/58, *1959 Television Commission Supplement* [unpublished report], p. 3.

34. Ibid., p. 7.

35. Ibid., p.10.

36. Ibid., pp. 12–13.

37. Ibid., p. 19.

38. Ibid., p. 25.

CHAPTER 10

Volte-Face

The strongest reactions to the Television Commission's report came from the Department of Finance and the Department of Posts and Telegraphs. Both initially chose to interpret the report in a manner that would best suit their particular interests. Finance and Posts and Telegraphs each sought to influence how the government would react to the final report, as both were concerned about steps that might be taken to inaugurate an Irish television service. The Department of Finance had long been opposed to the state becoming directly involved in financing television. However, in the summer of 1959 the department modified its position. This change in perspective had a tremendous impact on subsequent television policy.

Before considering the reaction to the final report, it is necessary to examine the report of another commission that was sitting while the Television Commission was in session. The Commission for the Restoration of the Irish Language had been formed to report to the government on efforts that had been made to revive the Irish language and to offer advice and recommendations on steps that could be taken to pursue the revival in a more successful manner. The Language Commission issued a special interim report, which was released to coincide with the publication of the Television Commission's final report.

The eight-page report was published in March 1959 and focused solely on the issue of television. The document was forwarded to the Taoiseach, Eamon de Valera, who sent a copy to the Minister of Posts and Telegraphs, Sean Ormonde, for his observations. The ensuing communications concerning the *Interim Report of the Language Commission* took place just prior to the Television Commission's issuance of its final report. One can sense in the exchange of memoranda that both the Department of Posts and Telegraphs and the Language Commission were under the impression that the service that was to be recommended and introduced would be a commercial one operated by a private program contractor.

The report raised familiar points that had been addressed by Irish-language groups in testimony before the Television Commission. These included concerns about the reception of British programs in the country and apprehension pertaining to the imminent opening of the new ITA station in Belfast. The report also expressed genuine fear that the government was about to make a grave mistake by allowing a foreign company to build and operate a commercial television station in Ireland.

The Language Commission advocated the creation of a national television service that would be sympathetic to the unique culture of the Irish nation and urged the government to support such a service. The report also maintained that the Language Commission was not interested in exploiting television to pursue a narrow political or cultural agenda. The commission denied wanting to use television, "continuously or even frequently for the purpose of propaganda or indoctrination." Instead, it claimed that a national television service should be used to "provide regular programmes portraying sympathetically the many facets of our native culture and our traditions."[1] The commission believed that the most important means of fostering a deep appreciation of Irish culture was by supporting the national language. It firmly believed that television should aid the efforts of the revival movement.

The commission criticized the state for what it considered its reluctance to earnestly embrace the language revival. This lack of support meant that the struggle to revive Irish "did not produce satisfactory results."[2] The Language Commission declared that the opening of a national television service presented a unique opportunity for the state to redress an injustice that it clearly considered to be a national disgrace. The commission recognized that for the first time since the establishment of Radio Eireann in 1926, the government had the chance to influence the development of a powerful form of media. It therefore urged the state to seize the initiative by creating a dynamic service that would help revitalize the national language. If the state failed to act in the interest of the revival, it warned, "We fear that the effort to save the language is doomed to failure."[3]

The commission was convinced that television could have a critical impact on efforts to resuscitate a language that was in decline. Critics dismissed the language lobby and the Commission for the Restoration of the Irish Language as an alarmist band of zealots who hoped, in spite of claims to the contrary, to exploit television for narrow political reasons. However, events would prove that the concerns of the Language Commission were well founded. The service that was established failed to incorporate a meaningful amount of Irish-language material into its programs. Advocates of the language continue to argue that the state has failed to produce a significant amount of quality Irish-language programming and that this failure has contributed to the decline of the native language.

The commission argued that the government should have in place an effective policy to ensure that when television was established, the Irish language would be employed in both the actual administration of the service and the programs broadcast. The report asked that the government ensure that the staff hired to operate the service be fluent in the native tongue. The commission also expected the state to encourage advertisers to broadcast their commercials in Irish. When addressing the issue of programming, the commission demanded a firm commitment from the state that a specific amount of airtime would be devoted to Irish-language broadcasts. The commission also wanted television to dedicate itself to reaching the young and argued that the majority of children's programs should be broadcast in Irish.

The Language Commission explained to the Taoiseach that it regarded these recommendations as critical and asked that all be incorporated into government policy. This was necessary

in order that the television public, including viewers, advertisers, administrators, artists, technicians[,] . . . may realise that the Irish language is to be accorded its due status as the national language. . . . The extent to which Irish is used in programmes and advertisements . . . should make it abundantly clear that Irish is, in fact, regarded as the first official language.[4]

The commission was clearly under the impression that Irish television would be overseen by a public authority and run by an independent program contractor. The report, therefore, focused on the authority that it presumed would oversee the service and interact with the program contractor. It argued that only Irish citizens who were sympathetic to the language in particular and Irish culture in general should be appointed to the authority. To guarantee a truly sensitive authority, it maintained that the majority of members should be Irish speakers. When considering the program company that would operate the television system, the commission maintained that its directors should be comprised of Irish nationals who appreciated the importance of the language. Although the Language Commission was sympathetic to the financial difficulties that challenged the state, it maintained that the government had a duty to protect a fragile native culture that was under tremendous "external" pressure. In such circumstances, the commission believed that the state should be prepared to provide the necessary financial aid to ensure that "programmes will not have a perverse influence, destructive of Irish nationality and of the Irish way of life."[5]

The commission's report was reviewed by Leon O'Broin and his department, which reported back to de Valera in May 1959. Posts and Telegraphs praised certain aspects of the commission's report while dismissing other segments that it found unrealistic. O'Broin exploited the urgent tone of the report to once again advocate the need for a publicly owned television service. Pointing to the dire warning issued by the commission concerning the failure of the revival, O'Broin maintained, "If that statement is correct, and if the whole or bulk of the Irish television programmes is to be operated by a commercial group, Irish or foreign, with financial profits as its primary objective, the revival movement might be regarded as dead."[6]

Posts and Telegraphs criticized the expectations of the Language Commission, which it regarded as unrealistic. The department explained to the Taoiseach that the critical challenge to an Irish station would be attracting an audience, especially in areas where viewers had the option of turning to British broadcasts. The role of the Irish language, though important, would therefore be limited, as Posts and Telegraphs maintained that to be a success, a station would have to offer popular programs at peak times. O'Broin considered himself a moderate who was genuinely sympathetic to the desires of the Language Commission. It was important that he and his supporters be seen as pragmatic, and therefore, the department did not hesitate to dismiss many of the recommendations that were considered quixotic. Recommendations stipulating that the television service and its authority be staffed by Irish speakers were dismissed as unrealistic. In reviewing the report, there is little doubt that O'Broin regarded the Language Commission as "completely out of touch with reality."[7]

O'Broin, with the support of his minister, advised the Taoiseach that no matter how impractical one considered the report of the Language Commission, it had raised critical issues that could not be ignored. The secretary understood that the fear expressed by the commission could be used to help advance the scheme outlined by his department. He argued that Irish-language programs would have a limited place in the type of service he envisioned:

It will probably be necessary as a token of the government's sincere desire to advance Irish that some programmes in Irish be broadcast even in the knowledge that their public will be extremely small. Gestures of this sort, though necessary, do little to advance the cause of Irish and it will probably be necessary to restrict them within reasonable limits.[8]

One noted historian commenting on the Language Commission has argued that it was established by a government that was well aware of the failure of the state's revival policy. When the full report of the Language Commission was published in 1963, few of its recommendations were accepted.[9] The commission's interim report suffered the same fate.

One applicant who accepted many of the concerns that had been articulated by the language commission was Gael-Linn. Gael-Linn had studied the *Report of the Television Commission* and submitted, directly to the government, a revised plan that tried to address the commission's recommendations. The fifty-page proposal dealt with issues that had caused the Television Commission concern in areas such as programming and finance. This revised proposal generated a great deal of interest, both among members of the government and in the national press. Gael-Linn underscored the importance of being the only company that was truly Irish and argued that it was the only applicant capable of building a service that would succeed in presenting programs to reflect and celebrate the unique culture of Ireland.

It is not surprising that Posts and Telegraphs was not impressed by the revised Gael-Linn proposal. A six-page *Memorandum for the Government* submitted to the Cabinet in July 1959 explained why the department believed the Gael-Linn proposal should be rejected. The fact that the memo was written at the request of the Cabinet indicates that the government believed the proposal should receive serious consideration. As has been seen, Posts and Telegraphs believed the group was simply not qualified to operate a television service. The department criticized the manner in which the proposed service would be financed and operated and portrayed Gael-Linn as an enthusiastic and sincere group of idealists who were plainly naive. The department concluded that the organization was simply not competent to assume such an important and complex task as running a national television service.[10]

The review that O'Broin had submitted to the government concerning the Gael-Linn proposal was thorough and highly critical. O'Broin was not hostile to the language and, in fact, was a bilingual scholar who had published material in both Irish and English.[11] However, his love for the language did not translate into support for a proposal that sought to exploit television for the purpose of propagandizing Irish. O'Broin recognized from the start that television, especially commercial television, could not be the primary vehicle for reviving the language.

Dónall Ó'Móráin, the Founding Chairman and Chief Executive of Gael-Linn, has argued that politicians were afraid of granting his organization the television franchise as they were concerned with his organization's political aspirations. Ó'Móráin maintained that there were "fears that awarding the franchise to Gael-Linn would have given us a special position in the community which could provide a political threat sooner or later. Many politicians cannot see that for some of us there are more things in heaven and earth than seats in parliament."[12]

Meanwhile O'Broin and his associates had submitted yet another *Memorandum for the Government*, once again proposing that "television be controlled and operated by a public service body."[13] O'Broin was still hoping that the government might have a change of heart and decide to support the state-owned public service that Posts and Telegraphs advocated.

Television received a good deal of attention in the Dail in July 1959. The report of the Television Commission became a subject of debate when the Dail began considering estimates for Radio Eireann. The Minister for Posts and Telegraphs introduced the budget for radio and therefore provided an opportunity for members to try to discuss the government's reaction to the recently released report of the Television Commission. Michael Hilliard, who had succeeded Sean Ormonde, introduced the budget for Radio Eireann and made only brief remarks about the status of television. Hilliard stated that the government had acted on the Television Commission's *Interim Report* by building a road and preparing the Kippure site for a Dublin transmitter. He mentioned that the Television Commission had issued its report and that most of it had been published. Beyond this, the minister simply stated that the government would consider the reports issued by the Television Commission.

Hilliard was not entirely successful in trying to exclude television from the debate. Gerard Sweetman, a Fine Gael member of the opposition who had been Minister of Finance in the Inter-Party Government from 1954 to 1957, insisted that the report of the Television Commission be discussed. As a former Minister of Finance, Sweetman was well aware of efforts made by Posts and Telegraphs to introduce television to Ireland. As has been noted, the Inter-Party government had opposed public spending on television and had adopted a hostile attitude toward efforts to get the state involved in the medium. The former minister had read the report and demanded that the government reveal its intentions concerning television.

As a senior member of his party, he also wanted to outline the Fine Gael position on the report and on television in general.

Sweetman's own ideas about television had not changed since serving as Minister of Finance. He remained the fiscal conservative he had been while in the Cabinet of the Inter-Party Government. He stated that he supported the terms of reference that had created the Television Commission and argued that the state should not become involved in financing television. Sweetman also made it clear that his party did not support the concept of the state supporting the establishment of a television service through an indirect subsidy extended by a government agency. This, he maintained, would ultimately involve public funds.

He urged the government to move carefully when considering television and expressed concern that the full report of the commission had not been published or made available to members of the Dail. He understood that the supplements contained sensitive information but still believed that the inability of the members of the Dail to have access to the unpublished material created a serious problem. He argued that without access to the unpublished supplements, the deputies could not critically analyze the commission's report.

Sweetman's apprehension was indicative of the anxiety held by deputies who were concerned with the Fianna Fail government's attitude toward television. He had a valid point in stating that it was difficult to gain a thorough understanding of the report without having access to the supplements that reviewed each proposal. Fine Gael was fearful that the Fianna Fail Government would simply select a private company to operate the service without allowing the opposition a say in who would be chosen. The former Minister of Finance predicted that charges of favoritism and even corruption might arise that would damage the television service.

Sweetman feared that television would become a "play thing of party politics," which might be changed or modified by subsequent governments.[14] He therefore called for the establishment of an all-party Dail committee that would examine the full reports of the Television Commission, including the confidential material that had been held back by the government. In this way he believed a bipartisan consensus could be nurtured that would separate party politics from television.

Labour, the second largest opposition party, also had an interest in the debate on television.[15] The man who would replace William Norton as the leader of the Labour party in 1960, Brendan Corish, advised the Dail of his party's position. Corish criticized the government for failing to define its position on the Television Commission's report or to make a conclusive statement concerning when a native television station would be built. He contended that he had concerns, not only for citizens, but for the domestic electronics industry, which was suffering financially because of government indecision.[16]

When debate resumed on July 22, 1959, Patrick McGilligan, another former Fine Gael Minister of Finance, addressed the Dail. He expressed frustration that the full report had not been made available to the Dail and commented on other aspects of the report that he saw as problematic. McGilligan examined the contradictions that were obvious in the report, focusing on the reluctance with which the commission had made its final recommendation. He pointed out that a close reading of the full report revealed that the members of the commission saw themselves as trapped due to the strict terms of reference that had established the body. McGilligan cited the passages in the report where the commission made it quite clear that their true sympathies lay with an Irish television service that would be publicly owned and operated.

McGilligan also commented on the Minority Report, stating that he generally agreed with its conclusions. He feared that if the government accepted a commercial proposal supported by the commission, such a service would be a mere extension of British television. However, even in agreeing with the opinion expressed in the Minority Report, McGilligan was frustrated by its support for what was described as "International Commercial Sound Broadcasting" (ICSB). He noted that the minority believed that this could offer an important source of revenue for a television service and that it required further investigation. However, he explained that he had no idea what this was as ICSB was never defined in the reports.[17] This was a reference to the proposals that had been made by the Michelson Group and the McLendon Investment Company. Since the details of these proposals were contained in the unpublished supplemental report, McGilligan and members of the Dail were unable to fully comprehend the report.

In spite of efforts made by opposition members of the Dail to entice Michael Hilliard into a debate, the minister avoided discussing the report. As the estimates under discussion did not request funds for television, Hilliard refused to respond to questions from the opposition. He ignored Sweetman's call for the establishment of a parliamentary committee to consider the full *Report of the Television Commission* and declared that all requests to see the unpublished reports would be refused. Hilliard advised the Dail that the government simply had not arrived at a decision on the nature and form of Irish television.

The voice of the television industry in Ireland, the *Irish Radio and Electrical Journal*, reviewed the published *Report of the Television Com-*

mission and complained that it was "exhaustive if not extensively enlightening."[18] It acknowledged that Irish television would be largely commercial, with a public authority that would supervise the service. The *Journal* remained unimpressed with advocates of public service television and was more concerned with getting a successful commercial service operational. The industry realized that demand and profits would not increase dramatically in Ireland until a service was broadcasting. The *Journal* was also wary of arguments that favored a station that would broadcast an abundance of cultural and educational material and warned that Irish television should not hide "behind a wall of complete nationalism."[19] The government was urged to make a prompt decision that would allow a television to be established without further delay.

O'Broin had also reviewed the Television Commission's report and was disappointed, though not surprised, that his proposal had been rejected. However, he did not give up hope that the commission's report could be used to advance the general scheme that he and his associates had designed. He recognized that the commission was greatly hindered by the terms of reference under which it labored and that many members had expressed a strong desire for a state-owned public service. The secretary hoped that these factors might help him convince the government to reconsider its position and ignore the commission's advice that the service be set up as a commercial service operated by a private company.

O'Broin had maintained a correspondence with Sir Ian Jacob, the Director General of the BBC, who remained committed to helping the Irish Secretary of Posts and Telegraphs. O'Broin had sent Jacob an early copy of the Television Commission's report and in June 1959 received a letter from the British Director General offering his observations on developments in Ireland.[20] Jacob recognized that the strict terms of reference given to the commission had restricted its ability to recommend the establishment of a public television service. He told O'Broin that the Irish Government had forced the commission to endorse a commercial service regulated by a public authority and concluded that such a service would fail. "Anyone who has experience in these matters will realise that the aspirations in the report cannot be realised."[21] He warned O'Broin about the prospect of television being operated by a private company. "The one thing that I am quite certain about is that if your television service is handed over to a commercial company, the safeguards proposed in the report will turn out to be impious [*sic*] ones. The company establishes such a strong position that it inevitably rides roughshod over the control in the interests of making money."[22]

O'Broin believed Jacob was correct and, as has been seen, tried in vain to get the Television Commission to support the scheme that his department had drafted. He wrote to Jacob thanking the Director General for his thoughts and told him that his government had still not arrived at a conclusive decision. He explained that he had tried to convince the government and the commission that the scheme his department had developed was the best alternative for the country. O'Broin acknowledged that in spite of his best efforts to convince the commission to accept his proposal, he had failed. "I was not successful . . . and I do not expect to have any more luck when decisions are being taken."[23]

O'Broin was despondent, feeling convinced that the television service that would be established in Ireland would be privately owned and overseen by a weak public authority. He realized that he would have to challenge the recommendations of the Television Commission and also battle the powerful Department of Finance if he was to have any chance of convincing the government to accept his proposal. He told Jacob that although he was not optimistic, he intended to keep fighting for the public service he had supported since the beginning of the decade. He referred to the commission's professed preference for a public service in advising Jacob that there were

indications that, were it not for the cramping effect of their Terms of Reference, they might have found in favour of a public service, and it is possible that since the Terms of Reference were drawn up things have changed economically for the better. That may influence the final decision, but it may not. The truth is I cannot tell; but I am not optimistic that my view of things will be followed.[24]

O'Broin explained to Jacob that the government was at the time distracted by national elections and an important referendum on proportional representation. Television was put on hold until these issues were decided. In these elections, Eamon de Valera, while still Taoiseach, was running for the office of president. The Taoiseach was also hoping that the electorate would veto proportional representation, a system he believed had hindered his party's efforts to gain clear majorities in Dail Eireann.

Sir Ian Jacob and the BBC were very sympathetic to O'Broin's plight and had tried to help the secretary in his efforts to influence the Television Commission. As has been seen, the BBC was alarmed at the possibility of a commercial company being granted the right to broadcast an international radio service from Ireland. Once that threat had seemed to pass, the BBC continued to do what it could to help O'Broin influence both the Television

Commission and the Irish government to accept television as a public service.

This is evident in an exchange that took place in March 1959, just prior to the Television Commission's issuance of its final report. On March 21, the Secretary of the Television Commission, Sean O'Droma, wrote to Sir Ian Jacob asking if a privately owned commercial service would enjoy the special affiliation with the BBC that Jacob had indicated an Irish public station might have.[25] (O'Broin had been working on an arrangement whereby an Irish public service would be able to receive BBC programs at specially discounted rates.) O'Broin was aware of O'Droma's request and intervened by contacting the BBC on several occasions to ask for assistance.

O'Broin telephoned Cyril Connor, the head of Overseas and Foreign Relations at the BBC, and asked how he intended to respond to the inquiry. Connor later reported that he explained to O'Broin

the lines on which we are thinking & he agreed that while it would be right for us to be fairly forthcoming in relation to an Irish public authority, he hoped that we would not make things too easy for commercial concessionaires. I told him we had this point in mind & promised to tell him the substance of our reply before it was sent off, so as to ensure that we were pulling in the same direction.[26]

Connor discussed the matter with Sir Ian Jacob and decided, "that while we must be reasonably forthcoming to an Irish public television authority we could not be expected to make things easy for a commercial concessionaire."[27] It is clear that O'Broin had an ally in the BBC; however, the British broadcasters had not been much help in influencing the final decision of the Television Commission.

The Department of Finance had monitored developments involving television and was aware that O'Broin would be launching yet another initiative to argue the case for a state-owned and -operated commercial service. Finance reviewed the *Report of the Television Commission* and submitted a formal *Memorandum to the Government* in July 1959. Louis M. Fitzgerald, who had been involved in developing Finance's policy on television throughout the 1950s, drafted the document. This was revised by the Secretary of the Department, T. K. Whitaker, and approved by the Minister of Finance, Dr. James Ryan, in July 1959. In reviewing the draft and the final memo that was sent to the Cabinet, one is not surprised at the conservative tone that characterizes the opening of the memorandum. As had been seen, the department had developed an effective obstructionist policy, which had not changed since Leon O'Broin was denied permission to purchase a television set in April 1950. Finance was still not convinced that television was something that the country really needed in 1959 and therefore pleaded patience, asking the Cabinet to consider whether television was a true national priority. Finance saw no reason to rush ahead with television and emphasized the financial drain that its introduction would cause. It predicted that a service would lead to the purchase of an additional 80,000 television sets which would drain £6.5 million from the economy.

Finance was at pains to explain to the Cabinet the difficult state of the Irish economy. It was clearly frightened of the economic consequences that it believed would result from the creation of an Irish television service. Once again it argued that the investment of even private capital into such a "luxury service" would damage the national economy and weaken the government's efforts to encourage savings, which it believed would assist in economic development. The Secretary of the Department of Finance, T. K. Whitaker, felt strongly about the issue and revised Fitzgerald's draft memorandum to include language that was more emphatic in detailing the department's objections.

As Ministers are aware, the 1959/60 programme of *public* capital expenditure (estimated at £45m.) is at the same level as the total *national* savings in 1958. Apart from the private capital needs it does not meet, the programme does not include provision for a television service and the question arises whether television is so beneficial as to merit insertion as a priority in a capital programme which is already so large in relation to the community's resources that a large deficit in the balance of payments is to be expected this year. The objections which are seen to capital expenditure at the present juncture on television would apply whether the capital is provided by Government sources or by private enterprise—there is only a limited pool of capital and any extra expenditure in the private sector would make less capital available for public borrowing and cause a heavier deficit in external payments. If, as it is reasonable to assume, the institution of television resulted in a large scale increase in the expenditure by private persons on television sets, private savings would be seriously affected, to the detriment of capital availabilities generally.[28]

The department believed that the introduction of television, financed by the state or by private investors, would upset the frail national economy. Finance concluded that if the state accepted the view that television was a national priority it would be guilty of hypocrisy as it would encourage consumer spending. Finance also raised familiar fiscal arguments that had been employed over the years to oppose the opening of a television service. It predicted a substantial decrease in the entertainment tax, due to cinemas losing business. The memorandum also warned that the items advertised on Irish television would be those of larger, wealthier firms, which would sell imported goods, further threatening the nation's balance of payments. It is clear that Finance did not want an Irish service established at any time in the near future. The government was advised that the Minister of Finance wanted the opening of an Irish television service postponed until the "Programme of Economic Expansion" was "well underway."[29]

To this point, Finance had articulated traditional department policy, and one would expect its memorandum to conclude here, having expressed itself in no uncertain terms. However, it was precisely at this juncture that Finance made a remarkable statement. The Department of Finance declared that it accepted that television was inevitable and announced that it would be willing to offer qualified support for the scheme that Posts and Telegraphs had recently submitted to the government. The memo reported that the Minister of Finance:

has some sympathy with the view of the Minister for Posts and Telegraphs that it is possible to regard the Television Commission as having construed perhaps too narrowly that portion of the terms of reference which requested them to make their recommendations on the basis that "no charge fall on the Exchequer." If a television service were to be provided, the Minister of Finance would be prepared to consider an arrangement under which the capital would be provided by the Government on a profit earning-basis. The Minister understands that the Minister for Posts and Telegraphs is strongly in favour of the recommendation made . . . that the Television Authority, which would be a state-sponsored body, would provide and operate the service, financed by licence fees and advertising revenue.[30]

Finance had relented and given its qualified support to the scheme proposed by O'Broin and his associates at Posts and Telegraphs. It is remarkable to note that Finance used the Television Commission as a scapegoat in declaring that it had interpreted the terms of reference in too strict a manner. Sean Lemass, under intense pressure from the Department of Finance, had drafted the terms of reference carefully and clearly intended the work of the commission to be limited. If blaming the commission allowed Finance to save face and make a 180-degree change, the Department of Posts and Telegraphs did not object.

Posts and Telegraphs responded quickly to the cautiously supportive memo from the Department of Finance. O'Broin immediately recognized that Finance had made a significant concession, which eliminated a major obstacle in his desire to keep television out of the hands of foreign corporations. A memo for the Cabinet was quickly drafted, which downplayed the anxiety exhibited by Finance. O'Broin dismissed Finance's skepticism regarding the urgency of television by noting that the government and the Television Commission had already made a commitment to setting up a service promptly. O'Broin dismissed as exaggerated Finance's concerns about the expected loss in entertainment revenue and fear of increased consumer spending. He was clearly pleased with the statement made by Finance that it was now willing to provide the capital needed to start a television service. He advised the Cabinet that this was "a valuable contribution on the part of the Minister for Finance because he is aware that to 'provide' the service by the Television Authority will involve the provision of capital from state sources."[31]

In the early summer of 1959, Posts and Telegraphs submitted a revised proposal to the government which contrasted sharply with the confused and contradictory report issued by the Television Commission. There can be little doubt that the three companies the Television Commission had put on the shortlist failed to impress Sean Lemass and other members of the Cabinet, including the Minister of Finance. O'Broin and his associates were able to put together a more detailed proposal, which requested financial support from the state but also promised a return on the government's investment. The proposal indicated that by accepting the principle that no ultimate charge should fall on the Exchequer, a state-owned service could quickly be gotten up and running. Posts and Telegraphs argued that this state-run service would be able to make a profit and pay back the loan that would allow it to get on the air.

The Department of Finance reluctantly acknowledged that it would support a service along the lines that had been outlined by Posts and Telegraphs. As the debates in the Dail had shown, the deputies realized that the Television Commission's Report was not an enthusiastic endorsement of a private commercial service. At this juncture O'Broin was perfectly positioned to try to persuade the government that a change in policy had to be made. To achieve this goal, he had to convince the most powerful member of the government, the new Taoiseach, Sean Lemass.

Sean Lemass had become Taoiseach on June 23, 1959, when de Valera assumed the presidency. Lemass realized that the Television Commission had been crippled by the strict terms of reference that he, with the support of the Department of Finance, had written. He was certainly impressed by the change in policy at the Department of Finance. Historians have commented on the marked difference between Sean Lemass and his predecessor, Eamon de Valera, in making important decisions. While de Valera opted to examine questions of policy from every conceivable angle and was reluctant to make quick, conclusive decisions, Lemass in many ways operated in an opposite manner. This interpretation is validated in the methodical manner in which de Valera had examined the question of television while he was Taoiseach.

Lemass has been praised for his ability to consider the arguments made by members of his government and quickly come to a decision on policy. One of his biographers, Brian Farrell, indicates that while Lemass was not a dictator, he was not afraid to exert his authority. "He saw himself as the man in the driving seat and was determined to direct the government and the country to its overdue rendezvous with the realities of the later twentieth-century world."[32] This explanation is also confirmed in the manner in which Lemass, once he was Taoiseach, decided how the television question would be resolved.

There is no doubt that the change in leadership enabled O'Broin to approach a Taoiseach who was much more inclined to reconsider what had become accepted government policy. Sean Lemass and Leon O'Broin met in July 1959 and discussed the future of Irish television. In this meeting, the Secretary for Posts and Telegraphs was able to put his case before the new Taoiseach. In his autobiography, O'Broin maintains that the change of policy endorsed by the government was due to Sean Lemass.

I can only surmise as to how the government's final decision was arrived at. Sean Lemass, who a couple of months before had taken over as Taoiseach from de Valera, had no doubt a lot to do with it. He asked me to go and see him. The interview was brief. I was concerned, I told him, about the quality of programmes. We were fortunately placed in close proximity to what was probably the best service in the world, the BBC, an entirely public service organisation, and I suggested that we might explore the possibility of a special arrangement for an extension of their service as a back-up to such programmes of quality that as we could produce at home on a similar public service basis. He made no comment, but as I spoke of the BBC I felt that the chauvinists among us would not take too well to any arrangements with the *British* Broadcasting Corporation.[33]

O'Broin's meeting with Lemass helped the Taoiseach come to a decision. O'Broin, who had believed that the BBC could be a valuable part of an Irish public service, recognized at this juncture that this would be very difficult for political reasons. However, this did not preclude the government from considering the Post Office plan *sans* BBC involvement. The government's ultimate decision surprised O'Broin, who described the announcement that was made in July 1959. "An extraordinary *volte face* occurred. The government, again without consultation with us, but obviously returning to our television committee's reports, rejected the view of the commission and proceeded to set up a statutory authority to run both television and radio without any commercial promoters whatever."[34]

The final decision had been made at a Cabinet meeting on July 31, 1959.[35] O'Broin had been successful in his persistent efforts to convince the government to accept the principle of a state-owned and -operated public television service. After years of difficult and challenging effort, he and his department, with the support of several ministers, had succeeded in convincing the government to adopt a proposal that had been tentatively outlined in the Television Committee's 1953 report. A formal public announcement was made by the Minister for Posts and Telegraphs, Michael Hilliard, in Cork in August.

There is little doubt that O'Broin was delighted with this decision. He wrote to Ian Jacob at the BBC shortly afterwards. "The change round in favour of a public authority, both controlling and operating, came to many people as a great surprise. . . . I am personally very happy about what has been decided, as I am sure you are too."[36] Jacob congratulated O'Broin and offered to assist in drafting the legislation that would establish the new television authority. He told O'Broin he was "delighted" by the announcement and commended him for his tenacity.[37]

The decision taken by the Lemass Government surprised observers who had expected the state to grant an exclusive contract to one of the applicants mentioned in the press. The *Irish Times* reported that the announcement "came as a big surprise to many people. . . . It had been expected, even by sources close to the Government, that a private company would be given the concession, at least for ten years."[38] The *Irish Radio and Electrical Journal*, long a critic of government inaction, was disappointed by the decision and wary of a public service that would be owned and operated by the state. It saw the announcement as a "considerable set-back to the industry" and argued that "Government Agencies are not always the best channels for progressing profitable enterprise."[39] Regardless, the voice of Irish retailers and manufacturers urged the government to act quickly in getting a service on the air.

The government had made an irrevocable decision to ignore the final recommendations of the Television Commission and accept the alternative outlined by Posts and Telegraphs.[40] O'Broin's department would oversee both the drafting of the legislation needed to establish the television authority and the building of the physical plant required for the service. It had taken the government nine years to decide on the basic structure that would be used to build and operate a national television service.

The decision made in July of 1959 represented the conclusion of an ideological debate that had taken place within the restrictive economic confines of Ireland in the 1950s. The dismal fiscal and economic realities that haunted Ireland throughout this period influenced the service that was established. While many both inside and outside government were inclined to support a state-financed public service, the grim realities of a state troubled by economic stagnation and relentless emigration forced a strict evaluation of priorities. The desire to avoid spending precious state funds on television when it was apparent that other, more critical issues had to be addressed had created strong opposition to state involvement in the new medium. This opposition came from the powerful Department of Finance, members of the Dail, editorial boards of the national newspapers, and leaders of both the Inter-Party and Fianna Fail Governments.

In spite of overwhelming odds, the efforts of the Department of Posts and Telegraphs prevailed. It is remarkable that a core of dedicated civil servants was successful in developing the state's television policy and in seeing their plans through to fruition. This had been done in spite of intense opposition from elected officials, wealthy industrialists, semistate bodies, national governments, and even the Roman Catholic Church.

The decision taken by the government must also be understood within the context of a nation undergoing fundamental change. The five-year Programme for Economic Development introduced in 1958 sought to develop the stagnant Irish economy by investing in infrastructure, encouraging foreign investment, and stimulating industrial output. These strategies were a significant departure from past economic policies, which had endorsed the Sinn Féin concept of protectionism and self-sufficiency. The new policies were also an important departure from the conservative economic orthodoxy long embraced by the Department of Finance. Seen within the overall shift in government thinking, the decision taken by the Lemass administration was not a radical departure in policy.

However, it is clear that this *volte face* could not have occurred without the efforts of two very unusual men, a dedicated and wily civil servant and a confident Taoiseach. Leon O'Broin remained an indefatigable champion of an Irish public service throughout the 1950s. Sean Lemass opposed O'Broin's efforts but displayed the courage and self-confidence to change his mind and admit that the best alternative lay in a state-owned and -operated television service.[41]

The final decision taken by the government did not give Ireland a true public service comparable to the British Broadcasting Corporation. However, in adopting a state-owned and -operated, commercial public service, Ireland had retained a certain degree of dignity and independence. This would not have been the case if the operation of Ireland's television service had been taken on by an American, British, or European corporation. One could also argue that turning over the service exclusively to Gael-Linn would have surrendered it to a sectional, or minority, group that was interested in pursuing a cultural and political agenda that may have alienated a majority of viewers.[42] The end result established a service that was by no means ideal. This would be proved as Irish television evolved and matured. However, one must carefully consider the economic, social, and political context within which the decision on the form and structure of Irish television was taken. Given the limited options confronting the state, it would be difficult to define the outcome as anything less than a victory for the Irish people.

NOTES

1. Archives of RTE 105/58 016A, *Interim Report of the Commission on the Restoration of the Irish Language*, March 20, 1959, pp. 2–3.

2. Ibid., p. 3.

3. Ibid., p. 3.

4. Archives of RTE, 105/58 017A, *Interim Report of the Language Commission*, March 1959, p. 5.

5. Ibid., p. 8.

6. Archives of RTE, 105/58 016C, memo from the Minister of Posts and Telegraphs to the Taoiseach, May 4, 1959. This memo was submitted to the government on May 5, 1959.

7. Archives of RTE, 105/58 016B. Draft memorandum for the Government prepared by Posts and Telegraphs, April 29, 1959, p. 3.

8. Ibid., p. 1.

9. Gearoid O'Tauthaigh, "Language, Literature and Culture in Ireland Since the War," in *Ireland 1945–1970* [Thomas Davis Lectures], ed. Joseph Lee (Dublin: Gill and Macmillan, 1979).

10. Department of Finance, S101/1/59, *Memorandum for the Government*, from the Minister of Posts and Telegraphs, July 16, 1959, p. 4.

11. O'Broin had been involved with *An Gum*, an organization committed to translating and publishing books in Irish. He translated *Kidnapped*, by Robert Louis Stevenson; *Three Men in A Boat*, by J. K. Jerome; and *Trent's Last Case*, by E. C. Bently; into Irish. He had also written several plays and short stories in Irish.

12. Dónall Ó Móráin, "The Irish Experience" *Irish Broadcasting Review*, no. 10 (Spring, 1981). This was confirmed in an interview conducted by the author with Ó Móráin in Dublin, December 14, 1990.

13. Department of Finance, S101/1/59, *Memorandum for the Government*, from Posts and Telegraphs, July 16, 1959, p. 1.

14. *Dail Debates* 176 (July 16, 1959); col. 1397.

15. The Labour Party held twelve seats after receiving 9.1 percent of the vote in the general election of March 1957.

16. *Dail Debates* 176 (July 16, 1959); cols. 1405–1406.

17. Ibid., 176 (July 22, 1959); col. 1687.

18. *Irish Radio and Electrical Journal* 17 (June 1959): 7.

19. Ibid.

20. BBC Written Archives at Caversham, E1/2,096/1, letter to Jacob from O'Broin, December 16, 1958.

21. BBC Written Archives at Caversham, E1/2,096/2, letter to Leon O'Broin from Sir Ian Jacob, June 9, 1959.

22. Ibid.

23. Ibid., letter from O'Broin to Jacob, June 12, 1959.

24. Ibid.

25. BBC Written Archives at Caversham, E1/2,096/1, letter from Sean O'Droma, to Sir Ian Jacob, March 21, 1959.

26. Ibid., memo from Cyril Connor, March 24, 1959, pp. 1–2. Note that "D. G." referred to Sir Ian Jacob, the Director General.

27. Ibid., memo from Cyril Connor, March 25, 1959.

28. Department of Finance, S101/1/59, *Memorandum for the Government*, July 1959, pp. 1–2.

29. Ibid., p. 3.

30. Department of Finance, S101/1/59, *Memorandum for the Government*, July 1959, p. 3.

31. Archives of RTE, 105/58 no. 18, July 23, 1959, pp. 2–3.

32. Brian Farrell, *Sean Lemass* (Dublin: Gill and Macmillan, 1983), p. 109.

33. Leon O'Broin, *Just Like Yesterday, an Autobiography* (Dublin: Gill and Macmillan, 1985), p. 210.

34. Ibid., pp. 209–210.

35. Department of the Taoiseach, July 31, 1959, S14996D, State Paper Office.

36. BBC Written Archives at Caversham, E1/2096/2, letter from O'Broin to Jacob, August 11, 1959.

37. Ibid, letter from Jacob to O'Broin, September 3, 1959.

38. *Irish Times*, August 8, 1959, p. 1.

39. *Irish Radio and Electrical Journal* 17 (August 1959): 9.

40. One former member of the Television Commission was not surprised by the Government's decision to ignore the recommendations of the Commission. Reverend H. R. McAdoo, the former Anglican Archbishop of Dublin, recalled his reaction to the announcement in Dalkey, County Dublin, December 12, 1990 interview with the author. In what may have been a reference to the fear that Gael-Linn would be awarded a license to operate television, the Archbishop stated that he was pleased with the decision taken by the Lemass Government:

As a matter of fact, given the situation . . . I think that was the right decision. Because Ireland was only just getting out of a sectionalist society and you would have a risk, if there was not government control, of various sections getting too much of a hold of television which would be in everybody's parlour . . . and that would be a bad thing. I think on the whole the right decision was taken.

41. One can only speculate how television may have been addressed had de Valera remained in power. He certainly did not appear anxious to involve the state in establishing a national television service, and his record in this regard is one of paralysis and procrastination. He had expressed the hope the state would be able to closely supervise the medium in a meeting held with the Comhairle in December 1957. Sean Lemass was also very uneasy about the advent of Irish television and the trouble it might cause the state. In 1960 he drafted very strict *policy directives* that he expected the new service to follow. Lemass, like de Valera, had very strong ideas about the type of programs that should and should not be broadcast. These *policy directives* were clearly designed to limit the independence of an Irish television service. They help explain his famous comment issued in the Dail in 1966 when he described RTE as 'an instrument of public policy.' (See S14996D, Department of the Taoiseach).

42. It should be pointed out that the efforts of the language lobby, including Gael-Linn, certainly helped defeat the efforts of foreign corporations interested in the commercial exploitation of Ireland's television and radio network.

Bibliography

PRIMARY SOURCES

State Paper Office at Dublin Castle, Department of the Taoiseach

Broadcasting Files

Broadcasting Authority Act 1960: S16748.
Broadcasting of Dail Debates: S14511.
Broadcasting, arrangements with Northern Ireland authorities: S10777.
Broadcasting, censorship: S16772.
Broadcasting, commercial: S9520; S10365; S10495.
Broadcasting, complaints: S5953.
Broadcasting, Great Britain: S3489.
Broadcasting, legislation relating to: S16748.
Broadcasting, political: S9908.
Broadcasting, programmes relating to Northern Ireland: S10779.
Broadcasting, scholarships: S10365.
Broadcasting, sports: S15666.
Broadcasting, use by political parties: S14204.
Broadcasts, from belligerent countries: S12109.
Broadcasts, vocational organisations: S10812.
Broadcasting service: S15443.
Broadcasting service, security arrangements: S15953.
Broadcasting stations, appointments: S7480.
Television: S14996.
Television broadcasting, European agreements: S16882.

Television programmes on Ireland: S16882.

Television censorship: S16772.

Television censorship untitled of films: S16772.

Additional files concerning radio and television broadcasting: S35321; S9520B;
   S60054; S2726A; S4550; S51114; S51111; S11838A; S7321; S1908;
   S7480C; S9092D; S14511; S14996A-E; S14996 Annex; S15580;
   S15666; S16699; S16867; S16882 b/61; S16882B; S16922; S16748A-B;
   S16772; S9520B; S9520D; S3532D; S3532; S3669; S5234; S7480;
   S9092; S9520A; S10436; S10795; S13299; S13325; S15580; S16212;
   S16699; S16867; S16922.

National Archives of Ireland

Áras An Uactárain

P5601; P502; 414/3/6.

Department of Foreign Affairs

414/3/6; 433/4/2.

Department of Communications

TV8204; TV8804; TV8990.

Archives of Radio Telefis Eireann

104/53 B1A, B4A; 105/58 no. 1; 105/58 no. 2; 105/58 no. 3 A-C; 105/58 no. 4
   A-15; 105/58 no. 4; 105/58 no. 4 A-E; 105/58 no. 5; 105/58 no. 9; 105/58
   012–A(1), 012–A(2), 012–B, 012–C; 105/58 no. 13; 105/58 no. 14;
   105/58 no. 16 A-D; 105/58 no. 18; 105/58 no. 19; 105/58 no. 20; 105/58
   no. 21; 105/58 no. 21 A; 105/58 no. 22.

Additional miscellaneous 105/58 files include: Seanad file: Minister's Speech for
   the Seanad; Maurice Gorham Files at RTE; Files numbered 1–44; 1608–
   1611.

Miscellaneous papers, articles, documents and pamphlets available at the Archives
   of RTE

Access RTE's Free Press. Archival press clippings, archival RTE chronology.

A View of Irish Broadcasting. Pamphlet, May 1971.

Citizens for Better Broadcasting, *Aspects of RTE Television Broadcasting.* Dublin:
   Citizens for Better Broadcasting, 1976.

Irish Marketing Surveys Ltd. *Joint National Media Research 1972/73* [survey of
   readership of newspapers and magazines, radio audience of RTE, and
   viewing habits in relation to RTE television]. Dublin: Irish Marketing
   Surveys, 1973.

Irish Marketing Surveys Ltd. *A Report on the Preference for a Second Television Channel*. Dublin: Author, 1975.

Peavoy, Diarmuid. *Access Broadcasting: A Report by Diarmuid Peavoy Containing a Personal Viewpoint, Some Philosophies, the BBC Experience and the Possibilities for RTE Radio*. 1978.

Radio Eireann Annual Reports. *RTE Radio Scoile, Report and Findings on the Pilot Broadcasts and Recommendations*. Dublin: RTE, 1975.

Television In Irish Society, A Report on a Research Project by Adrian Wells.

Union of Students in Ireland (USI). *Open Broadcasting: A Submission to the Minister for Posts and Telegraphs on the Final Report of the Broadcasting Review Committee*. Dublin: USI, 1974.

Unpublished Material

Doc. Gen. 1. "Report for the Television Commission," 1958.

Fogerty Report on Industrial Relations in RTE (confidential), 1978.

Workers Union of Ireland. *The Future of Radio: A Document Prepared by Radio Producers in the Workers Union of Ireland.*

Workers Union of Ireland. *Radio Dublin: A Discussion Document.*

Workers Union of Ireland: *Irish Radio: Possibilities for the Future*. Discussion document.

Working Party on Women in Broadcasting Report to the RTE Authority. Dublin: RTE, April 1981.

Young Fine Gael. *Local Radio*. Discussion document.

Department of Communications (at Scotch House)

TW 3756 Files; 1, 3, 7, 8, 9, 10, 11, 12, 13, 15, 16, 17; TV 6086; TV 11361; TV 10376; TW 40913/62; TW 894;1; TW 894;2; TW 894;3; TW 11292; TW 6291; TW 9821; TW 40657/62; C. and A. 27663/58; H.34713/60; H. 33780/60.

Department of Finance

S104/1/50; S101/1/59; S104/5/53; S38/1/59.

Archives of University College Dublin

Ernest Blythe Papers
Patrick McGilligan Papers

Archives of the British Broadcasting Corporation at Caversham

E1/2,089/1; E1/2,092/1; E1/2,092/2; E1/2,096/1; E2/2,096/2.

Dublin University Archives, Trinity College Manuscript Collection

Letters and Correspondences from the Denis Johnston Collection:
    10066/287/1259; 10066/287/1393; 10066/287/1394; 10066/287/1395;
    10066/287/2411; 10066/290/2116; 10066/290/2129; 10066/290/2136;
    10066/290/2143; 10066/290/2145; 10066/290/2151; 10066/290/2254;
    10066/290/2155; 10066/290/2156; 10066/290/2197; 10066/290/2201.
Bodkin Papers: 6934/100

Texas Tech University, Lubbock, Texas

The Gordon McLendon Collection, 1917–1979.

Official Government Publications

Dail Eireann, Parliamentary Debates.
Seanad Eireann, Parliamentary Debates.
Active or Passive? Broadcasting in the Future Tense, Green Paper on Broadcast-
    ing, Dublin, Stationary Office, 1995.
First, second, and third interim reports and the final report of the Special Commit-
    tee to Consider Wireless Broadcasting.
Minutes of evidence and appendices of the Special Committee on Wireless
    Broadcasting [Chairman: Padraig O'Maille]. Dublin: Stationery Of-
    fice, 1924.
Report of the Television Commission [Chairman: Justice George D. Murnaghan].
    Dublin: Stationery Office, 1959.
Inquiry into the Programme on Illegal Moneylending Broadcast on Television by
    R.T.E. on November 11, 1969, Report of Tribunal appointed by An
    Taoiseach December 22, 1969. Dublin: Stationery Office, 1970.
Broadcasting Review Committee Report [Chairman: Justice George D. Mur-
    naghan]. Dublin: Stationery Office, 1974.
Report of the Commission for the Restoration of the Irish Language 1958–1963.
    Dublin Stationary Office, 1963.
The Restoration of the Irish Language. Government White Paper, Dublin, 1965.

Private Collections

John Irvine. "Broadcasting and the Public Trust." Unpublished Thomas Davis
Lecture, Dublin, March 14, 1976.
The Papers of Edward Roth, Boston, Mass.
The Papers of Paul Warren, Dalkey, County Dublin.

Oral History

Interviews conducted by the author with the kind cooperation of: Paul Warren, fall
1990, Dalkey, County Dublin; John Irvine, October 25 and December 11,
1990, Dublin; Thomas Hardiman, December 5, 1990, Dublin; Dónall
Ó'Móráin, December 14, 1990, Dublin; Pádraig Ó'Rahilly, December
14, 1990, Dublin; Maeve Conway-Piskorski, December 13, 1990, Dublin; The Most Reverend Dr. Henry Robert McAdoo, December 12, 1990,
Dalkey County, Dublin; Áine Ní Channain, December 7, 1990, Dublin;
Emir O'Broin, 1990, Dublin; and Eilish MacCurtain Pearce, November
6, 1990, Dublin.

Periodicals

Newspapers

*Belfast Newsletter; Catholic News; Catholic Standard; Civil Service Review; Cork
Examiner; Evening Herald; Evening Mail; Evening Press; Financial
Times; Irish Catholic; Irish Independent; Irish Press; Irish Tattler and
Sketch; Irish Times; Manchester Guardian; Midland Tribune; Observer;
Standard; Sunday Tribune; Sunday Press; Sunday Review; The Tablet;
Times* (London); *Thom's Directory; The Western People.*

Trade Journals

*Broadcast; European Broadcasting Union Review; Irish Broadcasting Review;
Irish Electrical and Radio Trader; The Irish Electrician; Irish Radio and
Electrical Journal; Irish Radio Journal; Irish Radio News; Irish Radio
Review; Television Mail, Guide to Irish Television; RTE Guide (1961),
TV World.*

SECONDARY SOURCES

Adams, Michael. *Censorship: The Irish Experience.* Alabama: University of Alabama Press, 1968.
Akenson, Donald, Harman. *Conor, A Biography of Conor Cruise O'Brien.* Ithaca,
New York: Cornell University Press, 1994.

Andrew, Agnellus, O.F.M. "Television and Religion." *Irish Ecclesiastical Record*, 83 (1955): pp. 12–26.

Andrews, C. S. *Man of No Property*. Dublin: Mercier Press, 1982.

Andrews, C. S., et al. *Administration* [Special issue on RTE Dublin], 15, no. 3 (Autumn 1967): Dublin.

Andrews, Eamon. *This Is My Life*. McDonald Press, 1963.

————. "Mind-blowing Task!," *Comoradh 1962–1987*, Dublin: RTE, January 2, 1987, p. 5.

Barry, Michael. "In No Other Place," *Comoradh 1962–1987*, Dublin: RTE, January 2, 1987, p. 8.

Bell, Desmond. "Proclaiming the Republic: Broadcasting Policy and the Corporation State in Ireland." *Broadcasting and Politics in Western Europe*, 8, no. 2 (1985): p. 27.

Bew, Paul, and Patterson, Henry. *Sean Lemass and the Making of Modern Ireland 1945–1966*. Dublin: Gill and Macmillan, 1982.

Boylan, Henry. *A Dictionary of Irish Biography*. New York: Barnes and Noble, 1978.

Boyle, Andrew. *Only the Wind Will Listen: Reith of the B.B.C*. London, Hutchinson, 1972.

Brennan, Charles J. [Chairman of the Comhairle Radio Eireann]. *Radio Eireann Handbook*. Dublin: Stationery Office, 1955.

Brennan, Seamus. "Seven Years of Irish Radio." *Leader*, December 25, 1948–February 12, 1949.

Briggs, Asa. *The History of Broadcasting in the United Kingdom. Vol. 4: Sound and Vision*. Oxford: Oxford University Press, 1979.

Brown, Terence. *Ireland, A Social and Cultural History, 1922 to Present*. Ithaca, N.Y.: Cornell University Press, 1985.

Browne, Donald R. *Comparing Broadcast Systems, The Experience of Six Industrialized Nations*. Ames: Iowa University Press, 1989.

Browne, Noel. *Against the Tide*. Dublin: Gill and Macmillan, 1986.

Browne, Vincent, ed. *The Magill Book of Irish Politics*. Dublin: Magill, 1981.

Burns, T. *The BBC: Public Institution and Private World*. London: Macmillan, 1974.

Burrows, Wesley. *The Riordans, A Personal History*. Dublin: Gilbert Dalton, 1977.

————. "Tolka Row to Glenroe," *Comoradh 1962–1987*, Dublin: RTE, January 2, 1987, p. 12.

Byrne, D. "Ireland a Media History. *Admap*, 19, nos. 7–8 (July–August 1983).

Byrne, Gay. *To Whom It Concerns, Ten Years of the Late Late Show*. Dublin: Torc Books, 1972.

Campbell, James J. *Television in Ireland*. Dublin: Gill and Son, 1961.

Carlson, Julia, ed. *Banned in Ireland, Censorship and the Irish Writer*. Athens: University of Georgia Press, 1990.

Carr, Bunny. *The Instant Tree*. Dublin: Mercier Press, 1975.

Carty, Ciaran. *Confessions of a Sewer Rat*. Dublin: New Island Books, 1995.

Cathcart, Rex. *The Most Contrary Region, the BBC in Northern Ireland 1924–1984*. Belfast: Blackstaff Press, 1984.

Catholic Truth Society. "We Are Being Entertained to Death."

Catholic Truth Quarterly [Dublin], 2, no. 10 (July–September 1961): pp. 11–23.

Catholic Television Committee. *World Communications Day 1967, Notes for the Clergy*. Dublin: issued by the Catholic Television Committee, distributed by the Catholic Truth Society of Ireland, 1967. Pamphlet, National Library of Ireland.

Chubb, Basil. *The Government and Politics of Ireland*. 2nd ed. Stanford, Calif.: Stanford University Press, 1982.

Clarke, Paddy. *Dublin Calling, 2RN and the Birth of Irish Radio*. Dublin: RTE, 1986.

Cogley, Fred. "It's Bound to be 'On the Box,' " *Comoradh 1962–1987*, Dublin: RTE, January 2, 1987, p. 21.

Collins, P. *It Started on the Late Late Show*. Dublin: 1981.

Conway, Maev. "Children, Education and TV," *Comoradh 1962–1987*, Dublin: RTE, January 2, 1987, p. 22.

Coolahan, John. "The Dilemma of Educational Broadcasting in Ireland, Media and Popular Culture," *The Crane Bag*, 8, no. 2 [Dublin] 1984, 157.

Cronin, Adrian. "Cavalcade of Variety," *Comoradh 1962–1987*, Dublin: RTE, January 2, 1987, p. 18.

Culliton, James. "A Continuous Challenge," *Comoradh 1962–1987*, Dublin: RTE, January 2, 1987, p. 4.

Curtis, Liz. *Ireland, the Propaganda War, the British Media and the Battle for Hearts and Minds*. London: Pluto Press, 1984.

Davidson, Norris. "Radio in a Television Age," *Administration* [Dublin] 15, no. 3 (Autumn 1967): 189.

Devane, R. S. *The Imported Press: A National Menace—Some Remedies*. Dublin: Browne and Nolan Ltd., 1950.

Dillon-Malone, Patrick. "The Impact of Television, a Review of Research Findings." *Studies* [Dublin], 54 (Summer–Autumn 1965): 152–61.

Dodd, Fr. Romauld and Fr. Billy FitzGerald. "Religious Programmes on TV, Recollection . . . to Synod," *Comoradh 1962–1987*, Dublin: RTE, January 2, 1987, p. 23.

Dooney, Sean. *The Irish Civil Service*. Dublin: Institute of Public Administration, 1976.

Dowling, Jack. "Broadcasting: An Exercise in Deception?" *Aquarius* [Dublin] 1973: 123–33.

Dowling, Jack, Doolan, Lelia, and Quinn, Bob. *Sit Down and Be Counted*, the Cultural Evolution of a Television Station. Dublin: Wellington Publishers, 1971.

Dunn, Joseph. "The Clergy and Broadcasting: Some Personal Opinions," *Administration* [Dublin] 15, no. 3 (Autumn 1967: 233.

————. *No Tigers in Africa, Recollections and Reflections of 25 Years of Radharc*. Dublin: Columba Press, 1986.

Dwyer, T. Ryle. *de Valera The Man and the Myths*. Dublin: Poolbeg Press, 1991.

Edwards, Hilton. "Drama on Television," *Aquarius* [Dublin], 1973, 104.

Edwards, Hilton, Leonard, Hugh, Feehan, Fanny, McCarthy, Charles, Dowling, Jack and Hardiman, Thomas P. "RTE under Scrutiny." *Aquarius* [Dublin], 1973, 97–138.

Fanning, Ronan. *The Irish Department of Finance 1922–58*. Dublin: Institute of Public Administration, 1978.

————. *Independent Ireland*. Dublin: Helicon, 1983.

Farrell, Brian. *Sean Lemass*. Dublin: Gill and Macmillan, 1983.

————, ed. *Communications and Community in Ireland*. Dublin and Cork: R.T.E. and the Mercier Press, 1984.

————, "Getting People Involved in the Issues," *Comoradh 1962–1987*, Dublin: RTE, January 2, 1987, p.28.

Faupel, Luke, McRedmond, Louis, Himmelweit, Hilde, Kelly, John Kelly S.J., and Dunn, Joseph. "Dublin Discussion on the Media." *Christus Rex* [Dublin] 19, no. 1 (January 1965): 7–27.

Feeney, Peter. "Censorship and RTE, Media and Popular Culture," *The Crane Bag* [Dublin] 8, no. 2 (1984).

Finn, T. V. "A Sense of Excitement and Adventure," *Comoradh 1962–1987*, Dublin: RTE, January 2, 1987, p. 5.

Finn, Vincent. "RTE's Finances." *Management* [Dublin] 17, no. 12 December 1970. (Includes four additional articles under the title, "Television—The Old Novelty."; 1). *The Teleconomy*, by Patrick Dillon Malone, p. 9; 2). R.T.E.'s *Finances*, by Vincent Finn, p. 13; 3). *The Day the Guessing Had to Stop*, by Desmond B. O'Kennedy, p. 11; 4). R.T.E., *A Look to the Future*, by R. K. Gahan, p. 23.)

Fisher, Desmond. *Broadcasting in Ireland (Case Studies on Broadcasting Systems)*. London: Routledge and Kegan Paul in association with the International Institute of Communications, 1978.

Fitzgerald, Garret. "Radio Listenership and the TV Problem." *University Review* [Dublin], 2, no. 5: 38–45.

Fitz-Simon, Christopher. *The Irish Theatre*. London: Thames and Hudson, 1983.

Forristal, Desmond. "The T.V. Generation" *Catholic Communications Institute of Ireland* [Dublin], 1970.

Foster, R. F. *Modern Ireland 1600–1972*. Dublin: Penguin Press, 1988.

Foyle, Joseph. "The Mass Media Apostolate." *Capuchin Annual*, 1965, 356–64.

————. *The Switched Off*. Dublin: Foyle, 1971.

Gahan, Robert K. "The Commercial Break," *Comoradh 1962–1987*, Dublin: RTE, January 2, 1987, p. 7.

Garvey, Michael. "Neither Cut Nor Dried," *Administration* [Dublin] 15, no. 3 (Autumn 1967): 182.

————. "Battles and Balancing Acts," *Comoradh 1962–1987*, Dublin: RTE, January 2, 1987, p. 11.

Gibbons, Luke. "From Megalith to Megastore: Broadcasting and Irish Culture." In *Irish Studies A General Introduction*, ed. Thomas Bartlett, Chris Curtin, Riana O'Dwyer, and Gearoid O'Tuathaigh. Dublin: Gill and Macmillan, 1988.

Gordon, M. "The Impact of TV on Family Life." *Irish Monthly*, 82 (1954): 180–84.

Gorham, Maurice. *Forty Years of Irish Broadcasting*. Dublin: Talbot Press, 1967.

Gray, Ken. "Objectives Right But . . . ," *Comoradh 1962–1987*, Dublin: RTE, January 2, 1987, p. 30.

Grossberg, Lawrence, ed. *Cultural Studies*. New York: Routledge, 1992.

Hall, Eamonn G., and McGovern, Patrick J. C. "Regulation of the Media: Irish and European Dimensions." *Dublin University Law Journal*, 8 (1986).

Halton, Thomas. "Sponsored Radio and TV." *Studies* (1956): 233–38.

Hardiman, Thomas P. "Broadcast Engineering," *Administration* [Dublin] 15, no. 3 (Autumn 1967): 194.

————. "Communications: Social or Technical Imperative," *Aquarius* [Dublin], 1973, 134.

Harkness, David, *Northern Ireland since 1920*. Dublin: Helicon, 1983.

Havighurst, Alfred F. *Britain in Transition, the Twentieth Century*. Chicago, Ill.: University of Chicago Press, 1985.

Hickey, D. J., and Doherty, J. E. *A Dictionary of Irish History, 1800–1900*. Dublin: Gill and Macmillan, 1980.

Higgins, Michael D. "The Tyranny of Images, Media and Popular Culture," *The Crane Bag*, 8, no. 2 [Dublin 1984]: 132.

Hill, John, Martin McLoone, and Paul Hainsworth (eds.). *Border Crossing, Film in Ireland Britain and Europe*. Belfast, The Institute of Irish Studies, Queen's University, Belfast in association with the University of Ulster and the British Film Institute, 1994.

Hitchens, Christopher. "The BBC's Darkest Hour." *American Film*, 11, no. 3 (December 1985): 30–33.

Hoppen, K. Theodore. *Ireland since 1800: Conflict and Conformity*, New York: Longman, 1989.

Irvine, J. A. "A Look at USA Broadcasting," *Administration* [Dublin] 15, no. 3 (Autumn 1967): 241.

Jones, Harri Pritchard. *Wales/Ireland, A TV Contrast*. A talk given by the author to the Gaelic League, March 24, 1974. Pamphlet, National Library of Ireland.

Kearney, Richard, ed. A Debate on the Media and Popular Culture: Richard Kearney talks to Lelia Doolan, Nuala O'Faoláin, Ciaran Carty, and Luke Gibbons, "Media and Popular Culture. *The Crane Bag* [Dublin], 8, no. 2 (1984).

————. *Across the Frontiers, Ireland in the 1990s*. Dublin: Wolfhound Press, 1988.

Keating, Justin. "Telefis Feirme a 'First,' " *Comoradh 1962–1987*. Dublin: RTE, January 2, 1987, p. 29.

Kellner, Douglas. *Television and the Crisis of Democracy*. Boulder, Colo.: Westview Press, 1990.

Kelly, Anne. *Cultural Policy in Ireland*. The Irish Museums Trust. Naas, County Kildare; 1989.

Kelly, J. M. "The Constitutional Position of R.T.E.," *Administration* [Dublin] 15, no. 3 (Autumn 1967): 205.

Kennedy, Brian P. *Dreams and Responsibilities, the State and the Arts in Independent Ireland*. Dublin, Criterion Press, 1990.

Kennedy, Kieran A., ed. *Ireland in Transition, Economic and Social Change since 1960*. Dublin: RTE and the Mercier Press, 1986.

Kiernan, T. J. "The Developing Power of Broadcasting." Paper read to the Statistical and Social Inquiry Society of Dublin, Ireland, December 19, 1935.

Lee, Joseph, ed. *Ireland 1945–1970*. Dublin: Gill and Macmillan, 1979.

————. *Irish Historiography, 1970–1979*. Cork: Cork University Press, 1981.

————, ed. *Ireland: Towards a Sense of Place*. Cork: Cork University Press, 1985.

————. *Ireland 1912–1985, Politics and Society*. Cambridge: Cambridge University Press, 1989.

Lee, J. J. "Hard To Disengage Cause and Effect," *Comoradh 1962–1987*, Dublin: RTE, January 2, 1987, p. 7.

LeMahieu, D. L. *A Culture for Democracy: Mass Communications and the Cultivated Mind in Britain Between the Wars*. New York: Clarendon Press, 1988.

Leonard, Hugh. "Television and the Nation," *Aquarius* [Dublin]: 1973, 117.

Litton, Frank. *Unequal Achievement: The Irish Experience 1957–1982*. Dublin: Institute of Public Administration, 1982.

Lyons, F.S.L. *Ireland since the Famine*. London: Weictenfeld and Nicolson, 1971.

Mac Aonghusa, Proinsias. *Aeriris (Cnuasach aisti a chumadh don clar radio Aeriris, clar a craoladh ar Radio Eireann sna seascaidi)*. Dublin: An Clochomhar, 1976.

Martin, F. X. "The Thomas Davis Lectures 1953–1967." Reprint. *Irish Historical Studies*, 15, no. 59 (March 1967): 276–302.

McCarthy, Charles. "The Communication of Dissent," *Aquarius* [Dublin]: 1973, 111.

McCarthy, Colm, and Ryan, June. "An Econometric Model of TV Ownership." *Economic and Social Review* [Dublin] 7, no. 3 (April 1976): 265–77.

McCourt, Kevin C. "Broadcasting"—A Community Service," *Administration* [Dublin] 15, no. 3 (Autumn 1967): 173.

McCreesh, Gerald. "TV's Biggest Failure." *Everyman* [Dublin] 1 (1968): 127–30.

McGuinness, James P. "News Broadcasting," *Administration* [Dublin] 15, no. 3 (Autumn 1967): 200.

McLoone, Martin, and McMahon, John, eds. *Television and Irish Society, 21 Years of Irish Television.* Dublin: R.T.E., 1984.

McLuhan, Marshall. *Understanding Media.* London: Routledge and Kegan Paul, 1964.

McRedmond, Louis, ed. *Written On the Wind, Personal Memories of Irish Radio 1926–1976.* Dublin: RTE in association with Gill and Macmillan, 1976.

Meehan, J. *The Irish Economy since 1922.* Liverpool: Liverpool University Press, 1970.

Merck, Mandy. "This Is Not about Ireland." *New Statesman,* 110, no. 2839 (August 16, 1985).

Moran, Ciaran. "The Advertising Agency View of Ireland: Conservative Mono-Culture, Media and Popular Culture," *The Crane Bag,* 8, no. 2 [Dublin 1985]: 84.

Morris, Michael. *The Social Effects of Television Violence-the Irish Context.* Dublin: R.T.E., 1963.

————. *Broadcasting Research and Studies, A Study of Irish Broadcasting and Its Relationship to Irish Society and Irish Cultures.* Dublin: R.T.E., 1973.

————. *Towards an Anthropology of the Contemporary Arts, Cultural Implications of the New Media of Communication.* Dublin: R.T.E., 1973.

Moynihan Maurice, *Speeches and Statements of Eamon De Valera. Dublin: Gill and Macmillan Ltd., 1980.*

Murray, Joe. "Farming From First Night," *Comoradh 1962–1987,* Dublin: RTE, January 2, 1987, p. 29.

Murphy, John A. *Ireland in the Twentieth Century.* Dublin: Gill and Macmillan, 1975.

New Statesman. "The BBC Is Now an Arm of the Government" [editorial]. 110, no. 2837 (August 2, 1985).

Ni Chonmidhe, Meadhbh. "Broadcast Education," *Administration* [Dublin] 15, no. 3 (Autumn 1967): 226.

O'Brien, Connor Cruise. *States of Ireland.* London: Hutchinson, 1972.

O'Broin, Leon. "Amending Irish Broadcasting Law I." *European Broadcasting Union Review,* 25, no. 5 (September 1975): 39–41.

————. "Amending Irish Broadcasting Law II." *European Broadcasting Union Review,* 27, no. 1 (January 1976): 38–40.

————. "Amending Irish Broadcasting Law III." *European Broadcasting Review,* 28, no. 2 (March) 1977): 48–49.

————. *Just Like Yesterday, an Autobiography.* Dublin: Gill and Macmillan, 1985.

————. "The Legislative Origins," *Comoradh 1962–1987,* Dublin: RTE, January 2, 1987, p. 6.

O'Carroll, J. P., and Murphy, John A. *De Valera and His Times.* Cork: Cork University Press, 1986.

O'Donnell, James D. *How Ireland Is Governed.* Dublin: Institute of Public Administration, 1974.

OhAnachain, M. "The Broadcasting Dilemma." *Administration*, 28, no. 1 (1980).

O'Hehir, Michael. "A Night of Expectation and Celebration," *Comoradh 1962–1987*, Dublin: RTE, January 2, 1987, p. 8.

————. "The World of Sport is Now in Every Home," *Comoradh 1962–1987*, Dublin: RTE, January 2, 1987, p. 20.

O'Murchu, Liam. "Fiche Cuig Bliain Ag Fas!," *Comoradh 1962–1987*, Dublin: RTE, January 2, 1987, p. 26.

O'Reilly, P. P. "Starting a Revolution, Current Affairs on TV," *Comoradh 1962–1987*, Dublin, RTE, January 2, 1987, p. 28.

O'Sullivan, Michael. *Sean Lemass, A Biography*. Dublin: Blackwater Press, 1994.

Paulu, Burton. *Radio and Television Broadcasting on the European Continent*. Minneapolis: University of Minnesota Press, 1967.

Pettit, Philip. *On Popular Culture, a Criticism of Contemporary Communications*. 1969. Pamphlet, National Library of Ireland.

Pine, Richard. "After MacBride: Ireland and the New World Communications Order, Media and Popular Culture," *The Crane Bag*, 8, no. 2 [Dublin 1984]: 143.

Reith, John Charles. *The Reith Diaries, edited by Charles Stuart*. London: Collins, 1975.

Roche, Stephen. "Reading vrs TV." *Bell*, 17, no. 12 (March 1952): 91–95.

Rugheimer, Guynnar. "The 4 Minute Mile Twice," *Comoradh 1962–1987*, Dublin: RTE, January 2, 1987, p. 11.

Savage, Robert. *The Origins of Irish Radio*. Unpublished master's thesis, University College, Dublin, 1982.

Scannell, Paddy, and Cardiff, David. *A Social History of British Broadcasting: Vol. 1: 1922–1939, Serving the Nation*. Oxford: Basil Blackwell, 1991.

Sheehan, Helena. *Irish Television Drama*. Dublin: Radio Telefis Eireann, 1987.

Sheridan, Niall. "Irish Television Makes Its Bow." *Spectator*, April 27, 1962.

Skeffington, Andree Sheehy. *Skeff: The Life of Owen Sheehy Skeffington 1909–1970*. Dublin: Lilliput Press, 1991.

Stapleton, John. *Communication Policies in Ireland*. Paris: UNESCO Press, 1974.

Straschnov, Georges. "The Future of Television in the European and World Context," *Administration* [Dublin] 15, no. 3 (Autumn 1967): 249.

Sweeney, Maxwell. "Irish Television, a Compromise with Commerce." *Studies* [Dublin] 52 (1963): 410.

Thornley, David. "Ireland: The End of an Era?" *Studies*, 53 (1964): 1–17.

————. "Television and Politics." *Administration*, 15, no. 13 (1967): 217–25.

Tierney, Mark. "The Public and Private Image of the G.A.A.: A Centenary Appraisal, Media and Popular Culture," *The Crane Bag*, 8, no. 2 [Dublin 1984]: 161.

Tobin, Colm. "Gay Byrne: Irish Life as Cabaret, Media and Popular Culture," *The Crane Bag*, 8, no. 2 [Dublin 1984]: 65.

Tobin, Fergal. *The Best of Decades: Ireland in the 1960s*. Dublin: 1964.

Tracey, Michael. *A Variety of Lives, A Biography of Sir Hugh Greene.* London: The Bodley Head Ltd., 1983.

Walsh, James J. *Recollections of a Rebel.* Tralee: The Kerryman Ltd., 1944.

Walsh, Ronnie, ed. *Sunday Miscellany, a Selection from the Radio Eireann Series of Talks.* Dublin: R.T.E., in association with Gill and Macmillan, 1975.

——— . *Sunday Miscellany II.* Dublin: R.T.E., in association with Gill and Macmillan, 1976.

Ward, Alan J. "Parliamentary Procedures and the Machinery of Government in Ireland." *Irish University Review*, Autumn 1974.

Williams, Raymond. *Television, Technology and Cultural Form.* London: Fontana, 1974.

Woodman, Kiernan. *Media Control in Ireland.* Galway: Galway University Press, 1985.

Whyte, John. *Church and State in Modern Ireland 1923–1979.* London: Dublin, Gill and Macmillan, 1980.

Young, John N. *Erskine H. Childers, President of Ireland.* Buckinghamshire: Colin Smythe Ltd., 1985.

Legislation

Wireless Telegraphy Act 45, 1926.

Broadcasting Authority Act 10, 1960.

Broadcasting Authority (Amendment) Act 4, 1964.

Broadcasting Authority (Amendment) Act 7, 1966.

Broadcasting Authority (Offences) Act 35, 1968.

Broadcasting Authority (Amendment) Act 2, 1971.

Broadcasting Authority (Amendment) Act 1, 1973.

Broadcasting Authority (Amendment) Act 33, 1974.

Broadcasting Authority (Amendment) Act 37, 1976.

Broadcasting and Wireless Telegraphy Bill, 1979.

Index

About the Author

ROBERT J. SAVAGE, JR. is a professor at Boston College where he teaches Irish History.